How to Select & Use
HOME VIDEO EQUIPMENT

Marjorie Costello
and
Michael Heiss

HPBooks

About the Authors

Marjorie Costello is editor of **Videography** magazine, the leading source of information for video professionals. Her responsibilities keep her in touch with changes in the video industry on a daily basis. Ms. Costello has been in the communications and video fields for more than 10 years as a writer/producer for a large advertising/public relations firm, and manager of video services at a full-service production and post-production video facility in New York.

Ms. Costello has discussed home video on radio, written for **Home Video** and **Omni** magazines, and participated in seminars on the subject sponsored by United Business Publications and the National Academy of Television Arts and Sciences.

Michael Heiss has worked in broadcasting and consumer electronics for more than 10 years. He is west-coast editor for **Videography** and wrote for **Home Video** magazine. He has written about video for **Saturday Review, View** and **Creative Computing.** Mr. Heiss is an information provider on video hardware for CompuServe, a computer data-base service. He is entertainment account executive for Bell & Howell/Columbia Pictures Video Services in Los Angeles.

Previously, he was manager of creative services for the NBC Television Network in New York. He was also with Home Video Corporation, where he helped create the first national home video-cassette rental and home movie-to-cassette transfer services.

Mr. Heiss is a member of the Society of Motion Picture and Television Engineers (SMPTE) and Academy of Television Arts and Sciences.

Publisher: Rick Bailey
Editorial Director: Theodore DiSante
Editor: David A. Silverman
Art Director: Don Burton
Typography: Cindy Coatsworth, Michelle Claridge

Published by HPBooks®, P.O. Box 5367, Tucson AZ 85703   602/888-2150
ISBN: 0-89586-209-3   Library of Congress Catalog No. 83-82045
©1984 HPBooks, Inc. Printed in U.S.A.

How to Select & Use
HOME VIDEO EQUIPMENT

Marjorie Costello
and
Michael Heiss

You Ought to Be in Video 4
1 The Evolution of Home Video Recording ... 6
2 All About VCRs 16
3 All About Home Video Cameras 62
4 All About Videocassettes 95
5 Accessories 1O7
6 Buy or Rent? 116
7 How to Connect and Operate
   Your Equipment 121
8 All About Camcorders 139
  Source List 154
  Index............................ 157
  Buying Checklists 158

Front Cover
   Man with Camera: Courtesy RCA Consumer Electronics Division; Cassettes and
   Videocassette Recorder: H.P. Madden Photography, Equipment Courtesy Niles
   Radio & Television Center, Tucson AZ
Back Cover
   Courtesy General Electric Video

Introduction

You Ought to Be in Video

These are exciting times! Why? Because you've decided to join the *home-video revolution*. And, you're getting in on the action at the right time.

Today you have an amazing range of home-video equipment to choose from at almost every price level. Videocassette recorders (VCRs) and cameras, the mainstays of home-video recording, offer features that weren't available just a few years ago. We're overjoyed to see videotape technology move into the home. But we're also a bit concerned. That's why we've written this book.

We want you to know how to shop for your equipment. Then you can select what fits your needs and budget. And, we want you to understand home-video recording so you can get the most out of your equipment.

Imagine being able to make "home movies" of baby's first steps, or your child's first Little League home run! And then being able to go home and show it immediately, right on your TV screen! It's easier than ever with camcorders, which combine the camera and VCR in a single, compact, lightweight unit. Video is fun and exciting—and you'll want to be a part of it.

We've been working with and writing about video equipment for years. In that time, we've followed model changes, pricing and how the equipment is sold. We want to share what we've learned.

Once you understand the home-video industry, you'll be able to make an intelligent decision about what video equipment to buy or rent. The equipment is really very simple to operate, and lightweight, too.

WHAT DOES IT COST?

Of course, you must consider that initial outlay for equipment is high. Compared with super-8

Preserve the important events of your life by making your own home-video movies.

film, you may pay four times as much for a video tuner/timer, videocassette recorder and camera than you will for a super-8 camera and projector. Using a base figure of about $600 for purchase of super-8 sound equipment, you can expect to pay upwards of $2000 for a complete home-video setup—including portable VCR and tuner/timer package, and a color video camera.

But the excitement of instant gratification will probably be worth the initial cost of video. (It's *almost* instant—you have to rewind the videocassette.) You should also consider that you can record up to *eight hours* on one VHS T-160 videocassette recorded at the slowest speed—for less than $30. Using an L-830 tape with Beta, maximum recording time is five hours.

It costs almost $200 to purchase 20 rolls of super-8 film and processing for only *one hour* of film. And, you have to set up the projector and screen to show these separate three-minute segments. Your VCR is already connected to the TV, ready for showing the tape!

THE HOME-VIDEO SYSTEM

The first piece of equipment you may be considering for your home-video system is the video-cassette recorder. With a VCR or one of the new camcorders, you can record television programs as they're broadcast. You can do this while you're at home, or when you're not there. You can play back the shows at your leisure. This is called *time shift.* You can also view prerecorded video-cassettes of movies or instructional programs. These are available for purchase or rental.

When you also own a camera, you can make your own home-video "movies." With a camera and VCR, or one of the new camcorders, you can preserve electronic images of the important events of your life. And, you can have fun developing your skill as a *videographer.*

DON'T WORRY!

Many people are intimidated by electronic devices. When they first see home-video equipment, they're confused by all the cables, buttons and switches. In addition, they're baffled when they hear the names *Beta* and *VHS,* and learn that these are two incompatible home-video-recording formats. A third format, 8mm, adds to the confusion.

Although video-equipment manufacturers include instruction manuals with VCRs and cameras, many important questions are left unanswered. And, in spite of the many home-video magazines available, it's impossible to find all the answers in one place.

In this book, we provide what you need in a single volume. You'll find information about what equipment is available, a basic understanding of how it works, how to buy it, and how to hook it up and use it.

It's time to join the home-video revolution! With a setup like the Minolta video camera and portable VCR shown above, it's simple to shoot home-video movies of parties, sports activities or anything you want. Or, with a tabletop VCR like the RCA model below, you can become your own TV programmer by time-shifting and playing back movies on videocassettes.

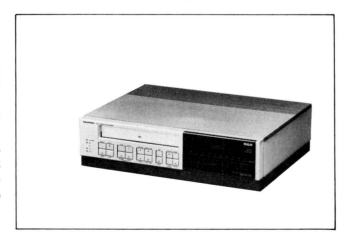

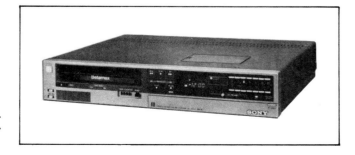

You can opt for a VCR that talks to you, too! Sony's E-Z Beta-max has a built-in voice synthesizer that tells you programming times and when you've made a control-setting error.

Chapter 1

The Evolution of Home Video Recording

The story of how video-recording equipment arrived in the home is almost as fascinating as the equipment itself. The present smashing success in home video was preceded by some embarrassing flops. You'll soon learn that today's VCRs and cameras for the home are the result of decades of research and development.

First There Was Television

The idea of sending pictures through wires or across space is one that scientists considered 100 years ago. The word *television* has been in the lexicon since 1900. Regular TV broadcasting began in the United States and England in the late 1940s. Then the new medium really began to grow.

Until the mid-1950s, television was a one-time-only phenomenon. It was live. You had to watch a program while it was being broadcast, or you missed it forever. When broadcasters wanted to preserve programs, they made *kinescopes*. These are films shot off a TV screen. Usually, kinescopes are poor quality.

TV broadcasters were interested in a high-quality method of recording and playing back shows. Years of research led to the introduction of the *videotape recorder* (VTR).

THE FIRST VIDEOTAPE RECORDER

The first videotape recorder was demonstrated in 1951 by the electronics division of Bing Crosby Enterprises. It used 1-inch tape at 100 inches per second (ips). It produced a dismal picture. On November 30, 1956, CBS used an Ampex 2-inch quadruplex format VTR for the first time to transmit a program, the delayed broadcast of *Douglas Edwards and the News* from New York to the West Coast.

But the early VTRs were hardly ready for the home. Early VTRs were immense compared to today's relatively compact units. The 2-inch-wide videotape ran at 7-1/2 and 15 inches per second, compared with Crosby's 100 ips on 1-inch-wide tape. The 2-inch-wide tape cost more than $250 for a one-hour reel. And, unless you had about $100,000 and a trained engineer on hand, you couldn't buy a 2-inch-format quad VTR for your TV station, let alone your home.

Live from the 1939 New York World's Fair! It was the first time television covered a news event: RCA founder General David Sarnoff's speech dedicating his company's pavilion.

VTR was first used by CBS and other networks to send delayed broadcasts to the West Coast.

In the next 10 years, engineers reduced the size and cost of VTRs.

GETTING SMALLER

With the development of transistorized parts and other electronic advances, VTR prices and complexity were reduced. Businesses and schools were able to afford the new video units that used 1-inch-wide and even 1/2-inch-wide videotape.

The possibility of video-recording systems for the home was considered. But there were still several major stumbling blocks: The machines had to be less expensive. Tape playing time had to be increased. Operation of the units had to be simplified for the average user.

The Evolution Begins—Two important advances led the way in the evolution of home-video equipment. Japanese engineers at Toshiba developed *helical-scan* recording techniques. This is discussed in more detail in Chapter 2.

In addition, helical VTRs required only two *video heads,* mounted on a rotating drum, to record or play back information. The 2-inch quad format had four. The results of helical scanning were a narrower tape width, slower tape speeds, still-frame ability and smaller machines.

Sony's Attempts—The first attempt at a practical home-videotape recorder came from Sony Corporation of Japan in the late 1960s. Sony introduced a unit using 1/2-inch-wide videotape on reels. The concept seemed right. This recorder was packaged in a console with a small TV set, and a tuner permitting "off-air" recording. But there were some inherent problems limiting the machine's appeal.

The Sony videotape recorder was simpler to operate than its big brothers in TV stations. But its tape-threading system proved too complicated for the "butter-fingered" public. Another drawback was that it was limited to one-hour recording. And, it only recorded in b&w. What's more, the price was too high for most people.

Sony kept on trying. The machine that didn't quite click with consumers in the late 1960s became the backbone of educational and corporate audiovisual departments. Later models recorded in color.

THEN CAME THE CASSETTES

To overcome some of the objections to these 1/2-inch-wide tape reel-to-reel videotape recorders, Sony developed a 3/4-inch-wide-tape format. This time the tape was contained in a cassette. Now there was no more fumbling with tape threading. And, the machine could record in color. Sony launched it in 1971 and called it the *U-Matic.* Once again, the company hoped their equipment would catch on in the home.

It didn't! The machines cost more than $1000 and the cassettes could record for only an hour. As with earlier 1/2-inch-wide-tape models, the U-Matic found its way into business and educational applications. It's still being used in these areas today.

To Sony's delight, the U-Matic also revolutionized TV news-gathering in the mid-70s.

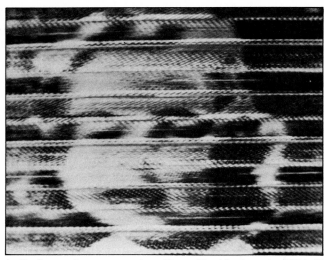 

Left: Ampex began experimenting with videotape in 1951. This is how a Shirley Temple film looked on tape when recorded on the Ampex Mark II VTR prototype using AM signal processing in late 1952. Right: Addition of FM signal processing and other improvements produced this quality by early 1955. Facing Page: By late 1955, Ampex engineers were able to produce quality such as this. (Courtesy Ampex Museum of Magnetic Recording)

Broadcasters began replacing 16mm film cameras with lightweight color-video cameras and 3/4-inch-tape VCRs.

While video was replacing 16mm in the newsroom, people began wondering when video was going to do the same to 8mm film in the home. The Japanese weren't the only ones working on home-video recording. American companies were also realizing the potential profits they could make.

Perhaps you remember *Cartrivision,* a 1/2-inch-wide-tape cartridge system built in the United States. It was developed by Avco and sold in the early 70s by retail outlets such as Sears. Unfortunately, image quality wasn't very good, the units weren't portable and the price was too high.

Meanwhile, in Japan, scientists and engineers were working with their marketing colleagues to come up with the right home system. The U-Matic proved to be a solid, dependable piece of equipment. It provided the technological basis for smaller and less expensive machines. In addition, the Japanese carefully studied what the public wanted in their home-recording system.

ENTER THE BETAMAX

In late 1975, Sony introduced the Betamax. At first it was available only in a $2220 console containing a VCR and TV. In February 1976, the Betamax recorder was liberated from its console. For less than $1200, the consumer could buy a VCR with a built-in tuner, clock-timer and one-hour recording capability — in color, of course.

Left: Videotape recording was only b&w until late 1957, when RCA announced the TRT-1AC, a color recorder. (Courtesy RCA)

Right: Helical-scan recording began in early 1961 when Ampex introduced the VR-8000, shown here. Sony started its video line a couple of months later with its SV-201. (Courtesy Ampex Museum of Magnetic Recording)

First Sony Betamax, a VCR and TV in a console, appeared in late 1975. It finally brought video "home."

Sony's engineers had developed a 1/2-inch-wide-tape videocassette recording format for the consumer. With the Betamax, you could record one program while watching another. With the tuner/timer, you could even record a show when away from home! Sony was selling what they called *time shift*—the ability to record programming you might otherwise miss. And they were selling it for a reasonable price!

Competition Arrives—Did Sony have a good idea? They must have. In the next year, other companies offered four different, incompatible formats. Price and emphasis on time shift appeared to be the keys in this successful introduction of home-video systems. In fact, Quasar called its home-video equipment the *Great Time Machine*.

All four formats did the same thing. But by doing it in a slightly different way, the foursome created chaos in the marketplace. Two of them—Quasar's Great Time Machine and Sanyo's V-Cord—survived little more than a year. Left to slug it out in the home-video marketplace were Sony's Beta format and the Video Home System (VHS) developed by the Japan Victor Company (JVC).

In the past few years, another format tried to break into the video world. The Compact Video Cassette (CVC) is made in Japan by Funai and sold in North America under the *Technicolor* brand name. Although CVC held some promise with its 1/4-inch-wide-tape videocassette and smaller VCR, it was less popular than Beta and VHS. The CVC is no longer sold in North America.

One more format, the V-2000, reached 20% market penetration in Europe. Its developer, Grundig of Germany, has kept it off the North-American shores.

Sony certainly had a good idea with the Betamax. Such a good idea, in fact, that there are more than 10 million VCRs in the United States alone. Beta and VHS are now so widespread that the likelihood of any new format pushing Beta and VHS off the market is slight, unless it offers a dramatic improvement in ease of use, is more portable and is compatible with other manufacturers' equipment.

Another Format—Such a format has been agreed upon by home-video manufacturers. It's called

Left: Sony's U-Matic brought the world a cassette containing 3/4-inch-wide videotape.

Right: This Panasonic 1/2-inch-format open-reel VTR required the operator to thread the tape on two individual reels.

This crew is carrying a lightweight professional Electronic News Gathering (ENG) camera, and 3/4-inch-format VCR.

8mm Video because the tape is 8mm wide. It is offered as a one-piece camera/VCR unit, geared for home-video moviemaking. We tell more about 8mm Video in Chapter 8.

We've Come a Long Way

Let's get back to the excitement surrounding the introduction of Sony's Betamax and JVC's VHS formats. Soon after the first introductions, other companies began to enter the competition. Under license from Sony and JVC, they either build their own VCRs or sell under their own brand name machines built by someone else.

So the competition is not only between the firms offering the two different formats, but among brands—both American and Japanese—offering a variety of models for home use.

MEANWHILE, BACK IN THE LAB . . .

As the competition intensified, there were more advances in VCR design and capabilities. Manufacturers began turning more attention to the other side of the home-video equation—the camera. Although time shift was first responsible for getting video recording into the home, the camera would get the entire family involved. Now you could shoot your own home-video movies.

In the next three chapters, we explain how the home-video system works. We also fill you in on the range of features available in current VCRs and cameras. In Chapter 8, we discuss the new camcorders.

Here's a sneak preview: Recording times per videocassette have increased. Tuners and timers can perform more functions and are easier to operate. VCRs are getting lighter and smaller. Many of the features offered today were unimaginable just a few years ago, both in terms of their sophistication and cost.

Technology has made it possible for you to have all these features at a cost that's actually lower than the first Betamax VCR. In this context, what's available today is also a real bargain when you consider inflation. For less than $2000, you can hang a portable VCR over your shoulder or use a camcorder to shoot action on location using a color camera with a zoom lens. Impressive!

VTR VS. VCR

Don't be confused by the terms *videotape recorder (VTR)* and *videocassette recorder (VCR).* Although some people and publications use them interchangeably, there is a specific difference between them.

VTR refers to recorders using two open reels of tape that must be threaded by the operator. *VCR* refers to the units containing two reels of tape in a sealed plastic case. The tape is threaded automatically by the recorder. All home-video recorders are VCRs.

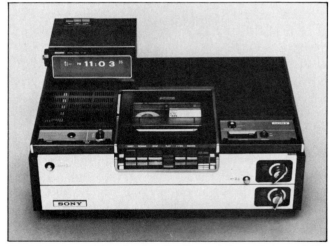

First tabletop VCR arrived in 1976, again from Sony, and the world started Betamaxing.

JVC's VHS hit the market in 1977. This format has outsold Beta over the years.

Here's the next generation of home-video-recording equipment. This is Eastman Kodak's Kodavision, an 8mm camcorder.

We've certainly come a long way from those rooms full of tubes, and heavy reels of 2-inch-wide videotape that weighed more than some of today's camera-and-VCR combinations. The incredible advances in consumer electronics have given us home-video systems that don't require an engineering degree or technician's certification to be understood. And you don't have to mortgage your home to take part.

TELEVISION STANDARDS

There are different television standards throughout the world. This is important if you're planning to use your VCR in another country. A TV standard is a set of technical specifications that define how the picture is created.

The United States, Canada, Mexico and Japan use the National Television System Committee (NTSC) standard. Two other major standards are Phase Alternation by Line (PAL) and Système Electronique pour Couleur Avec Memoire (SECAM). SECAM is used in France, Russia and Eastern Block countries, among others. PAL is the standard used in Britain, Germany, Scandinavia, The Netherlands, other European countries and parts of South America.

VCR and camera manufacturers build machines to be compatible with the TV standard used by each country selling their VCRs. The same holds true for TV manufacturers. Because the United States, Mexico, Canada and Japan use the NTSC standard, you can use the same type VCR in any of these countries. Videocassettes recorded on a NTSC VCR cannot be played back on PAL or SECAM VCRs and vice versa.

Despite the differences between NTSC, PAL and SECAM, many home-video marketers offer both Beta and VHS for each standard. Therefore, within the countries offering the different standards, you'll find both Beta and VHS machines.

You may be planning to live for an extended time in another country. If you're buying video equipment and pre-recorded tapes at home and bringing them with you, or buying them there and bringing them back, be sure to check if the standards are compatible. Equipment is sold in areas for use with the type of broadcast standard available locally. This may not be the same as your home location.

The State-of-the-Art

In our opinion, the best part of the video-recording evolution is that the systems have been designed to be easy to use. All it takes is a basic grasp of how the elements—VCR, videocassette and camera—operate. But before we get to that, we know you should have some appreciation of the state-of-the- art—what's available today.

TABLETOPS AND PORTABLES

Videocassette recorders are available in three basic types. One is the AC-powered *tabletop* model, sometimes referred to as a *home deck* or *console*. The tabletop has a built-in tuner.

The second category is the *portable,* a relatively lightweight, easy-to-carry battery-powered unit. When connected to a separate tuner/timer unit, a portable offers many of the features of a tabletop.

Quasar's Great Time Machine didn't survive the home-video-format wars.

Another also-ran format, the CVC, is no longer sold in North America.

Although popular overseas, Grundig's V-2000 format has never made it to North America.

As with other portable systems, the recorder section (right) of Hitachi's portable system VT-3 can record off the air and operate from AC house current when mated with the tuner/timer unit (left).

Portable packages, like this one from Zenith, provide a special "docking" feature. This allows you to connect the recorder to the tuner/timer without wires or cables.

Today, you can shoot almost anywhere with a camera and VCR.

Some people buy a portable as a second VCR. They add a simple AC-power adapter to charge the batteries or play back videocassettes when AC current is available.

The other type of VCR is part of a camcorder. More on that in Chapter 8.

You may be considering purchase of a separate home-video recorder. If this is for taping with a camera or copying material from a tabletop you already own, it may be best to buy a portable—without a tuner/timer.

If you want to tape broadcasts *and* shoot with a video camera, the fully equipped portable package—with a tuner/timer—is a wise initial investment.

Today, portables offer many of the special effects, such as fast-forward-with-picture, that were once the exclusive domain of tabletops. There are even lightweight portables featuring stereo sound and five heads for improved picture stability in still and slow-motion modes. A few models include a tuner/timer built into an easy-to-carry, battery-operated unit. We discuss these features in Chapter 2.

If you don't have plans for buying a video camera, you should probably stick with a tabletop. Of course, the prerecorded video-cassettes you can buy or rent can be played on either a tabletop or portable—as long as your unit is not a VHS-C VCR.

KEEPING UP

Manufacturers pay attention to the external appearance of their products. Units are becoming sleeker, slimmer and much more attractive. For example, front-loading VCRs require less operating space, so look neater in a wall unit. Manufacturers, with an eye on the concept of the "total home-entertainment system," are also coordinating the design of their VCRs, TVs and audio equipment.

Everyone is aware of the cable-television explosion. With it, an increasing number of channels is reaching the home. VCR engineers have made another improvement. They're building units with *cable-ready tuning*. This allows you to record programs from many of the channels you might normally need an external cable-converter box to receive. The cable-ready provision eliminates an extra piece of equipment and wires. It simplifies setup.

MORE FOR LESS

The many improvements made in VCRs doesn't mean you'll be forced to buy an expensive, high-tech, fully featured unit. You can

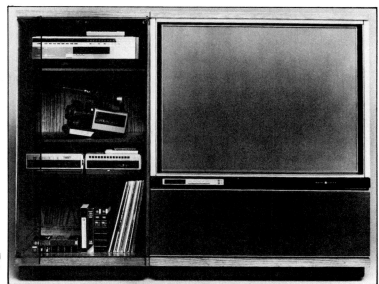

Companies such as General Electric are designing VCRs to fit neatly into total home-entertainment systems like this one.

also buy a more modest "no-frills" machine. It'll do an excellent job of recording off the air, using a simple one-day timer.

You should realize that it's not only the public that has been learning more about home-video recording. Technology has improved, so manufacturers are able to produce products that better serve the needs of the buying public.

Are you reading this book before buying your first VCR? Don't worry about being forced into buying something you don't need or can't afford. Read these pages carefully. You'll be able to deal with even the most aggressive salesperson. And you'll still get the best bargain for your money.

A PEEK AT CAMERAS

The video camera has advanced quickly, along with its partner, the VCR. As with VCRs, only a handful of OEMs make cameras. These are sold under many brand names.

Cameras today cost about the same as they did when the first home models were introduced in

1977. You can probably purchase older models for well below list price.

But for the same money, cameras now deliver far superior pictures. B&W cameras have almost disappeared from the market. The public, it seems, prefers to see the world in color and is willing to pay for this feature.

ABOUT BRANDS

Today, video equipment is sold under many brand names. Actually, only a few firms—located in Japan—build the video machines sold in North America. When a company buys a unit from a manufacturer, the manufacturer is called the *original equipment manufacturer,* or *OEM.*

We discuss buying a VCR in Chapter 2. We tell you more about OEMs there. We also include a chart listing brand names, OEMs and formats.

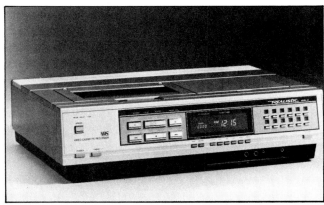

We've come a long way from the 2-inch-format VTR with its room full of tubes. This Radio Shack Realistic unit is sleek and compact. Today, Realistic and familiar brand names market VCRs made by companies called *original equipment manufacturers,* or *OEMs.*

There are several distinctly different styles and types of home-video cameras. They are discussed later in the book. The two pictured here are the Pentax PC-K030A (above) and JVC's GX-N70.

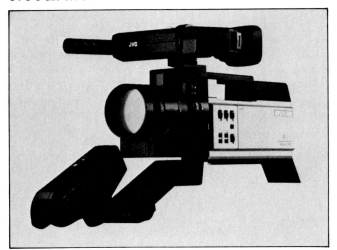

Many cameras feature a lightweight 6:1 power-zoom lens and electronic viewfinder, rather than a fixed-focal-length lens and simple optical viewfinder. Consumers are less inclined than ever to buy the cheaper stripped-down, color cameras.

For those willing to spend more, there are cameras featuring 8:1 or 12:1 zoom lenses, on-camera VCR controls and automatic focus. We explain these terms and features later.

We tell you more about video cameras in Chapter 3. Camcorders, which combine the camera and VCR in one unit, are discussed in Chapter 8.

WHAT ABOUT THE VIDEODISC?

With all of our talk about technology and the home-video revolution, you may be wondering why we haven't mentioned the videodisc player. The reason is simple. The videodisc player *does not record*. This book is about understanding and buying home-video *recording* equipment. Nonetheless, we would be remiss if we failed to tell you about this aspect of the home-video system.

Two incompatible videodisc formats have been available in North America. They are the optical, or LaserVision (LV), and the capacitance (CED) systems. Both are strictly playback devices. They use discs that look similar to audio records.

The systems differ in price and sophistication. The more expensive LV system scans the disc with a laser. CED players read the disc with a stylus, similar to the one in a record player.

(Above) Pioneer's LD-660 LaserVision videodisc player offers stereo sound and access to any of the disc's 54,000 frames in seconds. But alas, it can't record. (Right) RCA's CED player, no longer manufactured, also can't record.

Overall, videodisc players are less expensive than VCRs. And movies on discs cost less to buy than on videocassettes. Special programming has been created for the LV format. It capitalizes on the laser's ability to access, in seconds, any one of 54,000 frames on the disc.

With these special *interactive* discs, you can do everything from play a game to learn a new skill, all at your own pace. The CED format has also introduced players and programming offering interactive capabilities.

However, neither of the two videodisc formats has captured the imagination of the public. After spending millions of dollars developing and promoting the CED system, RCA has discontinued manufacture of videodisc players. However, the company will continue offering CED discs for a few years. The LV system is marketed by several companies, including Pioneer and Magnavox. Total sales of both format videodisc players in North America is less than one million.

One reason for the lack of popularity of videodisc players is that VCR prices have come down dramatically in the past few years. VCRs are only slightly more expensive than disc players. Renting videocassettes, rather than buying them, has also reduced the price of viewing prerecorded cassettes.

Perhaps the most basic reason is that the videodisc player can't do the one thing the public wants it to—record. In our opinion, a videodisc recorder will not be introduced for home use anytime soon. Prototype models have been demonstrated for industrial use. Prices for these will be extremely high.

BACK TO RECORDING

We can't predict with any great certainty how the videodisc player will fare in the years to come. But we do know that VCRs are here to stay. Many reliable sources are predicting that VCR sales are about to take off the way color-TV sales did in the mid-1960s.

Millions of people will be out looking for the right video-recording system for their needs. With this book in hand, you'll have a head start in the equipment hunt. To help you choose, set up and operate your equipment, first learn how all the elements in the home-video system operate.

In Chapter 2, we explain all about the VCR. Video cameras are explained in Chapter 3. And in Chapter 4, you'll learn how videocassettes are made and how they work.

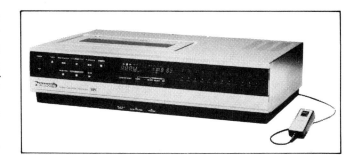

As with cameras, there are also many different styles of VCR. For example, this inexpensive no-frills top-loading Panasonic PV-1225 (top) allows you to record one event in a 14-day period, and has an electronic tuner and picture scan in forward and reverse. More VCRs are adding other features, such as front loading in this Toshiba (above). These and other features are explained later in the book.

Renting and buying a growing range of videocassette titles has made this Video Station store a popular hangout for VCR owners in the community.

Chapter 2

All About VCRs

It's time to find out how a home-video system works. In this chapter, we explain in detail the mainstay of the home-video recording system—the videocassette recorder (VCR).

You'll learn about the working parts, operation and range of features. In our discussion of recording techniques, we explain why the Beta and VHS formats are incompatible. We tell you the advantages of each, and make suggestions about which features we consider important.

Down to Basics

All modern home-video recorders are capable of recording and playing back in color. The same is true for videocassettes. Whether the image you see on your TV screen is b&w or color depends on several factors.

First, if you have a b&w TV set, everything you play back will be in b&w. Second, if you play back a movie shot in b&w, it will play back in b&w, even if your set is color. Third, even if you have a b&w TV, the VCR will still record a color program off the air in color. To view the tape in color, you must connect the VCR to a color TV. And, if you use a b&w video camera, the images will be played back in b&w.

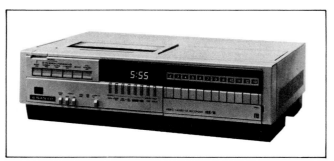

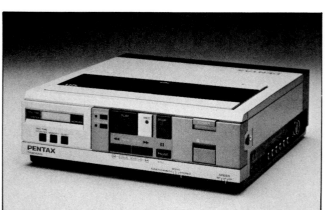

It's time to find out more about what's inside VCRs like the Sanyo (top) and Mitsubishi (right) tabletops and the Pentax portable (above).

COMPARISON OF BETA AND VHS		
	BETA	**VHS**
TAPE WIDTH	1/2 inch	1/2 inch
LINEAR SPEED	20mm/sec (X2)	33.35mm/sec (SP)
WRITING SPEED	6.69m/sec	5.8m/sec
HEAD OFFSET (AZIMUTH ANGLE)	+/-7°	+/-6°
CONTROL-TRACK WIDTH	.75mm	.75mm
AUDIO-TRACK WIDTH (MONO)	1mm	1mm
LOADING METHOD	U Tape Wrap	M-Load
CASSETTE SIZE	6.1x3.8x1 inch	7.4x4.1x1 inch
MAXIMUM RECORDING TIME	5 hours with L-830 tape (X3)	8 hours with T-160 tape (EP)

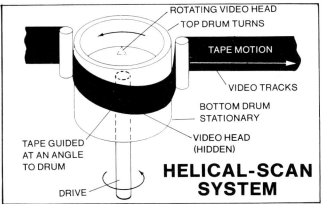

HELICAL-SCAN SYSTEM

ROTATING VIDEO HEAD
TOP DRUM TURNS
TAPE MOTION
VIDEO TRACKS
BOTTOM DRUM STATIONARY
VIDEO HEAD (HIDDEN)
TAPE GUIDED AT AN ANGLE TO DRUM
DRIVE

In helical-scan recording, a pair of rotating heads mounted on a drum record picture information in a diagonal pattern on the videotape.

Basically, all home-video recorders operate the same way. All formats record the image and sound on magnetic tape. One major reason that incompatibility exists is that each format records the image differently. See the accompanying box comparing formats.

Despite all the technical breakthroughs, it's still not possible to play a VHS cassette on a Beta-format VCR, and vice-versa.

HELICAL-SCAN RECORDING

All of today's machines, and those that will probably be introduced in the next few years, use *helical-scan* recording techniques. This is also called *slant track*. In helical recording, the VCR has a pair of rotating heads mounted in a small drum.

The rotating heads are arranged so they place the signal containing the image on the videotape in a long helical curve. Helical-scan recording maximizes the amount of information that can be recorded on the relatively narrow 1/2-inch or 8mm tape width of home-video.

Also placed on the tape with the picture are an *audio track* and a *control track*. The audio track consists of the sounds that accompany the action, or a narration. Think of the control track as the electronic equivalent of sprocket holes in motion-picture film. The control track keeps the tape running at the correct speed.

VCR heads that pick up the audio and control tracks are fixed. They resemble the audio heads in an audiotape recorder. However, video heads differ because they are not stationary. They spin as the tape passes over them.

VIDEO VS. AUDIO

It's a fact of life that the video signal contains too much information to permit the signal to be put down linearly. To accommodate the video signal's large information package, engineers use

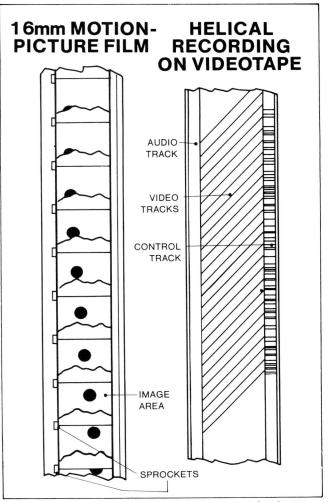

16mm MOTION-PICTURE FILM   HELICAL RECORDING ON VIDEOTAPE

AUDIO TRACK
VIDEO TRACKS
CONTROL TRACK
IMAGE AREA
SPROCKETS

Comparison of a 16mm motion-picture image (left) with a helical recording on videotape (right). In general, an advantage of film is that you can identify a shot easily by holding the film up to the light.

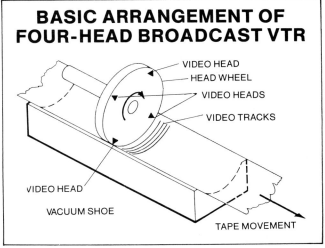

BASIC ARRANGEMENT OF FOUR-HEAD BROADCAST VTR

VIDEO HEAD
HEAD WHEEL
VIDEO HEADS
VIDEO TRACKS
VIDEO HEAD
VACUUM SHOE
TAPE MOVEMENT

In the original 2-inch-format VTRs, picture information was recorded perpendicular to the edge of the videotape. Development of the helical-recording technique helped pave the way for narrower tape and smaller recorders.

rotating heads. This eliminates the need for breakneck tape speeds and miles of tape.

The video signal isn't recorded in the same way as an audio signal. If it were, the videotape would have to move past the heads faster than 1500 inches per second (ips) to produce an acceptable picture. To record an hour, you'd need about 85 miles of tape!

Helical-scan recording, as mentioned in Chapter 1, was a major advancement permitting the development of smaller video recording devices.

THE AZIMUTH ANSWER

We noted earlier that many technological breakthroughs have simplified the video-recording process. For example, early professional-model VTRs required four video heads. But the simpler helical-scan technique, the precursor to today's home-video format, required only two for recording and playback.

You can now record at a choice of speeds because of improvements in heads and tape. This allows you to get more information on the tape in a videocassette. To really understand the nuts-and-bolts of how a VCR records, we'll point out another major breakthrough. *Azimuth recording* has helped make home-video recording possible.

Before azimuth recording was developed, there were empty tracks, or guard bands, between the video tracks recorded on tape. These kept the heads from picking up unwanted signals from adjacent tracks. Even though earlier systems offered good pictures, they required wider tape, and more of it.

The azimuth system records adjacent tracks at different angles. When the head passes over a recorded signal during playback, the head can only read the tracks aimed in its direction. If it's the correct direction, the head "sees" it; wrong direction, it sees nothing.

So, if Beta and VHS home-video formats use azimuth and helical-scan recording techniques, why are they incompatible?

THE COMPATIBILITY QUESTION

A quick glance at a Beta and a VHS video-cassette shows that Beta is smaller than VHS. If you measure the width of the tape inside each cassette, you'll find that both Beta and VHS are 1/2-inch wide. However, it's clear from the differences in dimensions of the plastic housing containing the tape that you couldn't possibly fit a VHS cassette in a Beta VCR.

But, you wonder, what if you spliced some tape recorded on a Beta cassette onto the tape in a VHS cassette? You would discover that not only are the cassettes different sizes, but the recording procedure used for each format varies, too.

You may also be wondering why the manufacturers didn't decide on one format for home-video recording. The reasons behind that could fill another book. It's only important to know that these incompatible formats do exist. It's of prime importance to recognize and understand the differences.

Recording Speeds—You don't have to worry about any serious incompatibility among today's home VCRs of the *same* format. However, you may find some incompatibility related to *recording and playback speeds*.

Early Beta VCRs for the home, and many professional Beta units, record in X1, the fastest speed. Today's Beta home units can only record in X2 and X3. Some home units can also play back cassettes recorded in X1. This is important to remember if you plan to use Beta cassettes produced for industrial or educational applications. Also keep in mind the recording speed if you use an older Beta home machine or borrow cassettes from someone who owns an early Beta tabletop.

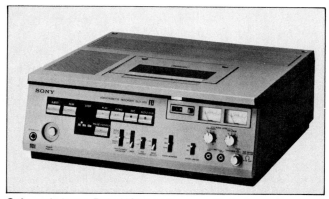

Only early home Beta VCRs and many of today's professional Beta units, like this Sony, record at X1 speed.

HOME-VIDEO RECORDING TIMES
(in minutes)

Beta (L-750 tape)* Speed (time)	VHS (T-120 tape)* Speed (time)
X1** (90)	SP—Standard Play (120)
X2 (180)	LP—Long Play (240)
X3 (270)	EP—Extended Play*** (360)

* T-120 and L-750 tapes are popular tape lengths for their formats.
** X1 is not a recording speed in modern home-video Beta units. Some home-video machines play back tapes recorded in X1 on older home models or professional Beta VCRs.
*** Older machines may use *SLP, super-long-play,* instead of current *EP* designation.

On the VHS side, none of the three recording speeds—SP, LP or EP (also called *SLP* for *super-long-play*)—has been "retired" from home use. However, early VHS machines didn't record in LP or EP. Most home VHS units record in SP and EP. Most professional machines record only in SP. Home machines that don't record in LP generally offer playback for cassettes recorded in LP speed. Professional VHS decks vary in the speeds offered for playback.

The VHS-C system, mentioned in Chapter 1, records and plays back only in SP. There really isn't a compatibility problem with the new VHS-C machines, either. Even though the cassettes are smaller than standard-size VHS cassettes, both use the same VHS recording technique.

The difference is that VHS-C machines use a cassette specially designed to fit in the smaller opening of a more compact VCR. The tape is the same as that in other VHS cassettes, but VHS-C videocassettes hold only 20 minutes' worth of tape at the SP speed. Although you can't fit a standard-size VHS cassette into a VHS-C machine, you can play or record a VHS-C cassette in a standard VHS machine by using an adapter.

The new VHS camcorder, VideoMovie, also records on VHS-C cassettes. More in Chapter 8.

BETA VS. VHS

Incompatibility between Beta and VHS goes beyond mere physical appearances. Essentially:
- Azimuth angle is different.
- Width of the video tracks is not the same.
- Color information is recorded at a different frequency.

So much for the electronics. There are also mechanical differences between Beta and VHS:
- Tape-running speeds used by the two formats are different.
- Diameter of the head drums isn't the same.
- Head-drum construction varies.

Loading and Threading Differ, Too—Look inside machines of each format and watch the tape thread through. You'll see that Beta machines draw the tape out of the cassette and wrap it around the head drum in a radically different way than a VHS VCR.

Beta VCRs use a loading or threading method that relies on a threading ring and guide rollers. It's called the *U tape wrap*. This method is also used in today's 3/4-inch VCRs. Some say that it's gentler because it doesn't stress the tape too much at any one point.

The Beta threading method also allows the tape to move across the head at fast and slow speeds in forward and reverse. This gives Beta units some special effects not available in VHS machines. More on this later.

VHS proponents argue that its loading system, dubbed the *M-load,* is simpler. This VHS threading technique uses a series of loading pins and stress guides. They lift the tape out of the cassette in a pattern that resembles the letter **M**. This gives a much shorter loading path than the one in Beta VCRs.

Basically, you want to know if the differences and incompatibility mean that one format is preferable over the other. VHS units typically outsell Beta by about three to one, but this shouldn't affect your decision about which format is best for you. We don't advise that you make your buying decision based on threading methods or

Beta cassette on the left is smaller than the VHS cassette on the right. Both use 1/2-inch-wide tape.

A VHS-C videocassette is only about the size of a deck of cards. It also contains 1/2-inch-wide tape. With an adapter, you can use the VHS-C cassette in a standard, full-size portable or tabletop VHS-format VCR.

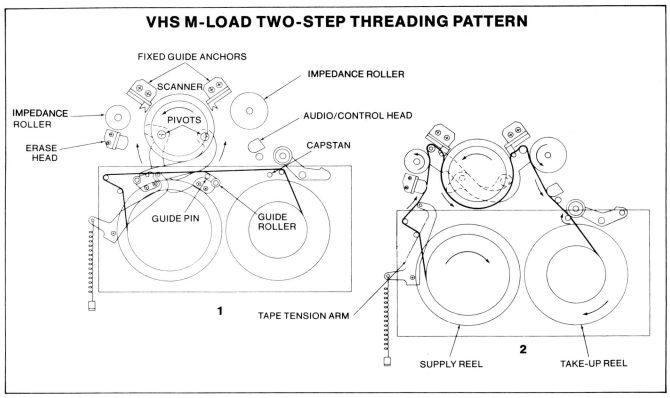

VHS M-LOAD TWO-STEP THREADING PATTERN

VHS M-load has a shorter threading path than Beta.

some of the other technical differences between Beta and VHS. Both formats have proved reliable. There have been no major complaints from the public about either recording method.

It's important to understand that VCR models in both formats are comparable. When choosing format, you should consider size, weight, price and maximum playing time, however. We'll discuss this more later.

In the rest of this chapter, we tell you more about the inner workings of VCRs of both formats. This will familiarize you with the increasing range of features available and what they can do for you.

Inside the VCR

You should understand how a VCR's basic parts function. This will help when you use the VCR.

THE SCANNER

This major VCR component is illustrated on pages 22 and 23. It contains a number of parts we discuss separately. The scanner is the surface over which the tape travels when the video signal is being recorded or played back. It must be correctly installed and aligned by the manufacturer

so the tape can pass over the heads at a specific location.

If there is something wrong with the scanner, the VCR won't be able to play back prerecorded cassettes you buy, rent or borrow. When the scanner is out of alignment, the signals can't be put down in the right place during recording. Nor can they be picked up properly during playback.

This technical problem is known as *poor interchange*. Basically, it means that the VCR has to go in for repair. *Never* try to fix the scanner yourself. You can only make matters worse and increase the expense of repairs.

HEAD DRUM

The head drum is at the top of the scanner. The drum rotates while the bottom of the scanner remains stationary to help guide the tape. Rotation speed is set by the manufacturer at the precise rate required for accurate recording and playback.

This complex assembly includes the video heads. It is balanced and aligned with great precision so the heads cross the tape where they're supposed to. If you have an opportunity to take a look at a head drum that has been removed from a VCR, you'll notice grooves along the edges. These are *air bearings*.

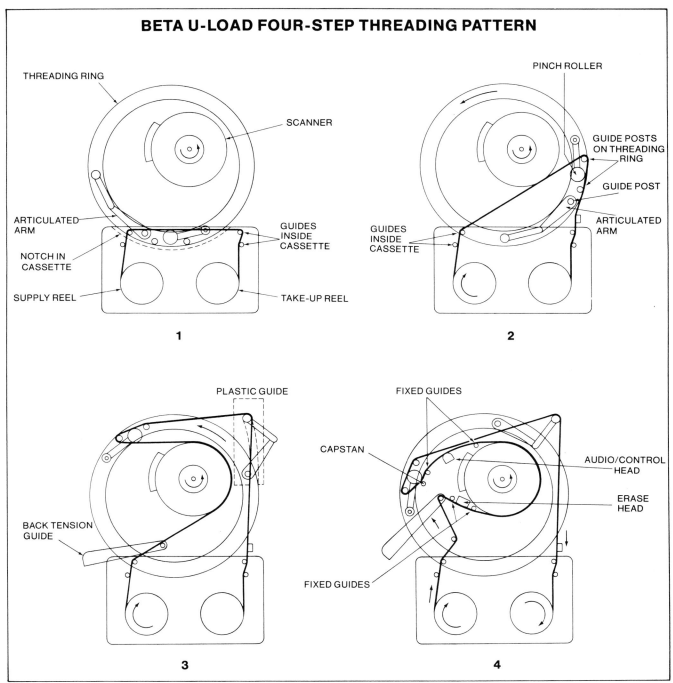

BETA U-LOAD FOUR-STEP THREADING PATTERN

1

THREADING RING

SCANNER

ARTICULATED ARM

NOTCH IN CASSETTE

SUPPLY REEL

GUIDES INSIDE CASSETTE

TAKE-UP REEL

2

PINCH ROLLER

GUIDE POSTS ON THREADING RING

GUIDE POST

ARTICULATED ARM

GUIDES INSIDE CASSETTE

3

PLASTIC GUIDE

BACK TENSION GUIDE

4

FIXED GUIDES

CAPSTAN

AUDIO/CONTROL HEAD

ERASE HEAD

FIXED GUIDES

Beta threading pattern looks like the letter U. This threading approach doesn't overstress the tape at any one point.

When the tape moves across the heads, rushing air lifts the tape off the drum. This is very slight—not so much that the tape loses contact with the heads that protrude from the drum. Air bearings make sure the tape is kept at just the right tension.

Look closely at the illustrations of Beta and VHS scanners on page 22. You'll spot one of the differences between the two formats. In VHS units, the heads are a part of the top of the rotating drum. In Beta machines, the heads are mounted on a ring-type assembly sandwiched in the scanner between two fixed cylinders.

VIDEO HEADS

The scanner contains a head drum containing the video heads. These heads contact the videotape. During recording, the video heads

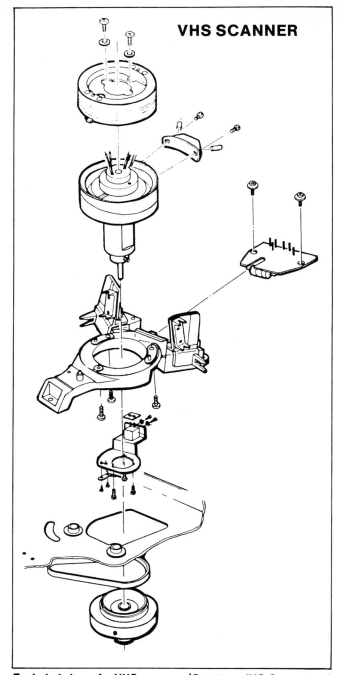

VHS SCANNER

Exploded view of a VHS scanner. (Courtesy JVC Company of America)

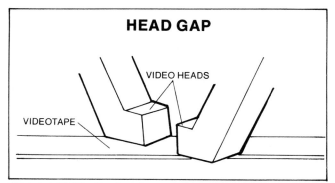

HEAD GAP

VIDEO HEADS

VIDEOTAPE

On many VCRs, the head gap at the center of the front of a video head is the same width as the video track.

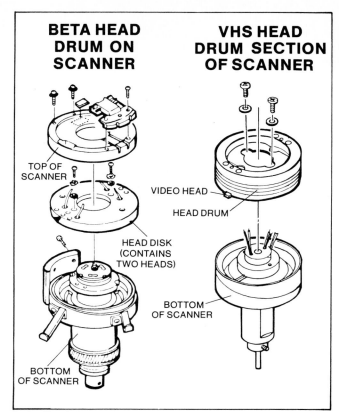

BETA HEAD DRUM ON SCANNER

VHS HEAD DRUM SECTION OF SCANNER

TOP OF SCANNER

VIDEO HEAD

HEAD DRUM

HEAD DISK (CONTAINS TWO HEADS)

BOTTOM OF SCANNER

BOTTOM OF SCANNER

Left: Head drum with the bottom of the scanner from a Sony VCR. Two heads are mounted in a ring assembly. (Courtesy Sony Corporation of America) Right: In VHS machines, the video heads are part of the drum. These parts comprise the scanner assembly. (Courtesy JVC Company of America)

magnetize the tape. In playback, they "read" the orientation of the magnetic particles on the tape. In two-head VCRs, video heads are mounted 180° apart in the head drum. Two heads are required to produce a picture. Each is responsible for 262-1/2 of the lines in each 525-line television picture frame.

When you look at a head drum, you see small tips projecting out of the side of the drum. These are the video heads. Look, but *don't touch!* They're fragile! If the heads have to be replaced along with the entire drum, it's an expensive repair job!

Video heads are small encapsulated electromagnets. They're composed of two pieces of ferrite metal with wire coils wrapped around each side. At the center of the front of each head is a tiny gap where the magnetic energy is concentrated.

This head gap is an open area through which the recording is made. The head gap is an area that gets clogged. When you clean the head, you are removing bits of tape oxide that have accumulated in the head-gap area. Oxide debris can prevent the heads from doing their job.

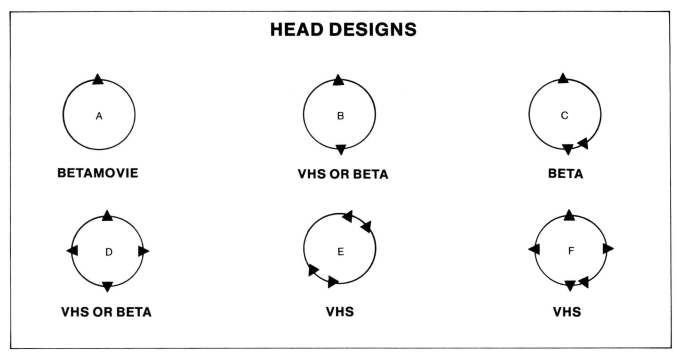

HEAD DESIGNS

BETAMOVIE   **VHS OR BETA**   **BETA**

VHS OR BETA   **VHS**   **VHS**

These illustrate the configurations of one-, two-, three-, four- and five-head designs.

(A) One head: Use of one head in a Beta machine seems contrary to the needs of the Beta helical system. Betamovie camera/recorder has a single head, but this single head is a *dual-azimuth*. Single head can record both azimuth tracks.

(B) Two heads: Most helical-scan machines use this format. Heads are 180° apart.

(C) Three heads: Some Beta machines use this approach for clearer playback in scan and still-frame modes. The third head, located slightly to the side of one of the standard heads, is a *dual-azimuth* head. One head can read both azimuth tracks.

(D) and (E) Four heads: To allow for "noise-free" still and scan viewing, many Beta and VHS machines are equipped with four heads. Depending on brand and model, heads may be placed either 90° apart (D), or as indicated in E.

(F) Five heads: Latest deluxe VHS machines have five heads. These machines offer even clearer images in still, scan and slow-motion modes.

Head-Gap Width — As just mentioned, the head gap should be the same width as the video track. Each speed records the video track with a different width.

The obvious solution is to have the head gap no wider than the smallest track. This way, you won't have any problems with a wide-track head picking up information from adjacent narrow, slow-speed tracks.

But this makes for compromises when a narrow head is used to try to pick up signals from the faster, wider-tracked speeds. You'll have trouble getting clear still frames. And, special effects like slow motion and fast scan can be a problem.

More Heads — The solution to the problem of clear still-frames and special effects is to use more heads. In addition to the required two heads, some manufacturers add an extra set for a second recording speed or for optimum playback of effects. The result is a four-head VCR. Some VCRs have only one additional special head. These are three-head units. Others have three special heads, resulting in a five-head VCR.

With an extra set of heads, the VCR can use two heads to do all the recording. Often, the other two will let you do freeze frames and picture search in all playback speeds. Therefore, you aren't limited to special effects in the slow speed for which the narrower record-head gaps are optimized.

In a four-head VCR, the special playback heads usually have a wider head gap. This is the area between the poles of the head. The head gap covers an area wider than the video tracks. This way, four-head machines can offer more features. That's also why they cost more than two-head models.

AUDIO AND ERASE HEADS

Video heads alone do not a VCR make. The role of video heads is to record and play back the picture. Other heads are required to record and play back the audio and control information. Additionally, there must be some way to erase it all when you want to. The ability to reuse a videocassette is one of the most important benefits of video over motion-picture film.

This illustrates the differences between audio dub and sound-on-sound, discussed in the text on page 45.

Audio- and Control-Track-Head Combination—In a VCR, the audio head is usually combined with the control-track head in a single "stack." To use as few parts as possible, VCR engineers combine the audio and control-track heads into one. This is accomplished easily because the tracks occupy different areas on the videotape.

Unlike video signals, which are recorded diagonally with a rotating-head assembly, audio and control signals are recorded parallel to the tape edge. This is the same method used in audiotape recorders.

Erase-Head Location—The erase head in a VCR is also similar to the one you'll find in audio recording. The erase head is positioned ahead of all the other heads in a VCR. Its job is to eliminate *all* information from the tape before it reaches

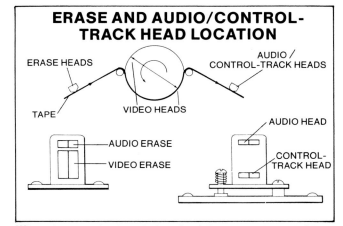

ERASE AND AUDIO/CONTROL-TRACK HEAD LOCATION

ERASE HEADS

AUDIO / CONTROL-TRACK HEADS

TAPE

VIDEO HEADS

AUDIO ERASE

VIDEO ERASE

AUDIO HEAD

CONTROL-TRACK HEAD

When the tape is threaded and moving through the VCR, it first passes over the video- and audio-erase heads. The video heads are next and then audio/control-track heads.

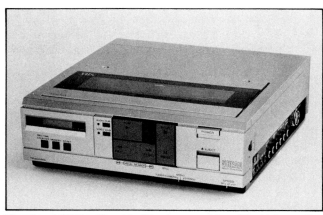

Five-head VCRs, like this Minolta portable, offer high-quality special effects.

Professional VCRs such as this VHS unit offer flying erase heads to avoid picture break-up. This feature may be added to home units in the future.

the recording heads. This includes visual, audio and control-track information.

There is a space in the tape path from the erase and video heads. As a result, a short length of tape is between the two heads when you start to record. This means that you won't be wiping the complete tape clean. The result is interference, called *break-up,* at the spot on the tape where the VCR goes into the record mode. It appears on the screen as a choppy picture.

To avoid picture break-up, manufacturers could add a special set of erase heads in the video-head drum. Today, you'll find these in professional recorders only because of price. They're called *flying erase heads* because they rotate with the video heads.

The erase head in a VCR is divided to allow erasure of only a portion of the tape. As a result, you can keep the visuals you've recorded on the tape while eliminating the original audio and adding a new sound track. You'll find this feature on most VCRs. It's called *audio dub.*

If you activate the audio head but *not* the erase head, you get a new sound track in addition to the old one on some machines. This results in a combination of both. It allows you to add music or commentary over the sounds originally recorded with the image. In a home VCR, this capability is usually referred to as *sound-on-sound.*

You may be wondering why we're telling you about features you may find only in professional video recorders. There are two reasons. First, you should understand that some limitations are inherent in the design of home-VCR equipment.

Second, we want you to be aware of features that may "trickle down" to home models. In fact, many of the impressive features we discuss in today's home units were once available only in professional video equipment. Home-video manufacturers are delivering as many features as possible at the most reasonable price.

MOTORS, DRIVES AND BELTS

We've been discussing tape and other things moving around inside the VCR. You'd think there would be a motor or two driving it all. You're right! In fact, there are many devices inside a VCR that must be driven by motors.

These include the supply and take-up sides of the cassette, and the scanner. There's also the *capstan,* a motor-driven roller that makes the tape pass the head drum at the correct speed.

All these items must be made to turn. And some of them must move in sync with the other devices for the VCR to operate properly.

Transport Motors—The jobs that motors have in a VCR depend on the design of the particular machine. If, for example, there is little space inside the VCR and economy of parts is important, two motors are used to drive almost everything. Various rotating components are connected by a series of belts and pulleys. This type of design has been used in the past for a number of machines, including the professional 3/4-inch-format decks.

This design has its drawbacks. Belts stretch,

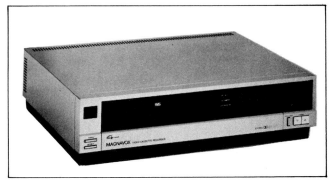

Front-loading is a feature of this Magnavox VCR. Some VCRs incorporate as many as six motors, one of which is used for loading.

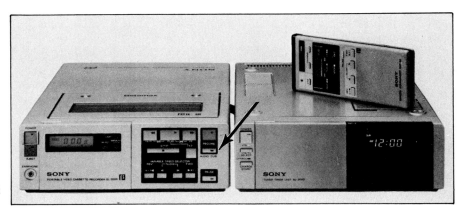

You'll find audio-dub capability on most home VCRs.

VHS BELT & PULLEY SCHEMATIC

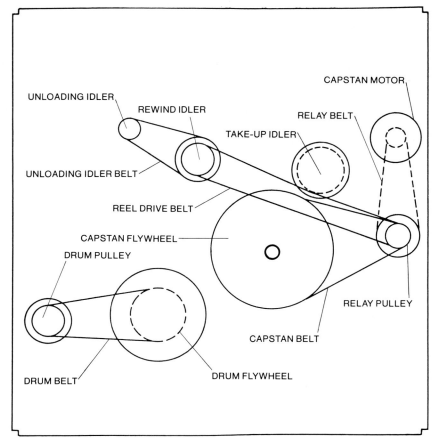

CAPSTAN MOTOR

UNLOADING IDLER

REWIND IDLER

RELAY BELT

TAKE-UP IDLER

UNLOADING IDLER BELT

REEL DRIVE BELT

CAPSTAN FLYWHEEL

DRUM PULLEY

RELAY PULLEY

CAPSTAN BELT

DRUM BELT

DRUM FLYWHEEL

(WITH VCR STANDING ON ITS END)

BETA SIX-MOTOR SCHEMATIC

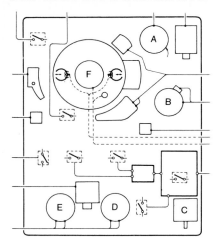

Above: Many current models use individual motors for specific jobs. You can see by the schematic that this front-loading VCR has six motors, including one for loading the cassette. A: Threading Motor. B: Capstan Motor. C: Cassette Loading Motor. D: Take-Up Reel Motor. E: Supply Reel Motor. F: Drum Motor. (Courtesy Sony Corporation of America)

Left: Older VCR models used belts and pulleys to drive the scanner and cassette reels because these VCRs had only one or two drive motors. (Courtesy JVC Company of America)

and must be replaced. As belts age, the VCR may begin to malfunction occasionally. For example, you might assume that you're making what you think is a fine recording. But then you discover that the cassette won't play back properly on another machine, or even on your own VCR after the belt is replaced! It's important that belts be in good condition to guarantee that everything in the VCR operates at the correct speed.

Multiple Motors—Just as higher-priced audio-tape recorders use three motors—one each for take-up and supply reel, with a third to drive the capstan—high-quality VCRs use multiple-motor drive systems.

In VCRs, there may be as many as *six* motors. The fourth can be used for threading. A fifth can drive the scanner. And the sixth can be used for loading. That way, belts are eliminated, making the machine more reliable.

Tuner and Timer

So far, we've concentrated on the inner workings of the recorder portion of the VCR. An all-important feature of home VCRs is their ability to record broadcast-television signals. A tabletop VCR can do this because it has a *built-in tuner and timer*. When a portable VCR is connected to a separate tuner/timer unit, it also can record broadcast signals. Some portables feature a built-in tuner/timer.

To simplify matters, we'll use the term *tuner* to refer to the separate tuner/timer used with a portable VCR.

There's nothing unusual about tuner operation in a VCR. It doesn't matter whether the tuner is a "click-type" mechanical tuner or one of the electronic versions.

Simply, you use the tuner to select the desired broadcast signal. The signal is then separated in the VCR's tuner and associated circuits into the audio and video signals and recorded on tape.

The new generation of tuners has cable-ready features. The tuner's range has been increased so you can select those extra channels that aren't used for conventional broadcast transmissions.

A video tuner serves the same function whether it's part of your TV, a large-screen projection

Few portable VCRs offer a built-in tuner as does this portable VCR in Sharp's My Video series.

Every component in this family's video home-entertainment center has a video tuner: the large-screen TV (right), tabletop VCR (center left) and portable tuner/timer (bottom left). The audio receiver on the top shelf next to the TV has an audio tuner. This means that each unit can be used individually to tune in broadcasts.

TV or VCR. It selects the signal that you wish to view on a screen. This signal can be sent over the air or through a cable. After the signal is selected, the tuner and its associated circuits convert the combined *radio frequency (RF)* signal into separate audio and video signals. These are processed and then either recorded on tape or viewed on a TV screen—or both.

Some Technical Talk—Video and audio television signals can't be sent over the air separately. They're added to a carrier frequency. They're modulated and combined for transmission as an RF signal.

To record the RF signal brought into your home via an antenna or cable wire, the VCR needs a tuner. The VCR can operate without a tuner. But you'd only be able to record separate audio and video inputs from a camera or another VCR. Portable VCRs generally don't have a built-in tuner. That's why a portable VCR is lighter and

easier to carry around than a tabletop deck.

For most VCR shoppers, however, a tuner is a must.

Every tabletop recorder has a built-in tuner. You can purchase a tuner as an add-on for a portable VCR. As noted earlier, some unique portables include a built-in tuner. The VCR tuner functions the same way as the one that's part of the channel selector on a TV.

TUNER TYPES

There are three types of tuners found in VCRs. They are *mechanical, electronic* and *frequency-synthesized.*

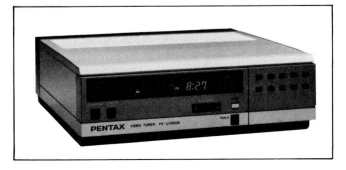

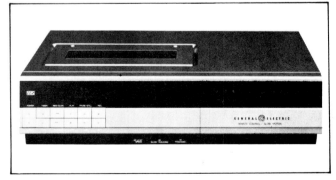

Left: Most portable VCRs can record off the air only when they're attached to a separate tuner/timer, such as this Pentax PV-U1000A tuner/timer. Above: With this General Electric tabletop VCR and similar units, you can arrange your favorite TV channels in any order, using the 12-position channel-selector panel on the right side.

27

Random access is a feature of this Quasar frequency-synthesized VCR. All you have to do is enter the channel numbers on the keypad in the center of the front of the unit. The channel you select will either be stored in the timer's memory, recorded by the VCR or viewed on the TV.

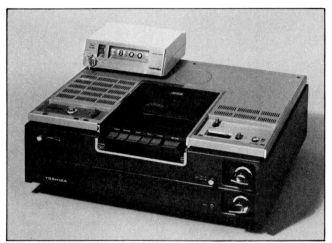

On early Beta home-video units like this Toshiba, the timer was separate from the VCR. Often, it was offered as an option and was plugged into the back of the unit.

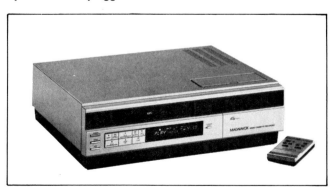

While you're away, you can record two events during a two-week period with this front-loading Magnavox tabletop.

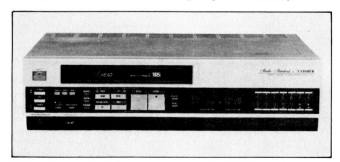

This cable-ready Fisher can tune in up to 105 channels.

You can spot a VCR with a mechanical tuner by its characteristic dials—one for UHF and one for VHS.

Mechanical Tuner—A mechanical tuner in a VCR works the same way as the identical mechanical tuner would if it were installed in a TV.

A series of metal contacts—arranged around a circular hub—is connected to electrical components that tune the specific channels. Movement of the tuner arm across these contacts gives the mechanical tuner its characteristic click.

Mechanical tuners are found on some low-end VCRs. There's nothing wrong with having this type. But a mechanical tuner limits your use of the VCR's potential.

Its timer can program the VCR to record only one event in advance in a 24-hour period. With a mechanical tuner, you can record one program while watching another. You can do the same with an electronic tuner. However, an electronic tuner allows you to preset the VCR to record a number of events over many days.

An electronic tuner is more reliable than its mechanical counterpart. It has fewer parts subject to wear. It allows you to change channels using a remote control. Generally, with a mechanical tuner, you use the remote only as a pause control.

High-end models, an increasing number of step-up models and even some leader models offer an electronic tuner.

Electronic Tuner—In both TV and VCR technology, the mechanical tuner is gradually being replaced by the electronic tuner. This uses a series of variable electronic devices—often with

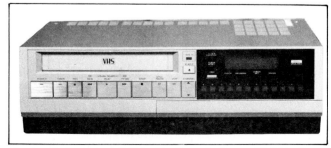

Electronic tuner/programmable timer in Sears 53161 allows for unattended recording of up to four events in a two-week period.

the aid of quartz crystal—for better frequency stability.

Each channel position on an electronically tuned VCR is a *separate* tuner. Therefore, with this feature, you can select any available TV channels that you like. And, you can have them appear on the channel-selector panel in any order you desire. So, if you're tired of seeing TV channels listed in standard numerical order, you can now start from 13 and work backward on your VCR tuner. You can also mix and mingle VHF and UHF stations on the VCR tuner.

When shopping for a VCR, compare the location of channel-setting controls. Are the controls convenient and easy to use? How do you make settings? Some machines are more confusing to set than others.

Frequency-Synthesized Tuner—Another feature, *random access,* is the latest and most advanced use of electronic tuning. With random-access-equipped tuning, you can enter the channel number into a keypad directly, instead of selecting the number on the channel-selector panel. This type of tuner is called *frequency-synthesized.*

This top-of-the-line tuner is quartz controlled. It offers simple access to a channel. All you do is press the number on a keypad. There's no need for fine-tuning or fooling around with all those little thumbwheels found in most electronic tuners.

Using the frequency-synthesized tuner's remote control is the ultimate in state-of-the-art, easy-chair tuning from across the room. You'll never run out of channel presets!

Automatic Fine Tuning (AFT)—AFT is important on all VCRs that don't have a frequency-synthesized tuner. This is found in many TV sets and FM radios. You need AFT because it helps tune a channel even if you haven't been exact in your tuning. It also automatically adjusts tuning on an older machine with a tuner that has drifted slightly. Typically, to use AFT, you turn a thumbwheel until reception is better.

Although most VCR tuners include AFT, some don't have a switch that turns the AFT off. Make sure the unit you buy has this switch. It'll help you tune a station accurately.

TIMER

The timer includes microprocessor chips of the same type that control automobile fuel-injection systems or microwave-oven timers. In a VCR, the timer is connected to a clock and a memory. You use pushbuttons to indicate the various time settings on the timer, and channel selections on the tuner. The timer sends your instructions from its memory at the appropriate time.

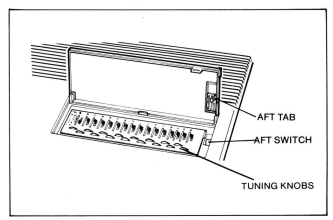

AFT TAB
AFT SWITCH
TUNING KNOBS

If you don't have a frequency-synthesized tuner, be sure the tuner has an AFT (also called an *automatic fine setting)* switch that you can turn off. With AFT, you can bring in a better signal. (Courtesy Minolta Corporation)

Some VCRs have a quartz timer. This type is precise. It requires resetting only twice a year.

Hitachi VT-7 portable package lets you tune in as many as 133 channels by using ten buttons on front of tuner/timer.

For manufacturers, it was simple to add a timer to the tuner and VCR package. Basically, all they did was slightly modify a simple clock circuit and attach it to a VCR. The clock then tells the VCR when to turn on and off.

Because early home VCRs had mechanical tuners, the user had to change channels manually. Therefore, the timer could turn the VCR on and off only once in a 24-hour period for a pre-set channel.

This is simple and effective. It's still found today in some basic VCRs. However, this design isn't very flexible. There's no way to record more than one program on more than a single channel with only one setting.

That's where the electronic tuner came to the rescue. It doesn't require manual switching to change channels. So the electronic tuner can be connected to a timer controlled by a microprocessor chip. The chip can store information to record as many events as its designers wish.

When you push the correct buttons, you can leave and let the VCR's memory do the rest. Your instructions can be for the unit to record several different shows. They can even be on different channels and at different times! This is called *multi-event programmability.*

Electronic Clock—The timer gets its instructions from the built-in memory. The timer's electronic clock does the prompting. VCR manuals often refer to the clock separately, so it's worthy of discussion here.

The clock is similar to electronic clocks found in cars or clock radios. It's part of the timer chip.

How does it keep track of time? Most clocks base their timing circuits on the 60-cycle AC-power standard in the U.S., Canada and Mexico. This 60-cycle frequency is quite stable. Because it has the same number of cycles as there are seconds in a minute, you have a hint as to how the clock in a VCR functions.

JVC front-loading D-series HR-D225U VCR is cable-ready. It also offers stereo sound and Dolby noise reduction. All controls are on the front panel.

The microprocessor chip counts these cycles. In effect, it calculates time from them. As long as the power is stable, the clock will be accurate. Unattended recordings are then made at the correct time. Many machines offer a battery backup system that retains the information in the timer's memory for a short time if there's a power failure. Sometimes this backup can last as long as one hour.

Some VCRs don't use an AC-timed clock. Instead, they feature a *quartz clock*. In this, the timing pulses are derived from the vibrations of a quartz crystal fed from the VCR's DC power supply. This is the same technique that operates digital watches.

Which is better? It depends on how much of a stickler you are about exact timing. Quartz timers are more accurate. You have to adjust them once every six months, as opposed to once a month for AC-timed clocks.

CABLE-READINESS

An important part of the tuner/timer discussion is a feature that's increasing home-VCR capabilities. Some machines feature a tuner that can also pick up signals from channels used by cable-television systems. These models are called *cable-ready.*

With a cable-ready VCR, it is easier to use your VCR to record cable-TV programs while you're away from the machine. Channel selection is limited if you use a unit with a mechanical tuner.

When your home is connected to a cable-TV system, a cable-ready tuner in your home-video recording system offers more flexibility. It allows tuning in a number of the mid-, super- and sometimes hyper-band channels used to transmit special signals without a cable-converter box.

A non-cable-ready tuner will record programming on these bands only when the cable company's converter box is used. However, you may not be able to use some of the tuner's remote-control capabilities when the converter box is connected.

You don't need a cable-ready tuner to use your VCR to record off the air if you have cable-TV service. But it's easier when the VCR is cable-ready.

Don't think you're getting something for nothing with a cable-ready unit, however. A cable-ready tuner won't decode scrambled channels used for pay-TV services such as Home Box Office (HBO). You need a special hookup. We discuss connecting your equipment to cable systems in Chapter 7.

Cable-readiness is something you should consider when shopping for a video tuner. But you may not have cable now. Or it may not be offered in your area. If this is the case, you might not need to spend the extra money for a cable-ready tuner. You can always use a non-cable-ready tuner with the converter box supplied by the cable company. Don't buy something you don't need just to have the latest equipment.

Keep in mind, too, that although all cable-ready tuners are electronic, not all electronic tuners are cable-ready. Be sure to read the specifications. Salespeople don't always know or understand which capabilities the equipment offers. If you're not sure about a particular model, contact the distributor direct. Addresses are in the Source List.

There may be many more cable channels available on your cable system than there are channel presets on the VCR you're considering. If you're one of the growing number of people receiving dozens of channels from a cable system, you might consider a VCR with a frequency-synthesized tuner.

A further complication is that some cable companies are converting their equipment so a special converter box will be *required*. As a result, even if your equipment is cable-ready, you may still have to use a supplied converter. Because this is happening *now,* we can't make a definitive statement.

When you're ready to go shopping, contact your local cable service and tell them your plans. Ask for advice. There's certainly no need to purchase a more-expensive cable-ready VCR if you can't take advantage of that capability without a cable-company-supplied converter box.

How to Choose a VCR

We've discussed some of the basic details about VCR design. Now we get into more specifics about standard features on basic VCRs and those found only on higher-priced machines.

We provide you with a buyer's guide and answer many of the questions you no doubt have. We offer pointers to keep in mind when you're ready to buy so you'll get the best deal for your money. As you read this information, keep the checklist on page 143 handy.

Wondering whether to buy or rent? We discuss that in Chapter 6. There, you'll also find a brief look into the future. By the end of Chapter 6, you'll have a better idea if the time is right for you to invest in home video. And, you'll know more about the type of equipment for your needs and budget.

VCRs are available with many brand names and model designations. In the VCR world, there are differences, not only among brands, but model lines, too.

OEMs

Although VCRs are sold under a variety of brand names, there are actually very few manufacturers. When a distributor buys a model for marketing, the manufacturer is called the *original equipment manufacturer,* or *OEM.* It's important to know something about OEMs when shopping for a VCR.

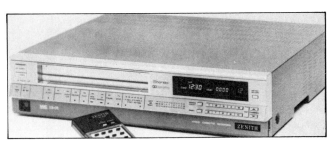

JVC Hi-Fi HR-D 725U VCR (top left) is basically the same machine as Zenith's VC4000 (top right). JVC builds both of these VHS units. The only differences between General Electric's 1CVP4022X (left) and Magnavox VR8471 (right) are cosmetic. Matsushita is the OEM for both VHS portables.

VCR OEM AND FORMAT CHART

BRAND	FORMAT	OEM	BRAND	FORMAT	OEM
Aiwa	Beta	Aiwa	Olympus	VHS	Matsushita
Akai	VHS	Akai	Panasonic	VHS	Matsushita
Canon	VHS	Matsushita	J.C. Penney	VHS	Matsushita
Curtis Mathes	VHS	Matsushita	Pentax	VHS	Hitachi
Emerson	VHS	Mitsubishi	Philco	VHS	Matsushita
Fisher	VHS	Sanyo	Pioneer*	Beta	Pioneer
General Electric	VHS	Matsushita	Quasar	VHS	Matsushita
Hitachi	VHS	Hitachi	Radio Shack	VHS	Sanyo
Jensen	VHS	JVC	RCA	VHS	Hitachi
JVC	VHS	JVC	Sansui	VHS	JVC
Kenwood	VHS	JVC	Sanyo	Beta	Sanyo
Konica*	VHS	JVC	Sears	Beta	Sanyo and Toshiba
Magnavox	VHS	Matsushita		VHS	Hitachi
Marantz	Beta	Toshiba	Sharp	VHS	Sharp
Minolta	VHS	Hitachi	Sony	Beta	Sony
Mitsubishi	VHS	Mitsubishi	Sylvania	VHS	Matsushita
Montgomery Ward	VHS	Various	Teknika*	Beta	General
Nakamichi*	Beta	Nakamichi	Toshiba	Beta	Toshiba
NEC	Beta	NEC	Video Concepts	VHS	Mitsubishi
	VHS	NEC	Zenith	VHS	JVC
Nikon*	VHS	Matsushita			

* Licensed, proposed, reported or announced but not imported or sold in North America as of 3/84.

A VCR may appear under eight or more different brand names, with minor technical or cosmetic differences, although manufactured by the same company, You may be able to buy your dream machine for less money under a different brand than the one whose advertising originally caught your eye.

If the lower-priced VCR looks the same and the specifications are the same, odds are it's the same machine. Check the dimensions, number of heads and tuner/timer capabilities.

The accompanying chart tells you about OEMs. Recently, American marketers have been asking their OEMs in Japan for special features. These engineering "exclusives" help differentiate the brands made by the same OEM.

When you know the name of a brand's OEM, make sure the models you're comparing are the same. After you've done that, you can throw brand loyalties aside because—even with some cosmetic differences—a Matsushita is still a Matsushita, for example. That's true whether the VCR is carrying the Panasonic, Quasar, Philco or some other brand name on the outside.

One thing to note is that mass merchandisers such as Sears Roebuck, Montgomery Ward and J.C. Penney may change their OEMs more frequently than the major brands. Also, some companies marketing VCRs use different OEMs for their tabletop and portable units.

VCR MARKET SHARE*

1983 Rank	Brand	Format	1983 % Share	1982 Rank
1	RCA	VHS	16.0	1
2	Panasonic	VHS	15.0	2
3	Sony	Beta	7.0	3
4	General Electric	VHS	5.5	4
5	Fisher	VHS	5.0	12
6	Sanyo	Beta	5.0	7
7	JVC	VHS	5.0	5
8	Sears	both	4.65	10
9	Magnavox	VHS	4.65	8
10	Quasar	VHS	4.6	9
11	Hitachi	VHS	4.0	11
12	Sharp	VHS	3.0	14
13	Zenith	Beta	2.6	6
14	Mitsubishi (MGA)	VHS	2.0	16
15	Sylvania	VHS	2.0	13
16	Montgomery Ward	VHS	1.5	18
17	J.C. Penny	VHS	1.5	15
18	Toshiba	Beta	1.2	17
19	Curtis Mathes	VHS	1.0	19
20	Philco	VHS	0.9	21

TOP 20 Brands   TOTAL   92.1

* These are the latest figures available at time of printing. Information supplied is an indicator of relative sales for 1982 and 1983. As you can see, the market changes from year to year. In 1983, VCR sales totaled 4,091,000, double 1982 sales. Projected sales for 1984 are 5,500,000 units. (Chart used with permission of Television Digest, Inc. Copyright 1984. Sales figures from EIA.)

TABLETOP VCR CONTROLS

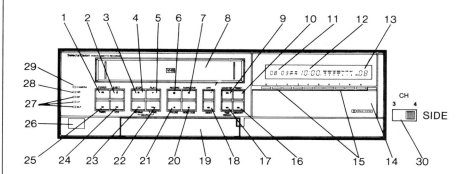

FRONT

1. POWER
2. EJECT
3. STOP
4. DEW INDICATOR (ON STOP BUTTON)
5. PLAY
6. RECORD
7. AUDIO DUB
8. TAPE SLOT (FRONT-LOADING)
9. COUNTER-DISPLAY BUTTON
10. COUNTER RESET
11. TIME-REMAINING/COUNTER DISPLAY
12. ELECTRONIC-CLOCK DISPLAY
13. CHANNEL-INDICATOR DISPLAY
14. TIMER CONTROLS DOOR
15. CHANNEL-SELECTOR BUTTONS
16. MEMORY SWITCH
17. TIME-REMAINING DISPLAY BUTTON
18. INDEX (OR TAB) MARKER
19. SECONDARY CONTROL DOOR
20. VIDEO DUB (INSERT EDITING) CONTROL
21. PAUSE
22. FAST-FORWARD/SEARCH
23. REWIND/SEARCH
24. VCR/TV BUTTON
25. TIMER SWITCH
26. REMOTE RECEIVER
27. RECORDING-SPEED DISPLAY
28. DOLBY NOISE-REDUCTION LIGHT
29. CAMERA-INDICATOR LIGHT

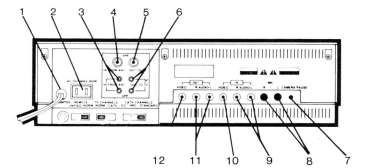

REAR

1. AC POWER CORD
2. AC OUTLET
3. UHF INPUT
4. VHF INPUT
5. VHF OUTPUT
6. UHF OUTPUT
7. CAMERA REMOTE-PAUSE INPUT
8. MICROPHONE INPUT (LEFT AND RIGHT)
9. AUDIO INPUT (LEFT AND RIGHT)
10. VIDEO INPUT
11. AUDIO OUTPUT (LEFT AND RIGHT)
12. VIDEO OUTPUT

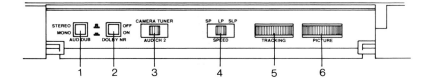

CONTROLS BEHIND SECONDARY CONTROL DOOR

1. AUDIO DUB (STEREO/MONO)
2. DOLBY NOISE-REDUCTION SWITCH
3. CAMERA/TUNER SWITCH (WITH STEREO-INPUT CHOICE)
4. RECORDING-SPEED SWITCH
5. TRACKING CONTROL
6. PICTURE ADJUSTMENT

Diagrams of controls for a high-end tabletop stereo VHS VCR. (Courtesy RCA Corporation)

PORTABLE VCR CONTROLS

VCR
FRONT

1. RECORDING TIME/COUNTER DISPLAY
2. CASSETTE HOLDER
3. AUDIO-DUB BUTTON
4. PLAY BUTTON
5. RECORD BUTTON
6. STOP BUTTON
7. POWER SWITCH
8. TAPE-SPEED SELECTOR
9. EJECT BUTTON
10. AUDIO-INPUT SELECTOR SWITCH
11. PAUSE BUTTON
12. FAST-FORWARD BUTTON
13. REWIND BUTTON
14. VIDEO-DUB BUTTON
15. RESET BUTTON
16. COUNTER-MEMORY BUTTON
17. RECORDING-TIME/COUNTER-SELECTOR BUTTON
18. TRACKING-CONTROL KNOB

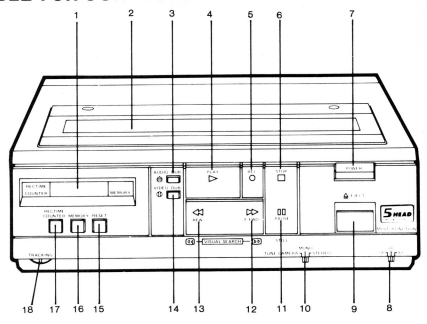

SIDE

19. DATE-SELECT BUTTON, DATE-ADVANCE BUTTON
20. NOISE-REDUCTION/SOUND-WITH-SOUND/DATE-SELECTOR SWITCH
21. REMOTE-CONTROL JACK
22. MICROPHONE JACK
23. AUDIO IN
24. AUDIO OUT
25. VIDEO IN
26. VIDEO OUT
27. EXTERNAL-BATTERY (DC) JACK
28. CAMERA JACK
29. RF-CONVERTOR SWITCH

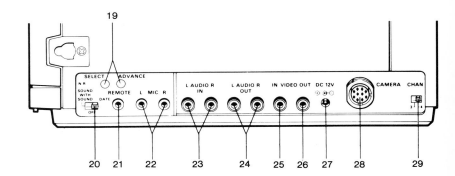

REAR

30. BATTERY-EJECT BUTTON
31. BATTERY COMPARTMENT
32. RF-OUT/TUNER-JACK COVER
33. TUNER JACK
34. RF OUT
35. VERTICAL-JITTER CONTROLS

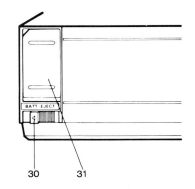
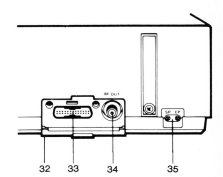

Diagrams of controls for a high-end portable VHS VCR and tuner/timer. (Courtesy Minolta Corporation)

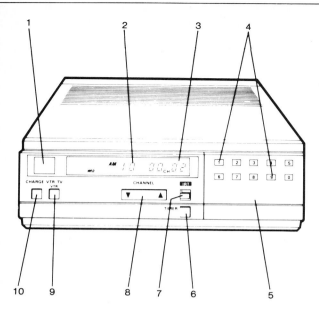

TUNER/TIMER
FRONT

1 INFRARED RECEIVING SECTION
2 DIGITAL-CLOCK/TIMER DISPLAY
3 CHANNEL DISPLAY
4 CHANNEL-SELECTOR BUTTONS
5 TUNER/TIMER CONTROLS COVER
6 TIMER SWITCH
7 INSTANT-RECORDING TIMER (IRT) BUTTON
8 CHANNEL-SELECTOR BAR
9 VCR/TV SELECTOR
10 CHARGE SWITCH

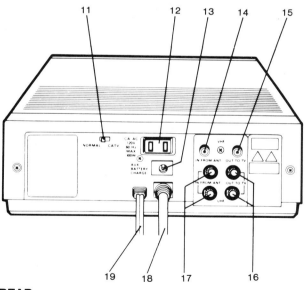

REAR

11 NORMAL/CATV SELECTOR
12 AC OUTLET
13 AUXILIARY BATTERY-CHARGE TERMINAL
14 VHF-ANTENNA INPUT
15 VHF-ANTENNA OUTPUT
16 UHF-ANTENNA OUTPUT
17 UHF-ANTENNA INPUT
18 VCR CONNECTOR CORD
19 AC-POWER CORD

Many leader models offer electronic tuning.

General Electric's top-of-the-line VHS Hi-Fi VCR offers almost every feature you'll ever want.

Tabletop vs. Portable

The first question you may be asking yourself is whether to buy a tabletop model or a portable. Here's a rundown of the general price classes found in each of these two VCR types. In this description, we mention many of the features offered with these models. We'll explain more about the specific features later in this chapter.

If the first question you want answered is whether to buy a camcorder, read Chapter 8 now.

TABLETOP

Tabletop models operate with household AC current. The tuner/timer is built in. The tabletop is designed to be left in place. You can't conveniently carry it around with you. If you want to connect a camera to most tabletops, you need a special adapter.

With this in mind, here's what you can expect in various price-range tabletop VCRs.

Leader Models—In VCR advertisements, you'll notice that dealers often lead off with the lowest-priced model. This is called a *leader,* or a *stripped-down* model. The dealer does that to attract your attention and draw you into the store. Once you're there, he may insist on showing and demonstrating more-expensive models.

You'll see front loading on many step-up models.

Above: Sharp VC-381 front-loading tabletop has a built-in seven-day, one-event tuner/timer. Below: Hitachi's high-end four-head VT-19A includes stereo-sound and Dolby noise-reduction capability.

The least-expensive VCRs generally have the fewest features. You may not find fast-picture scan on all of these machines. They may include a mechanical rather than electronic tuner.

Most feature a built-in clock, but are limited to one-day/one-event programming. With this, you can set the machine to make only one unattended recording in a 24-hour period.

Leader models usually offer a remote control. But it's almost always wired. Rarely does it offer more than pause and sometimes channel-change or scan buttons.

Higher-priced models offer wireless, infrared remote control, offering more functions. More on this in the next sections, on *Step-Up* and *High-End Models.*

Look closely at brand names on the leader models. Depending on the types of VCRs a brand name is buying from the Orient, you may find some units with scan capability and an electronic tuner. Often, companies such as RCA and Zenith will market a VCR with these added features to meet competition from higher-priced units sold under Japanese brand names.

Depending on where you shop, you should be able to find leader model tabletop VCRs for less than $400.

Step-Up Models—Dealers use this mid-range line to move the buyer up from the leader model. They hope the customer will step up to a higher-priced VCR. Step-up VCR models fall somewhere between leader models and the ones with all the "bells and whistles."

Step-up models usually feature an electronic tuner with multi-day/multi-event programmable tuner/timer. In mid-range VCR lines, you'll even find some front-loading and cable-ready models.

Fast scan is standard in step-up models. The remote control may include stop, start and channel-change functions in addition to pause. And, although the remote is usually wired, there is often a wireless remote-control option. The dealer may throw in this wireless control on a special sale.

High-End Models—These VCRs are the luxury models. They're at the top of the price and features scale. High-end machines usually offer most of the features mentioned later in this chapter.

What this means is that you'll find a full-capability wireless remote control, multi-day/multi-event programmable timer and cable-ready tuner. Some offer stereo sound with noise reduction, others are Hi-Fi. And, they may feature an electronic tape-time counter and tab marker.

These VCRs generally have four heads and offer special effects for playback of material recorded at any speed. Some include a fifth head for better images and more effects.

PORTABLE

Shopping for a portable VCR system is at the same time easier and more confusing than buying a tabletop. It's simpler because most companies offer only one portable VCR in their model lineup at a given time. But, there are more components and features to consider.

A complete portable system includes a recorder and separate tuner/timer. The recorder is either the leader model or high-end. This depends on its weight, size and number of heads. When portables were first introduced, they weighed about 15 pounds with the battery. Today, that has been reduced to about 10 pounds or less.

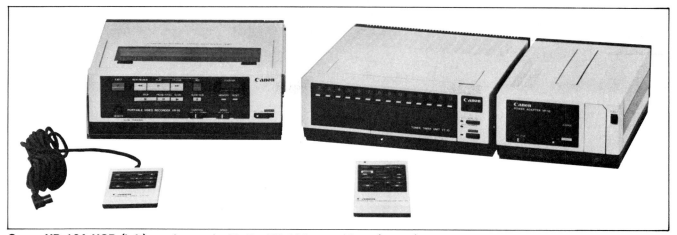

Canon VR-10A VCR (left) can be used with the VT-10A tuner/timer (center) or the VP-10A power adapter/battery charger (right). When connected to the tuner/timer, the VCR can use the tuner/timer as an AC power source or battery charger. VP-10A can recharge the battery, or acts as a power source if AC-power is available and you don't need mobility. To record off-the-air or cable signals, the VR-10A must be mated to the VT-10A. Also shown are the two types of remote control, one wired for the recorder, and one wireless for the tuner/timer.

Manufacturers generally ask you to pay more for a lighter VCR, and for the special effects delivered by a recorder with four or more heads. A company may offer more than one complete portable package—VCR and tuner/timer—within a price range. If so, the differences generally are in the design of the tuner/timer. Although the recorder is usually the same in each package, this isn't always the case.

Purchasing a portable can be even more confusing when a manufacturer offers more than one recorder. However, this practice is not common.

Leader Models—The lowest-priced portables allow recording only from a camera or another VCR. You can't record off the air because there's no tuner/timer.

The price of a leader-model portable usually includes a separate AC adapter/battery charger. With this charger, you can charge the batteries and operate the portable from household AC current.

Step-Up Models—These feature a recorder with two heads, similar to the leader-model package. However, a step-up package usually includes a *separate* tuner/timer. In most cases, the tuner/timer offers only one-day/one-event programming. It allows you to operate the portable from household AC current. And, because

Right: Toshiba's high-end Beta package, V-X34, includes a recorder that weighs only 5.5 pounds. Eight-event, 14-day timer is cable-ready. It accepts 105 channels. Far Right: Marketers are adding stereo recorders with Dolby noise reduction to their portable VCR lines. This is the Olympus VC-103.

Magnavox VR8470BK is sold with a plug-in AC adapter as part of the package. The VCR also works on battery power.

the tuner/timer includes a built-in AC adapter/battery charger, it'll charge the batteries, too.

High-End Models—To record more than one TV program in a 24-hour period when you're not at home, you'll probably have to buy a high-end portable. Some high-end portable VCRs offer stereo with noise reduction.

The tuner/timer in a high-end portable system is more versatile than the one you'll find in step-up packages. It can be programmed to record as many as eight or more events over a two- or three-week period.

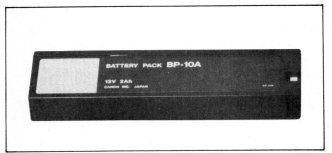

On the outside, most standard batteries look the same. They are not necessarily interchangeable from one VCR to another, however.

Above: Piano-key approach used on this early Magnavox VCR has given way to an easier and more efficient way to select functions. Below: Many current models, such as this Zenith VCR, offer soft-touch electronic controls.

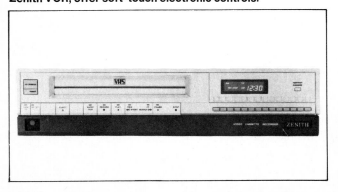

Compare the packages you're interested in. Do they all include the same basic recorder—remembering our earlier discussion about OEMs—with a different tuner/timer? Use the information in this book as a guideline in your search.

Batteries—Before we explain VCR features, we should mention that a battery is a critical part of the portable system. This is what makes the VCR truly "portable." However, to discuss batteries in any detail here would require a lot of information geared toward specific VCR makes and models.

As we explain in the specifications section later in this chapter, some VCRs consume more power than others. There are low- and high-capacity batteries, too. A portable VCR comes with one battery. Typically, this will power the VCR and camera for about 30 to 60 minutes before requiring recharging.

You can recharge the battery in the VCR, or purchase an accessory AC adapter/battery charger. The charger also acts as a power source for the VCR by transforming standard AC house current into the DC current required by the portable VCR and video camera.

You can buy additional batteries with the same brand name as your VCR, but there are also many types and styles available from aftermarket suppliers. These include low- and high-capacity types or belt, shoulder or backpack types. We illustrate some of these in Chapter 5. For more information about batteries for your specific model, ask your video dealer or contact the suppliers listed in the Source List at the back of this book.

Which Features Do You Need?

We've discussed some of the most important features of today's VCRs. But there are many others to consider. The question still remains: Which ones do you *need?*

Here, we tell you about what's available. It's up to you to decide which ones you need. It's also important to realize that, to get one particular feature, you may have to choose a model with a feature you're not interested in. Manufacturers offer a "package" of features in each of their lines. You must search until you find the package that fulfills your needs.

Use the *VCR Buying Checklist* on page 158 to indicate those features you'll be looking for in your dream machine. You can separate which ones are musts and which are nice to have but not essential.

MECHANICAL FEATURES

Not all VCR features operate electronically. Many are still basically mechanical.

Loading—Basically, there are two types of loading: *top-loading* and *front-loading*. With top-loading models, you slip the cassette into the machine by placing it into a holder that rises out of the top of the VCR. Typically, you pop out the holder by pushing an eject button. This can be either a mechanical or electronic control. After loading the holder, you press it down to insert the cassette into the VCR. Top-loading machines require about six inches of clearance at the top.

Another aspect of top-loading is how the machine slows the rise of the cassette out of the VCR when the holder opens. The cassette elevator in some machines may be air-damped with a pneumatic system. In many, it's fluid-damped with a small, sealed hydraulic cylinder.

Both operate the same way as the standard, spring-loaded system. The damped method is gentler. It results in less vibration jarring the inside of the VCR.

A relative newcomer cropping up on some basic units and top-of-the-line models is *front-loading*. Essentially, this system eliminates the loading elevator. Instead, you feed the cassette into a slot in the front of the VCR. The cassette passes a sensor switch. Then a motorized system takes over and eases the cassette into the VCR. It drops the cassette gently into the transport

With solenoid controls, a machine can provide remote control for many VCR functions. Many VCRs offer wireless infrared remote capability, such as shown here.

Akai's VPS-7350 VHS model was introduced in 1980. It was the first home-video stereo VCR.

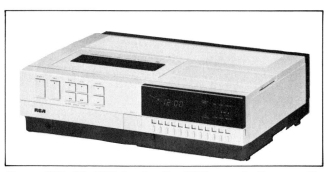

Above: With this RCA top-loading VCR, you slip the cassette into the platform that pops up when the eject button is pushed. Then push the platform down into the machine. Below: Cassette is inserted into the slot covered by the door on the front of this Sony front-loader.

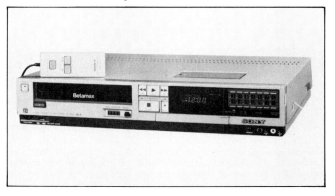

Many machines offer a four-digit mechanical counter. The counter is located below the loading slot on this NEC front-loader.

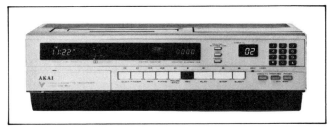

You can use an electronic real-time counter to check time used on a tape—something you can't do with other counter types. This is an Akai VCR.

mechanism. Although this system is more complicated mechanically, it is reliable.

Front-loading VCRs offer an important advantage. Less space is required above the top of the machine. If you plan to put your VCR in a cabinet or on a shelf with little top clearance, consider a front-loading machine.

There are also side-loading models, usually found only in upright-style portables. They operate much like the top-loaders.

Remember that the VCR's electronics generate heat. Be sure to leave at least one inch on all sides for ventilation—regardless of loading method.

Multi-Motor Transport—We discussed this subject briefly earlier. Multi-motor transports—the use of several motor transports and direct-drive systems—are becoming more popular. Motors do many things in a VCR, including driving the capstan and scanner, moving the reels on the cassette and threading the tape.

A VCR can get these jobs done with just two or three motors and lots of belts and pulleys. But it can work more reliably if one motor is used for each function. Although such machines are slightly more expensive, you may get your investment back in the long run because the model has fewer parts that can break or wear.

Counter—There are three different types of counter. One is mechanical and two are electronic. The mechanical type, discussed here, is driven by the transport.

Many VCRs offer a mechanical counter resembling the one found on audiotape recorders. The mechanical counter doesn't measure footage. Nor do its numbers correspond to any commonly used time or space measurement. The mechanical counter has three or four digits. We prefer the four-digit type. The counter is driven by a belt attached to the VCR's drive system.

An electronic counter uses a liquid-crystal display (LCD) or light-emitting diode (LED). It may be more reliable in the long run because it isn't driven by a belt. Instead, an electronic counter gets information from a photocell sensor.

Both mechanical and electronic counters generally count mysterious *arbitrary increments,* not tape length or time. What they do provide is a reference point for gauging videotape movement.

Some VCR models feature a *real-time counter,* also called *linear time counter.* This is explained under *Electronic Features.*

Counter-Memory—Counter-memory is a common feature. It lets you rewind the cassette to a specific point by zeroing the counter before you start recording or playing back. When you're finished, you simply turn on the counter-memory and put the VCR in rewind. When the counter reaches the 0000 spot you "marked," the VCR stops rewinding. This returns the tape to the marked point.

VCRs with this feature store only one location. When you remove the tape from the machine, the setting is no longer valid. The setting isn't a mark on the tape; rather, it's a function of resetting the counter.

It's a good feature if you plan to study a segment over and over. With counter-memory, you won't have to keep writing down the counter number. The machine will keep track of the beginning of a section you wish to see again.

Some VCRs combine counter-memory and auto-rewind. With this added feature, the VCR will go into rewind at the end of a cassette. But instead of stopping or playing back from the beginning, the machine will start up at a spot you've previously marked by zeroing the counter. It's useful if you plan to study specific parts of your tapes.

An electronic version of counter-memory is *tab marker,* explained under *Electronic Features.*

ELECTRONIC FEATURES

Some VCR features are electronic. Others, described in the next section, combine mechanics and electronics.

Audio balance control, auto rewind and stereo sound with Dolby noise reduction are features of Sylvania VC3630.

Canon portable recorder offers stereo-sound capability, Dolby noise reduction and four video heads for better special effects.

COMPARISON OF STANDARD AND HI-FI AUDIO SPECIFICATIONS

CONVENTIONAL AUDIO CHARACTERISTICS

	S/N	FREQUENCY RESPONSE	WOW AND FLUTTER	DISTORTION
BETA X2 AND VHS SP	MORE THAN 40 dB	50Hz to 11KHz	0.3%	3.0%

HI-FI AUDIO CHARACTERISTICS

	DYNAMIC RANGE	FREQUENCY RESPONSE	WOW AND FLUTTER	DISTORTION
BETA Hi-Fi (X2, X3) AND VHS Hi-Fi (SP, LP, EP)	MORE THAN 80dB	20Hz to 20KHz	LESS THAN 0.005%	LESS THAN 0.3%

Beta Hi-Fi and VHS Hi-Fi offer quality audio in all recording speeds.

Stereo Sound—When the first home VCRs were introduced in the late 1970s, their main selling point was time shift. Initially, buyers were using their VCRs to record their favorite broadcast-TV shows. They could then watch them when it was more convenient.

These machines, and many still offered today, had one audio channel. The two audio channels necessary to record and play back stereo weren't considered a desired feature because broadcast TV was transmitted with a single audio channel.

In the past few years, however, things have changed. Cable television has increased its reach. In some cities, cable companies offer programming channels transmitted with stereo sound. With the growing use of VCRs to play back prerecorded cassettes, it was only a matter of time before there was a demand for musical and other types of programming offering stereo soundtracks. Of course, you must have a stereo amplifier and speakers to take advantage of this feature.

It should come as no surprise that there is a growing number of stereo VCRs. VHS stereo machines have accommodated two audio tracks similar to audio-recording techniques. The stereo audio heads simply divide the track in half. This creates two audio channels instead of one.

A more recent development has been the arrival of Hi-Fi stereo VCRs. These machines, in both Beta and VHS, provide excellent audio reproduction. Sound fidelity approaches that of digital, audiodisc systems.

Beta Hi-Fi, introduced in 1983, achieves this high-quality audio by mixing the stereo tracks as part of the video signal during recording. No additional audio heads are required. A standard fixed audio head is included for compatibility with existing mono Beta VCRs.

The VHS approach doesn't record the audio tracks as part of the video as in Beta Hi-Fi. Instead, to record the audio, VHS uses a set of rotating heads mounted on the same drum as the video heads. The video signal is recorded *over* the audio. But because the audio and video signals are recorded at different azimuth angles—30° for audio and 6° for video—there's no interference between the two during playback. They are compatible with other stereo and mono VCRs because they are still regular audio tracks.

Some VCRs with stereo-sound capabilities include a switch that allows you to select which channel you record on. But if you want to change or add audio if you're considering a single-

Beta Hi-Fi is available in several VCR models. This is Sony's SL 2700.

channel machine, you'll want to look for audio dub or sound-on-sound capability.

Before you decide whether stereo sound is important, consider a few factors. First, if you want to use the stereo capabilities of the VCR, you must connect the unit to a stereo system. That means that you have to place the VCR near an audio receiver, amplifier or component-TV

You can benefit from the full effect of Dolby B noise-reduction-encoded prerecorded videocassettes only if you connect your home stereo system to a VCR with Dolby B noise-reduction circuitry.

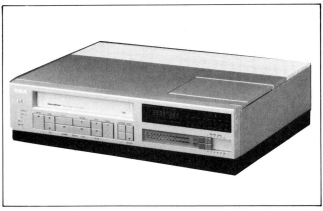

RCA and other companies offer near-digital-quality audio with their VHS Hi-Fi models. This is RCA VKT550.

system. The TV and speakers have to be in the same room so you can view the image while listening to the stereo sound.

Check the back of your audio receiver. Be sure there's an extra set of input jacks to accommodate the cables you need to connect the VCR to your audio equipment. If all the jacks are already in use, you'll have to juggle the wires around when you play back the VCR's soundtrack through your stereo system. Or you have to find another way to connect it.

Second, decide if you actually plan to use the stereo capabilities enough to justify the extra cost. If you're going to use your VCR primarily to record broadcast-TV programming, you'll have little use for stereo at this point. If your home is wired for cable-TV reception and the cable service offers stereo-sound programming, stereo-recording capability is something to consider.

Many prerecorded videocassettes are available with stereo sound. This is in anticipation of an expanded market resulting from introduction of stereo VCRs. So if you plan to buy or rent a lot of prerecorded cassettes, you might want to consider stereo capability.

You may plan to use the VCR primarily for taping with a camera. If so, stereo sound may not be a feature you want to pay more for—unless, of course, you're going to shoot a lot of musical groups.

While you're considering features such as stereo sound, remember that you may not need it *now*. But what do you think *may* happen in six months, a year or two years? Is there even a *possibility* that your interests or needs might change to the point that your equipment won't be satisfactory?

Noise Reduction—Dolby noise reduction (NR) is the most popular type of noise-reduction system. Two types are offered in VCRs: Dolby B NR and Dolby C NR.

Dolby B NR is in almost universal use among stereo VHS VCRs. Most prerecorded musical

Panasonic portable package incorporates stereo-sound capability with Dolby noise reduction.

You'll find this logo on all equipment and videocassettes recorded using Dolby noise-reduction systems. (Courtesy Dolby Laboratories Licensing Corp.)

programming and an increasing number of movie titles are recorded with Dolby B NR. The Dolby NR system in most standard split-track stereo VHS models (not the super-high-fidelity models) is the same Dolby B NR system used in audio recording and FM broadcasting.

With a split-track system, the mono track is recorded with two distinct tracks for stereo. A non-stereo VCR reads this split track as one, similar to how a mono audio recorder plays back a stereo audio tape.

It lowers high-frequency noise, which you hear as hiss. This hiss is common, especially on tapes recorded at the slow, extended-play speeds offered by VCRs. In the record mode, noise-reduction systems boost the higher audio frequencies. The amount of boost increases as the audio-signal level decreases. In playback, the system does the reverse. It restores the original frequency response by lowering the high frequencies in proportion to signal strength.

The effects of the boosts and cutbacks cancel each other. But the signal-to-noise ratio may be 5 to 10 decibels (dB) better than you would have had without an audio noise-reduction system.

An important note: Basically, all these systems do when recording is boost the high frequencies. As a result, you can play a Dolby NR-encoded tape on any non-Dolby-NR-equipped VCR, stereo or not. You'll notice only a slight increase in the high frequencies.

It's easy to remedy this: Turn down the treble control on the stereo receiver. This must be connected to the VCR to get the full effect of the two audio channels recorded on the videocassette.

When a Dolby NR-encoded tape is played back through a standard TV speaker using a VCR without a decoder, you probably won't notice any change. That's because of the generally poor sound quality from those built-in speakers.

There are other noise-reduction systems, although Dolby B NR is the most common. Dolby A NR is much more complex than B. It reduces noise across the entire frequency bandwidth, not just at the higher frequencies. Its complexity

makes it more expensive. Therefore, its use in video is limited to professional recorders.

Dolby C NR was added to some Beta machines. It uses two sets of encoders and decoders. These achieve even higher levels of noise reduction. This is an advantage when you do original recordings. Although the C system is better than B, it's intended for use when making original recordings. A VCR featuring Dolby C NR won't enhance the audio quality of a prerecorded videocassette using Dolby B NR.

Hitachi Hi-Fi VHS VT-88A records the video signal on top of the audio signal.

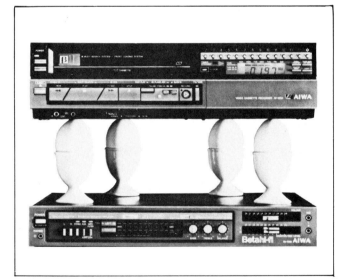

Aiwa entered the video market in 1984 with this unique approach to Beta Hi-Fi. The company's V-5 system includes a 13.7-pound portable with built-in tuner/timer (top) and a Beta Hi-Fi adapter with built-in amplifier (bottom).

 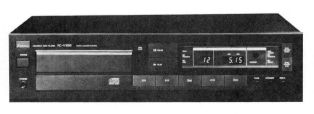

Sansui SV-R9000 stereo VCR is designed to look like the company's audio hardware. Note the similarity between the VCR at left and Sansui compact digital audio disc player at right.

Some VCRs have other noise-reduction circuits that operate only during playback. These circuits reduce noise on any cassette, regardless of the presence or absence of noise-reduction encoding on the videocassette.

Beta and VHS Hi-Fi VCRs include automatic integrated noise-reduction systems. You don't have to worry about choosing a noise-reduction system to "mate" with your Hi-Fi VCR. Some VHS Hi-Fi machines offer Dolby B NR for the longitudinal audio.

You may have heard of another noise reduction system called *dbx*. This *companding* system works by *com*pressing the entire signal during recording and then ex*panding* it again during playback. Recordings made with dbx generally don't play back well without a decoder. Therefore, although dbx is used in audiotape recording and on special records, it has not been used in home VCRs.

You may read more about dbx in the future because dbx will be used with stereo broadcast television signals. It's not important if your VCR isn't equipped with a decoder. Special stereo adapters will include a decoder, so you can provide normal audio to your VCR's inputs.

The final noise-reduction system we'll mention is the *CX system*. You may hear about it in connection with the CED and LV videodisc players. This has features more suited to videodisc technology.

It's possible that special adapters may be offered in the future. These could be for dbx, CX or other noise-reduction systems for use with specially packaged "audiophile" VCRs.

Some stereo portables don't use Dolby NR because of weight and power considerations. These units usually use other, less-complicated noise-reduction systems.

Do You Really Need Noise Reduction?— Consider how important good sound is to you. This is something only you can decide. Have the dealer play a videocassette for you on a VCR with noise reduction and then on another without it. Ask for a demonstration with a cassette recorded with noise-reduction encoding. Then try a cassette without it. If a videocassette is Dolby NR-encoded, this will be indicated on the label. Listen for the difference.

A Word to the Wise—When testing a VCR for stereo or noise reduction, make sure the dealer uses a good amplifier or stereo receiver and quality speakers. Remember, you must own this type of equipment if you want to be able to appreciate the capabilities of a VCR with stereo and noise reduction. You also have to keep in mind that the sound will be affected by the room containing the speakers. The demonstration room may be considerably different than the room used for your sound system.

Don't do your in-store sound tests through a TV set's tiny speaker. It'll be hard to hear the differences, regardless of which set of noise-reduction combinations you ask the dealer to demonstrate.

Electronic Counter—An electronic counter displays tape movement with an LED or LCD. Like its mechanical counterpart, the electronic counter is neither a footage counter nor a time counter—unless specifically listed as such in the manual. We'll get into that under *Linear Time Counter*.

Electronic counters can display letters in addition to numbers. If a manufacturer uses sensors such as moisture (dew detector), low-battery and tape-supply warnings, among others, in its VCRs, the electronic-counter display is a good way to send those messages to you.

The advantage of an electronic counter is that it's easier to read and use with functions like tab marker. It also looks more impressive and "high-tech." An electronic counter is an interesting and attractive feature, but clearly not a vital one.

Linear Time Counter—This is really the good

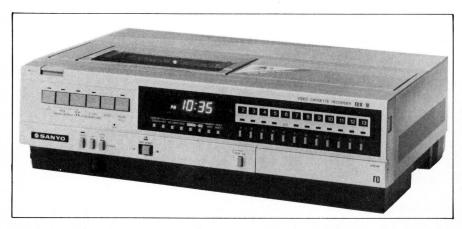

Sanyo VCR4400 is one of the least-expensive VCRs. Unit has nine-times-normal picture-speed scan in forward and reverse in Beta X3 mode and a four-digit electronic tape counter.

one. A mechanical or electronic counter measures arbitrary units. Unlike them, a linear time counter measures the real thing. It reads out directly in minutes and seconds while the tape moves in standard playback, slow-scan or fast-scan modes.

It has a special circuit that counts pulses on the videotape control track. From that, it derives the actual running time of the tape. It's a tricky and expensive bit of electronic magic. But it's a feature you'll want once you've tried it.

It's important to know that most linear time counters *don't* function in fast-forward or fast-reverse.

Audio Dub—This feature is found in VCRs in all price ranges. But many people never use it. Audio dub allows you to play back a previously recorded picture while erasing the original audio track and adding a new one. When the VCR is in the audio-dub mode, only the portion of the erase head that covers the audio track is activated. It eliminates the old track while the audio head adds a new one. During the process, the picture track is not affected.

If you like adding your own soundtrack to late-night movies recorded off the air, or providing your personal commentary to vacation footage shot with your camera, audio dub is a must. But before you decide on audio dub, read the next section discussing sound-on-sound. Then make your decision.

Sound-on-Sound—Some machines offer sound-on-sound. This is similar to audio dub except that you can add a second track without altering the original one. You're still not affecting the picture.

Sound-on-sound lets you keep the original audio track while you add your commentary, special music or other sounds. Here's an example: You've videotaped a family gathering and want to add a description of the people and the event without losing any of the chatter. To do this, the machine activates the record functions of the audio head without turning on any part of the

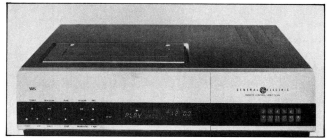

This GE VCR offers an electronic counter. It replaces the number wheels with LEDs or LCDs.

erase head. This also leaves the video portion of the tape unchanged.

Machines with sound-on-sound always include audio dub. However, machines with audio dub don't always offer sound-on-sound.

Audio-Level Control Defeat—Most VCRs automatically adjust audio-recording level. The automatic control is called *automatic gain control (AGC)* or *automatic volume control (AVC)*. This control lowers the incoming signal if it gets too loud or increases it if it's too low. The result is a consistent sound level.

However, if you plan to do a lot of music recording, you may want to be able to set audio levels as you would with your audio recorder. You can do this with a VCR if you *defeat* or work around the automatic-level control. This defeat function isn't found on many VCRs today. It may become more common with the advent of Hi-Fi VCRs.

If you want a machine with defeat capability, make sure it also includes an *audio-level indicator*. This is a set of meters or electronic bar graphs. Without a meter, the audio-level controls are useless.

Pause—All machines offer this function. **PAUSE** stops the VCR momentarily. The pause described here doesn't produce a picture on the screen from the videocassette in the VCR at the time. Still- or freeze-frame, discussed under *Special Ef-*

JVC D-Series HR-D120U has a tape-run indicator. Auto rewind, a tape counter and memory search are also offered.

fects on page 47, does provide a screen image.

The pause control lets you stop and start the VCR more quickly than would be possible by activating the **STOP** or **PLAY** buttons. After the VCR has been put in **PAUSE**, it can then be started again, almost instantly. It returns to the function the machine has been set to perform. Many people use **PAUSE** to stop the VCR from recording commercials during a show they're watching and taping at the same time.

Tape-Remaining Indicator—This is useful if you have a tendency to pop a tape into the VCR without checking to see how much is left for recording. VCRs offering this function typically have a series of indicator lights. The lights count off, in five-minute increments, the last 15 to 30 minutes left on a cassette. This is not common on VCRs. But a tape-remaining indicator might come in handy if you're absent-minded.

Sleep Switch—Do you doze off while watching TV, or consider yourself forgetful? If so, this feature may be important. With a sleep switch on the VCR, you can set the machine to turn itself off automatically at a predetermined time.

If this sounds similar to the standard timer function found on most VCRs, it is. The difference is that you don't have to fool around with timer settings. You just turn on the sleep switch and the machine does the rest.

PCM Output—You'll find this legend above a switch on the back of some VCRs. There may even be a special socket near **PCM OUT**. Do you need it? Should you look for one? What does it mean?

PCM stands for *pulse-code modulation*. This is a type of digital-recording technique. It produces very high-quality audio. PCM requires more signal bandwidth than a normal audio recorder can accept. Because of video's wider bandwidth, PCM has been incorporated into the video-recorder design. It takes up the *complete tape width,* so you cannot use this with the video picture.

By attaching a special external indicator to the VCR, you can turn the VCR into a digital audio recorder. There are a couple of important points to remember. The required adapter may cost as much as the VCR itself. And, you'll only be able to record audio on the videocassette if you use the VCR as a digital audio recorder. There won't be any room on the tape for visuals.

To optimize your VCR for this type of recording, flip the PCM switch if it has one, and connect the adapter. This causes internal adjustments in the VCR's recording process.

Suffice to say, the PCM switch is not one that many VCR buyers look for. This is especially true today with the Hi-Fi VCRs that deliver near-digital audio quality *and* pictures. And the Hi-Fi units do this without a special, separate adapter.

The adapter can be connected to the video output of any VCR. However, a PCM adapter works best with a VCR that has a PCM switch.

Timer Back-Up—Hour/minute, time and channel settings for off-air recordings are held in a volatile microprocessor memory. This is a computerlike circuit chip. The volatile memory requires continuous power to store information. If the power goes off, the memory is wiped out—even if you restore power immediately.

To prevent the VCR from losing its volatile memory, some manufacturers have added a timer back-up feature. This was originally introduced in clock radios. Timer back-up prevents loss of the memory if there's a short power outage or if you unplug the tuner/timer for a brief period.

When the AC power is on, a battery charges constantly. When the power goes off, the timer chip keeps its memory intact by drawing voltage from the battery.

Some VCRs offering this feature substitute a

Tuner/timer in JVC portable package features eight-event/two-week unattended programmability. It also has one-hour memory backup in case of power failure—a good feature to have, especially if you live in an area that has frequent blackouts.

capacitor for the battery. This is an electronic component that stores an electrical charge. Capacitors lose their charge after about 10 minutes, though.

This could be a problem if you live in an area where brownouts or blackouts are common. In this case, shop for a VCR that uses a battery for its timer back-up. If you plan to move your machine from one AC outlet to another, a timer back-up with a capacitor may suffice.

To find out exactly how long the system will retain its memory, examine the equipment literature or ask a salesperson.

Channel settings on your tuner/timer are stored in a non-volatile device. This is a diode or resistor that doesn't lose this information if the power is off.

Channel Lock—If you have small children or pets in your home, you might consider a machine with a channel lock. This prevents the channel you set from being changed accidentally when the machine is in the record mode.

It operates regardless of whether the machine is triggered by the timer or started manually. With channel lock, you'll be assured that carelessly placed fingers or paws don't replace your long-awaited recording of *Casablanca* with a cassette filled with a late-night talk show.

Stereo Adapter Output—Now that stereo TV broadcasting is almost here, VCR makers are getting ready. To make sure you can use VCRs designed before the stereo broadcast system was set, some stereo VCRs have a plug for connection to an adapter.

With this adapter, you'll be able to use the VCR to record stereo TV broadcasts. This plug is a good feature to look for on stereo or Hi-Fi VCRs.

ELECTRO-MECHANICAL FEATURES

Now it's time to explain all those other features you're anxious to hear about. We've left them for this final section because they operate as a result of a combination of the VCR's electronic and mechanical parts.

Special Effects—This term has become an important part of VCR vocabulary. Actually, it's a misnomer. What's called *special effects* is the fast and slow scan-with-picture *playback* feature in many VCRs. It's sometimes called *picture scan* and other names. This feature is found on most VCRs above leader-model level. With scan, you can view a picture faster or slower than normal speed. Actual special effects involve the *manipula-*

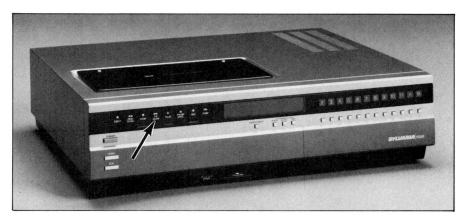

On some models, special effects are called *scan.*

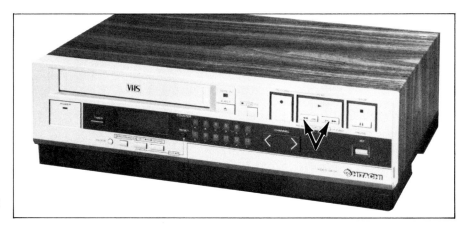

On others, special effects are referred to as *visual search.*

tion of the picture itself, or the various images. That can be done only with expensive professional equipment.

Now that we've set the record straight and corrected what we know to be a semantic injustice, we'll proceed to call them . . . *special effects.*

Early home VCRs offered a simple pause function. This halted tape movement by stopping the take-up and supply-reel motors, while releasing the tape from the capstan and pinch rollers. People used the pause function to avoid recording commercials, or to stop playback for a short time.

During pause, the tape is not in contact with the head drum. The result is no picture in pause mode. Machines with electronic functions keep the tape against the heads while maintaining the tape at a steady tension. This "frozen" image, called *still-frame* or *freeze-frame,* is visible on the screen. It's possible because each scan of the

video head is a full picture. When tape movement halts, the head just keeps "looking" at the same picture over and over.

This allows you to study a single frame. For example, perhaps you want to see if a football player's feet were really in bounds when he caught the ball. Or you may want to identify one of the individuals in a crowd scene. Basically, freeze-frame can enhance your enjoyment of home-video recording.

But not all freeze-frames are created equal. Some don't look as good as others. This is where head gaps come into play. When a VCR has a set of heads properly matched to the width of the video track, you get a better picture. That's why three-, four- and five-head VCRs produce better freeze frames.

Head gaps can't be matched to all speeds on a VCR with only one pair of heads. There's either

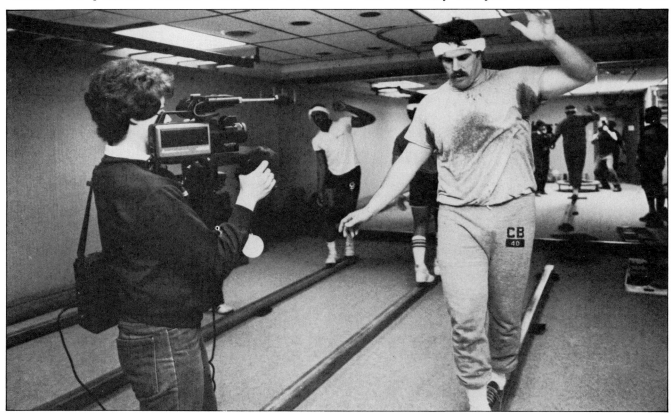

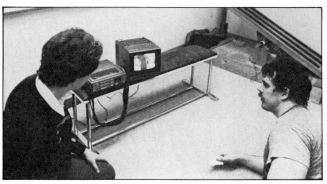

You can use a VCR's slow-scan capability for immediate analysis of many different types of activities. These can include sporting events, checking dancing technique or watching baby's first steps.

no freeze-frame at other than the slowest speed, which is the narrowest track, or you get a poor freeze-frame effect. You must decide how important this feature is to you. Then audition some VCRs to see if the freeze-frame is clear enough to meet your needs.

Freeze-frame capability was taken one step further in the lab to give you still another feature. Designers positioned the drive system for linear movement so it can move the tape along the length of only one video frame. With this feature, you step through the images one at a time. It's called *frame-advance*. There are 30 frames in each second of material recorded on a videocassette, regardless of the speed used to make the recording.

Frame-advance is of special interest to sports fans. You may want to see a player as he caught the ball during a close call, for example. Others like to study golf swings in great detail. For these and similar needs, frame-advance is a handy feature.

If the heads move at their correct fixed rate, but the speed at which the tape moves past them is varied, you'll either have more or fewer images per second than normal. More pictures per second is called *fast-scan, visual search, shuttle, cue and review.* The term could also be another combination of terms that usually includes one of these words.

When using the fast-scan mode, you see a fast-moving image on the screen. This is reminiscent of the Keystone Kops movies of years ago. You can use fast-scan to locate the point on a videocassette where a specific recording began. In the simple fast-forward mode, you don't see an image.

You may have several TV shows or segments recorded on the same cassette. It's easier to use the fast-scan feature to find the beginning of each

recording than keeping track of counter numbers every time you record. If you don't like commercials, you can use fast-scan to whisk by the ads when playing back recordings of TV shows.

Fewer pictures per second, or *slow-scan,* results in slow motion. This is a favorite of sports fans who like to analyze plays or see if the referees were right or wrong. Amateur athletes use slow motion to study their tennis serves or golf swings. And some parents can sit still all evening, watching baby's first steps over and over in slow motion.

Some VCRs offer more than one scan speed. When using the scan control, if you move the tape in its normal direction, you obviously will get either fast-scan or slow-scan in the forward mode. Running the tape backward, you get these effects in reverse. Some higher-priced VCRs offer variable-speed controls for these speed effects.

All of these effects may seem simple to achieve. But they really aren't. The tension of the tape across the drum must remain correct for proper scanning to occur. The tape must be fed out at just the right speed. In VHS machines, the slow-motion reverse function is difficult to achieve. This is a result of the tremendous tension that exists when the tape runs backward in an M-type loading system.

Multi-head scanners, mentioned earlier, are required to produce acceptable scan at all speeds and in both directions. If the head is narrower than the tracks, it won't pick up all the picture information. The result is poor-quality pictures.

If the head has too wide a head gap for the width of the track, it will pick up the information for more than one picture frame. That's obviously not good, either. Therefore, multi-head scanners are required to provide these effects. As a result,

Panasonic tabletop VCR offers pause/still and frame advance that can be controlled from both the remote control and front panel. With many units, some special effects can be controlled only from the remote control.

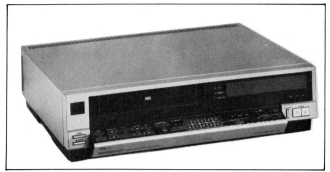

Tab marker is one of the many features of Magnavox VR8440BK. It also includes stereo capability with Dolby NR.

VCR cost and complexity increase.

Some VCRs offer scan in forward only. Others have it in both forward and reverse. Some give you special effects for videocassettes recorded at only one recording speed; others at all speeds.

As in the case of freeze-frame, fast-scan and slow-scan capabilities can enhance your enjoyment of home video.

When choosing a VCR, you'll have to base at least part of your decision on which combination of scan features you need. Think about what you want a VCR to do. Do you want the simple capability to move quickly through commercials on cassettes you've recorded off the air at the slowest speeds? Then you need only simple, *fast-scan forward.* Or, you may need to be able to scan cassettes recorded at other speeds. To go one step further, look for a machine that can scan in reverse.

Some VCRs allow control of the scan feature from both the front panel and the remote control. With others, you can only operate scan with the remote control. Keep these considerations in mind when choosing a particular model.

If you'll be using your VCR to examine shows such as sporting events, choose a high-end VCR featuring *slow-speed scan.*

Know how to describe the type of special effects or scan you need. Balance what you would like to have with what you have in your pocket to spend. Many people come to the conclusion that fast-scan forward is a special effect they can't live without. We tend to agree.

Automatic Pause Release—Pause and freeze-frame are nice to have. But they put stress on the videotape and the machine's fragile video heads. If you leave these functions engaged for longer than a few minutes, the result may be a hole in the tape or a ruined head. That's because the rotating head drum is continuously tracing the same path over the stopped tape.

If you tend to be careless with machines, investigate units featuring an automatic-release function. This special circuit puts the VCR back in the play mode for a brief time after it has been stilled for five minutes.

Editing—If you have ever edited motion-picture film, you know that it's a tedious, manual process. You hold the film up to the light or run it through a viewer to find the place where you want to make an edit. You physically cut the film on the frame line. Then remove or add a section of film and cement or tape the pieces back together. You have an edit. Depending on your prejudices, video editing is either much easier or much more difficult.

The first difference is that you can't see images on tape by holding the tape up to the light. Be-

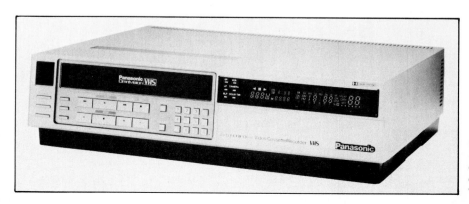

Panasonic PV-1720 tabletop offers insert-editing and stereo-sound capability with Dolby NR. Ten-pin camera input is not common on tabletops. It eliminates the need for a separate camera-power supply when shooting with a camera.

cause you can't tell where the frame lines are located on a piece of videotape, you don't know where to make splices.

A special fluid develops magnetic images on videotape but it won't let you see the pictures. However, it shows you where the magnetic track lines are located. You also see the very recognizable spike-like pulses on the control track. These indicate the start and end of each picture frame.

If you were to cut on these lines, you would have a perfect picture edit. This technique was once used by professionals. No one edits videotape this way any more. Electronic-editing technology is used instead.

Here's some advice: Don't ever physically splice a piece of videotape. In addition to finding it extremely difficult, you also run the risk of ruining the video heads if a splice hits them at the wrong angle. Fortunately, there's an electronic alternative.

Crude electronic edits are possible with almost any VCR. You can play the tape, pause it at the edit point and then put the VCR in the record mode to pick up information fed by a tuner/timer, camera or another VCR.

The problem with this method is that the tension holding the tape on the head drum might slip. Then the second picture may not start precisely where the first left off. The result is *picture break-up,* a choppy image. It happens because the machine hasn't quite found the beginning of the next picture on the tape. You can think of this as the equivalent of a splice in the middle of a film frame.

One solution is to have the VCR stop at the desired point and back up a short, measured amount. Then start the machine and go into the record mode at the beginning of the frame. This is called *assemble editing* because it consists of building a picture on the end of another.

A VCR can perform assemble edits. It uses a combination of electronic circuits that read the control-track frame-start pulses and then roll the

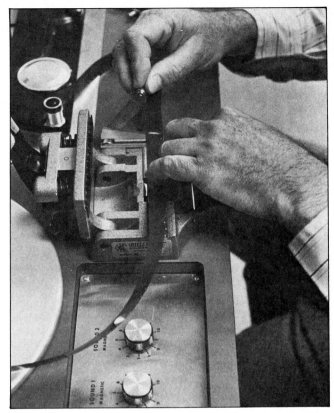

Film editing involves manually cutting the film on a frame line and cementing the pieces together. (Courtesy Eastman Kodak Company)

ASSEMBLE EDITING

ORIGINAL RECORDED MATERIAL	SEGMENT A	SEGMENT B	SEGMENT C	SEGMENT D

INSERT EDITING

ORIGINAL RECORDED MATERIAL	SEGMENT A	ORIGINAL RECORDED MATERIAL	SEGMENT B	ORIGINAL RECORDED MATERIAL

In *assemble editing,* the end of the original recording is followed by a series of edits that insert new material. It's a simple linear assembly of sequences. In *insert editing,* you insert new material into the original material.

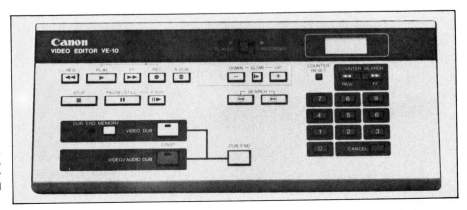

With an accessory video editor, you can do insert and assemble editing, and dub audio. You must have two VCRs for editing images on two prerecorded videocassettes.

tape. The VCR goes into the record mode only at the precise end of one frame and the precise beginning of another.

This feature is most likely to be found in portable VCRs. People tend to use cameras with these. They do a lot of starting and stopping when shooting. You may see assemble editing referred to as *backspace editing.* That is really what it is.

Assemble editing is a handy feature. But what if you want to do more? What if you want to drop a new bit of picture into a previously recorded program? Here again, the challenge is to be certain all pictures begin and end at the proper points.

It takes a fancy combination of electronic circuits and mechanical controls to perform this more-sophisticated type of editing, called *insert editing.* You won't find this capability on any but the most deluxe VCR models.

Insert edit is a desirable feature if you plan to add new material to recordings you've already made. Without this special insert function, you can still add the new recording to the tape. But there will be electronic noise at the beginning and end of the new recording. You may also see picture break-up for a few moments.

The insert function doesn't put the VCR in record the moment you press the button. Instead, it waits for the end of a video frame. Then it starts recording an incoming frame to give you a smooth transition, free of break-up. The same thing happens at the end of the recording.

However, even with this feature, some models still show residual color bars creeping into the picture at edit points. But the bars disappear quickly. If you're really interested in insert edit, test a few different VCR models to see how they handle this function.

A VCR with the insert-edit function is impor-tant if you plan to do a lot of editing into previously recorded materials.

An alternative to purchasing a VCR with built-in editing capability is to buy an accessory editor that can perform insert and assemble edits, and dub audio. You still need two recorders with an accessory editor.

Cue and Locating Systems—These are provided by making another combination of mechanical and electronic items work together. The joint effort makes it possible to get to a specific point on the tape in a videocassette without referring to the counter.

Counter memory, discussed as a mechanical function, is used by setting the counter to zero at the beginning of a specific scene or program. To get back to that point after the program is over, you put the VCR in the reverse mode and turn on the memory switch.

An attachment to the mechanical counter or a circuit in the electronic counter looks for 0000. The VCR stops automatically when that point is reached. It's a simple function. But it works only when you keep the same tape in the VCR. When you remove it, you have to play the cassette to the desired point and zero the counter again.

A more advanced solution to the locating problem is called *tab marker* or *electronic-cue stop.*

With this feature, an inaudible signal is placed on the tape each time the VCR is in record mode. If you set the appropriate switches and put the VCR in fast forward, the audio head will listen for that signal. When it hears the signal, the transport is stopped. Tab marker offers a convenient way of locating the start of each program on a cassette containing a number of different recordings.

Once again, it's a feature that will be used more by those who plan to watch their cassettes over and over. It's of special importance if you'll be recording many separate segments on a videocassette. You're more apt to do this if you also have a camera.

One-Touch Recording—One-touch recording sounds self-explanatory. But it might make you wonder if there are two- or three-touch recording models. That's a good question.

Many VCRs take a cue from the audio-recording systems. Typically, you have to press the **RECORD** and **PLAY** buttons simultaneously to start recording. The two-touch approach isn't a bad idea. It prevents you from accidentally putting the VCR in the record mode.

But some people think the two-button approach is inconvenient. Now there are VCRs that can be placed in the record mode with the push of just one button.

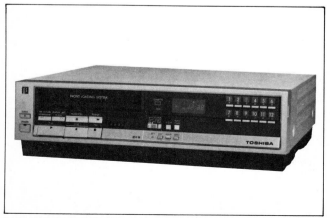

Toshiba's V-M40 has a one-touch record button.

In some models, one-touch recording goes a step further. Every time you press a button, the VCR goes on for an increment of 30 minutes or another set interval. Be sure to check which type of one-touch recording is in the VCR you're considering.

If you're confident about operating your equipment, a single-touch recording control may be preferable. But, if you have a young child or pet around the house, the two-button approach may be best.

Dew Warning—Changes in temperature and humidity can cause condensation inside the VCR. This is especially true with a portable. A portable is often moved from one environment to another—from your warm home to the chilly outdoors and vice versa. Therefore, its susceptibility to moisture is further increased.

You don't want moisture in the VCR. If it forms on the tape and head drums, it can lead to poor playback quality. It can even damage the machine!

To alert the user, VCRs have a dew-warning system that senses moisture-forming conditions. An indicator light warns you when not to use the machine. In some machines, the dew-warning system prevents you from operating the VCR. It may trigger a small heater. When the light goes off, conditions have returned to normal, and you can use the VCR again.

A dew-warning system is a definite plus. It's standard on most VCRs.

Remote and Other Controls—Early VCRs used mechanical controls only. This meant that when you pushed one of their "piano-key" buttons, you were actually tripping a series of switches and mechanical levers. When the levers were in place, the transport made the machine do what you wanted—go forward or backward, record or stop. The buttons were simple and inexpensive.

But they limited what the VCR could do when it was set for unattended recording.

Enter VCRs incorporating *soft-touch controls*. When you push a soft-touch button, it engages a solenoid. This is an electromagnetic-circuit control system that pulls levers inside the VCR. The levers then actuate various transport functions. Solenoid controls permit and improve expanded remote-control operation.

Until recently, the remote-control switch was at the end of a wire. It allowed you to put the VCR into pause mode only. Remote-pause control interrupted the power to the motor, stopping the tape at a specific point. With mechanical controls, that was about all you could do when using a remote control. Anything else required a lot of force to move levers.

Because a solenoid does much of the work for you, it's a simple matter to use different electronic switches. Now you have remote-control capability for all transport functions at the end of a wire.

After solenoid controls were introduced, it didn't take long for engineers to build VCRs offering *wireless* remote control. This is similar to that used for remote-controlled TV sets. You can send signals across the room to the VCR and tell it to start, stop, record, pause or perform other functions, usually by infrared beam.

The newest type of remote control is the *unitary remote*. It allows use of a single remote-control unit to activate not only a VCR, but also a TV, video projector and a videodisc player.

If you don't want to juggle two, three or four different remote controls in your home-entertainment system, this is for you. However, unitary remote only works with components of the same brand. This type of remote control is generally found only on high-end models.

RCA VKP900 convertible portable uses a wireless remote control to set the clock and timer. It allows preprogramming as many as eight programs up to one year in advance! It displays programming commands on the TV screen, with a menu. It can be controlled with RCA's Digital Command Center remote, which works with the company's color TV monitor/receivers.

Before buying video equipment, read video magazines. They offer up-to-date information on the newest innovations. Check models and current prices in magazines such as those shown here, and in newspapers from large cities.

Getting Ready to Buy

You're getting closer to an actual shopping expedition. You know how a VCR works, the range of features you can expect to find at various price levels and what these features can do for you.

You've probably formulated a list of the features you "can't live without." And, you have some idea how much you can afford to spend. The next step is to examine available VCR models carefully.

DO YOUR HOMEWORK

You can check what's available without leaving your home. All you have to do is read home-video magazines. Examine product test reports. In some magazines, you'll find reader-service cards. Use them to ask for more information. The manufacturers will send you free literature and specification sheets.

Another way to do your homework is to speak with acquaintances who already own home-video equipment. Ask what format and model they own, and what they think of their equipment. Try the equipment.

If you're concerned about the reliability of a certain machine and know a TV/video service-man, ask his opinion.

Visit local video-equipment dealers. Ask questions. Pick up brochures. And don't be afraid to ask something that may sound silly. If it's important to you, that's what counts.

A salesperson may try overwhelming you with technical information. He'll quote strange numbers and terms listed in specification sheets, brochures and test reports. What do these terms mean? Can they help you in your decision? Here's where you find out.

How to Read a Specification Sheet

When you look at a *specification,* or *spec sheet,* the first thing you'll see is a list of general specifications. Some spec sheets are more complete than others. Just because a company has a more comprehensive sheet doesn't mean its video products are better. Conversely, some spec sheets don't include all the information we describe here. Don't figure that the company is selling inferior equipment.

SAMPLE VHS VCR SPECIFICATIONS

Tape Format: VHS 1/2"-width high-density videocassette tape
Power Source: 120V, 60 Hz
Power Consumption: Approx. 43 watts
Video Recording System: Rotary four-head helical-scan azimuth
Video Signal: EIA standard (525 lines, 60 fields); NTSC color
VHF Output Signal: F-type connector, 75 ohms unbalanced
Tape Speed: SP: 1-5/16 ips (33.35mm/s), LP: 5/8 ips (16.67mm/s), EP: 7/16 ips (11.12mm/s)
Video Input: 0.5—2.0V p-p 75 ohms unbalanced
Video Output: 1.0V p-p 75 ohms unbalanced
Audio Input: Line —20dB (78 VRMS) high impedance; Microphone —69dB low impedance
Audio Output: Line —6dB (388m VRMS) low impedance; Earphone 26dB 8 ohms
Horizontal Resolution: More than 240 lines (in SP mode)
Record/Playback Time: 8 hours max. with T-160 used in EP mode
Heads: Video: 4 rotary heads; Audio: 2 stationary heads; Control: 1 stationary head; Erase: 1 full track
　　erase, 2 audio track erase for audio dubbing
Audio Frequency Response: SP: 50 Hz—10 kHz
Signal-to-Noise Ratio: Video: better than 45dB; Audio: better than 40dB
Operating Temperature: 32—104F (0C—40C)
Relative Humidity Range: 10% to 75%
RF Channel Output: Channels 3 or 4, switchable
RF Input/Output: VHF: F connectors/75 ohm; UHF: screw terminals/300 ohm
Weight: 8.4 lbs. (3.8kg) (with internal battery pack)*
Dimensions: 9-3/8" (W), 3-5/8" (H), 9-1/2" (D)*
Program Timer: 14 day, 1 event programmable; 24 hour digital synchronized with power-line frequency
Fast Forward & Rewind Time: Under 4 min. (T-120)

Supplied Accessories:
　　Videocassette (1)
　　Antenna selector (1)
　　75-ohm coaxial cable (2)
　　Shoulder strap (1)*
　　External antenna connectors: 75-ohm-
　　　to-300-ohm matching transformer (1);
　　　300-ohm-to-75-ohm matching transformer (1)
　　Earphone (1)*

Optional accessories:
　　Videocassette
　　Video head-cleaning cassette
　　AC-power adapter*
　　Tuner/timer*
　　Color video camera
　　Battery pack*
　　Car battery cord*
　　Connecting cord*
　　Carrying case*
　　Carrying handle*

Specifications are subject to change without notice for further improvement.

*Listings found only on spec sheets for portable VCRs.

These are specifications compiled from specification sheets supplied by several brands and manufacturers. This listing isn't meant to be complete, nor do the figures necessarily go together. We just wanted to illustrate here the variety of information you can expect to see. Some spec sheets are more detailed, and others are more graphic. But they all give you at least the minimum information required, such as format, recording speeds, power requirements, video and audio input and output, signal-to-noise ratio, weight and size.

GENERAL SPECIFICATIONS

The general specs lead off with the format. Most commonly, this is Beta or VHS. You already know about these.

Video Recording System—Following the format listings, you'll probably notice the category, *Video Recording System.* It may read ". . . rotary, slant-azimuth, two-head helical system." Don't be thrown by that one. It's a specification that has to be there if you're looking at a VHS or Beta machine. These terms briefly describe the method used to record the signal.

Occasionally, however, the terms just mentioned are followed with a note. It may state that the VCR has a "third head for special-effects playback," or "with two pairs of video heads, one exclusively for the SP mode and one pair for the EP mode."

This tells you that the machine—VHS in this case—is one of the more-expensive multi-head VCRs. It also indicates that it offers superior pictures, especially in fast-scan, slow-scan and freeze-frame modes. You'll find similar notations for extra heads on the spec sheets for many Beta VCRs.

Recording Speeds—Under the system description, you may see a listing of recording speeds and tape width. Width will be shown as either 1/2 inch or 12.7mm. As far as recording speeds go, we wish we could tell you that all spec sheets list all the recording-speed capabilities of the VCR. They don't.

The three VHS recording speeds are SP, LP and EP. You may see SLP instead of EP. Beta offers X1, X2 and X3. Today, X1 recording speed is found only on professional Beta-format VCRs. It was the original home-VCR Beta speed. X1 is available on some Beta models for playback only.

Some VCRs allow playback of a tape recorded in a speed in which the machine can't record. You have to examine brochures, read magazine test reports or consult a salesperson to find out the recording-speed capabilities of different machines.

The spec sheet may list the speed in inches or millimeters-per-second without giving the exact name of the speed. But you don't have to worry about all the millimeters and inches. As in the case with tape width for VHS and Beta machines, each speed is fixed according to the format. These listings are really a formality. They help make spec sheets look more impressive.

Then, you may find information about storage and operating temperatures. Unless you plan to keep your VCR in conditions that you wouldn't stay in yourself, you can skip these lines. Besides, there's little difference in this spec from one VCR to another.

VIDEO SPECIFICATIONS

Next on the spec sheet is the video-specifications section. This usually leads off with video-input and -output levels. Here, too, standards are limited by the format.

You'll see input listed as "0.5 to 2.0 volts peak," "1 volt -0.5/+1" or something similar. This is the type of video signal the VCR receives from the camera, tuner/timer or another VCR. The output will almost always be listed as "1 volt." This means that the VCR is designed to operate, with some tolerance, at the industry standard for a video signal of 1 volt.

Next come the specs for items that may vary—but not significantly—from machine to machine.

Video Signal-to-Noise (S/N) Ratio—You may understand this one if you're familiar with audio-tape recorders and their specifications. As in audio, the higher the number, the better the performance. In video, this means clearer pictures. You'll see it listed on spec sheets as "Video Signal to Noise," "Video Recording S/N" or something similar.

Unlike audio, where there are different types of design approaches, the video signal-to-noise figure is limited by constraints of the Beta and VHS recording systems.

The video signal has two components: *Luminance* is the brightness/b&w component of the video signal. *Chrominance* is the color portion. Video signal-to-noise measurement can be made on either the luminance or the chrominance.

Figures for the luminance S/N are usually about 10dB higher than the chrominance. You may assume that if the figures aren't specified as one or the other on the sheet, you're looking at a luminance figure.

As a guideline, expect a range of 40 to 47dB for the luminance S/N of a 1/2-inch VCR. *Don't accept* anything less than 40dB! These days, we'd be surprised if you see a rating less than 42dB.

The norm is 45dB for the fastest recording speeds of SP in VHS and X2 in Beta. Anything much more than that is advertising hype that should arouse your suspicions. In the rare case that you see a figure quoted for chrominance, look for something in the 35dB range.

Note that S/N figures quoted are usually for the fastest speeds. This is a result of lower performance at the slower recording speeds. A VCR with a 45dB figure in SP, for example, should give about 40dB in EP.

We mention this so you'll observe the most important rule in reading spec sheets: You must compare apples with apples and oranges with oranges. Be certain the figures you're comparing are for the same speed or the same signal component—luminance or chrominance.

If you are a keen observer of spec sheets, you may have been puzzled by the names *Rohde & Schwarz* often listed next to S/N figures. No, it's not the name of Sony's law firm or a deli where video people hang out.

Rather, it's the name of a high-quality brand of German test equipment used to measure signal-to-noise ratios. We don't understand why some brands list this on their spec sheets. But in case you wondered what it was, now you know!

Horizontal Resolution—This is sometimes called *picture resolution*. The figure is given in lines. Because this spec is expressed in lines, the listing is often confusing to nontechnical readers.

Here's why it may be confusing. Many people know that the NTSC television standard used in the United States, Canada and Mexico uses 525 lines to create a TV picture. But, they forget that these are *horizontal,* not vertical lines. So, when they see a spec sheet figure of 240 lines, they wonder what happened to the other 285!

Actually, nothing has happened to them. The 525 horizontal scanning lines are all there. Otherwise, you wouldn't be able to produce an acceptable picture with your VCR. The horizontal resolution figure on the spec sheet refers to the number of *vertical lines visible within a given picture area.* It's a technical measurement of the VCR's ability to show picture detail.

We suggest that you look for a VCR that offers horizontal resolution in the 240- to 270-line range. That's the norm. You should also know that even the best TV set available won't give you a resolution figure of more than about 330 lines.

A horizontal resolution of more than 270 lines isn't possible in home VCRs. This is due to the inherent limitations of Beta and VHS recording systems.

You'll also usually find a dual measurement here. Again, the luminance, or monochrome, numbers will be higher than the chrominance, or color, figures. If there's just one number, it's for the monochrome or luminance, not the color or chrominance.

To sum up the figures on video specifications, we must emphasize that most specs are fixed by the nature of the 1/2-inch recording system. Once you look over enough spec sheets, you'll get a feel for the state-of-the-art. It'll be represented by the figures you see most often.

AUDIO SPECIFICATIONS

You don't have to be an audiophile to understand figures relating to a VCR's audio performance. If you plan to add new sound tracks to your videotapes, you'll want to buy the correct plugs and cables.

Inputs and Outputs—These numbers generally don't vary much from VCR to VCR. Home machines are designed so they can be used with all types of consumer audio equipment.

The Line figure with Audio Input/Output gives you information about connecting the VCR to an amplifier, audiotape deck or external tuner. Microphone Input is also mentioned.

Spec sheets sometimes list the type of connector that should be used. Video connections on VCRs are typically made with RCA phono plugs. Audio hookups require either RCA phono plugs or mini plugs. You may see this type of plug listed as a *pin-plug* in some literature.

Frequency Response—The wider the range, the better the quality of the response. Be certain, once again, that you compare figures for the same recording speed. A range of 50 to 10,000 hertz (Hz) is a good norm to follow for SP and X2, the fastest VHS and Beta recording speeds in home video. This may also be expressed as 50 Hz to 10 kHz or 50 to 10 kHz.

Audio Signal-to-Noise (S/N) Ratio— Remember, we're talking about *audio S/N.* Once again, the higher the number the better. Be sure you're comparing apples with apples.

To record off-the-air broadcasts with most portable VCRs, you must have a separate tuner/timer unit. On the far right is a Panasonic portable VCR. To its left, connected by wires in the back, is the companion tuner/timer.

Check to see that you're comparing the audio figures with other audio numbers and not to the video S/N information. Also, be certain that you're not comparing the S/N at SP on one VHS machine, for example, with the S/N of another in the LP speed. It should be about 40dB for the slow speed and in the low 40s for the fastest recording speed.

If the VCR includes a noise-reduction encoding system such as Dolby NR, check the S/N numbers carefully. These specs apply only to tapes encoded and played back with the particular noise-reduction system built into the VCR.

Don't be alarmed if the VCR's audio specs are lower than in your stereo system. This is the inevitable result of the relatively slower tape speeds used in home-video recording. However, specs for Beta and VHS Hi-Fi will be *better* than most stereo systems.

SPEC VARIATIONS

So far, most of the specifications we've discussed are basically fixed in a certain range by the limitations of the 1/2-inch formats. Now it's time to talk about the specs that differ significantly from machine to machine.

Size and Weight—Some VCRs are larger and weigh more than others. When you examine the figures for portables, see if they include the weight of the battery and case. This may add a pound or two to the unit slung over your shoulder. Again, when comparing two machines, be sure that the information is consistent.

Usually, manufacturers are accurate when indicating height, width and depth of a VCR. But typically they don't mention the amount of clearance needed for the VCR.

This can be important, depending on where you plan to use the equipment. You should take into account if there is sufficient room on the sides and top for ventilation. You need about one inch all around. If the VCR loads from the top, you need at least another two to three inches so the tape compartment can pop up. However, a three-inch clearance may not be adequate when using a VCR with channel-selection switches on the top.

You must allow for space at the back of the VCR to make connections. These include the AC wall outlet, television, antenna or cable, and your stereo when you have the proper equipment. Some of these connectors extend at least an inch or two behind the back of the machine. Generally, you can't position video equipment where there is no place for the connecting wires to run out the back.

Power Consumption—We know that energy conservation is on everyone's mind. Don't worry. A VCR doesn't require a lot of electricity. The power figure for most AC-powered tabletops reveals that they generally use less power than a 75-watt light bulb.

Power figures become important in portables. The lower the power consumption, the longer the battery will run on a charge. Pay special attention to the mode listed. Are the figures for the standby or pause mode, in which the motors aren't running, or for full-power mode, when the motors are running?

Low power consumption is a plus. But if it's tied in with a low-capacity battery, the two can cancel each other out. Check to see how long the supplied battery will power the portable unit.

The same could be said of a portable with higher power consumption and longer-lasting battery. Yes, there are tradeoffs everywhere. The longer-lasting battery will weigh more, although it may not be much of a difference. We advise you to go beyond the spec sheets and sales pitches. Ascertain your needs by asking questions.

Tuner/Timer—You'll find listings of the number of days and events the VCR's tuner/timer can be set to record. The VCR's ability to tune in cable-TV's mid-, super- and hyper-band channels may or may not be noted on the spec sheet. Regardless, the spec-sheet comparison is the best way to see how each VCR you're considering stacks up.

Rewind Time—A good spec sheet will also provide you with a listing of the amount of time it takes to rewind or fast-forward a videocassette. Remember, these figures must compare cassettes of the same length. When no cassette length is noted, the figures are usually for a VHS T-120 or Beta L-500 videocassette.

Standard Accessories—These are the extras that come packed with the equipment. They're included in the purchase price. In the brochure, you may also see a listing of optional accessories available at extra cost.

VCR marketers typically give you just enough in the way of accessories to connect the VCR to most antennas. They include the wires needed for hooking the tabletop or portable to a TV. If you have a portable VCR, you get the cables required to attach the tuner/timer to the VCR.

We tell you more about how to use these standard accessories for connecting your VCR in Chapter 7. You'll also find out about items you may have to purchase separately when making some of the more complex cable-TV hookups.

To make the best buying decision, you must do some research. Start by reading video magazines written for the home user. Request information from manufacturers. Talk to friends about their experiences with home-video equipment. Then go to different stores and ask questions. Here, a salesman demonstrates a VCR to a prospective buyer. (Courtesy Electronic Industries Association and Crazy Eddie)

Warning—One last word about standard accessories. Some unscrupulous dealers may try to sell a VCR at a low price without standard accessories. If the spec sheet tells you certain items are included with the VCR, *make sure you get them all.* If you're not sure what's supposed to come with the VCR, even after reading the spec sheet, go to another dealer and compare what he delivers with the unit. There's no need to guess.

Going Shopping

Now that you've digested all this information, you're ready technically to buy a VCR. You know generally how home VCRs operate. And you've decided which features you must have and the ones you'd like if the price is right. You've read the test reports, spoken with people and compared spec sheets.

By now, you've decided on a price range and given serious thought to whether a tabletop or portable is in your future.

Now comes the hard part: Where do you buy and how much do you pay?

CHOOSING A DEALER

It seems that everyone is selling home-video equipment these days, including department stores, audio retailers and photo shops. Video specialty stores are popping up all over, too. In addition, you may have seen mail-order ads in magazines. Where's the best place to shop? Maybe you should rent a VCR instead of buying one?

We'll talk about the rental option in Chapter 6, *Buy or Rent?* Depending on your interests, you may want to skip to that chapter now, before reading the rest of this. Once you've made that

decision, you can come back here and shop with us.

Hands-On May Be Best—You have to make your decision where to buy based on a combination of factors. Just how much help do you need with the purchase? Even though we'd like to believe you'll get everything you need to know from this book, there's no substitute for handling the real thing.

If you want a complex demonstration, or still have questions that need answers, by all means seek out a video-specialty shop. Because video is their business—their only business in some cases—they'll have well-trained salespeople. But, you'll probably pay more for your equipment in this type of store or in a photo store that concentrates on video.

However, you may be confident that we've helped make you somewhat of an expert. In that case, don't be afraid to buy from a bare-bones discount store or mail-order outfit. Be careful, though, when buying by mail or phone.

Make sure you find out what type of shipping method is used and how much it costs. Some people use mail order to beat state and local sales taxes, only to find out that the shipping charges cost more than any tax savings.

Once again, make sure the discounter or mail-order house is including all the standard accessories listed in the VCR's spec sheet. Be sure you receive a properly filled-out bill of sale. You'll need this if the machine needs service during the warranty period.

Service and Warranties—If the machine doesn't have a warranty card, either the factory forgot to include one or someone has sold you a used or improperly imported machine.

We discussed OEMs earlier. You now know

VCR CARE AND USE

● Buy or make a cover to protect the VCR from moisture and dust. Keep the unit covered when not in use. When carrying the VCR on location, keep it in a carrying case. Be especially careful when near the ocean or any other salt-air or sandy environment.

● Don't place liquids or other substances on or near the VCR. If liquids spill inside the VCR, take it to an authorized service outlet before attempting to use it again.

● Allow adequate ventilation behind the VCR to prevent overheating.

● Never operate a tabletop in other than a horizontal position.

● Use in a cool, dry location. Don't expose to direct sunlight or heat.

● Save the original packaging in case the equipment has to be shipped for repair.

● Don't attempt to service the VCR yourself. You may void the manufacturer's warranties. If any problems develop with the equipment, first be sure all connections have been made correctly and that no wires or connectors are faulty. Also, check the video-cassette and incoming signals. Re-read the instruction manuals. If you still have a problem, ask your dealer or authorized repair outlet for assistance.

● Clean heads only when necessary. Use procedures and equipment recommended by the manufacturer.

PORTABLE VCR BATTERY CARE AND USE

● Charge batteries before the first use.

● Recharge batteries after every use, or every six months if not used.

● Don't subject batteries to temperature extremes. Remember that batteries don't work well at low temperatures.

● Remove batteries from equipment if you aren't planning to use the equipment for a long time.

● Follow manufacturer's recommendations when charging batteries. *Most* charging units automatically stop charging when the process is completed to avoid overcharging.

● Use care when handling fragile connecting points and wires.

that many VCRs selling under different brand names are actually the same machine, with a few cosmetic variations. It's also important to know that some machines offer longer warranties than others. This depends on the marketing company's repair policies.

When comparing warranties, see if they refer to *parts and labor* or *parts only*. And, check to see *which parts* are covered. In many cases, not only does the length of the warranty vary, but also what's covered.

As far as service goes, it's reassuring if the store that sold you the video equipment also has a service department. This is not always the case. But the video-equipment repair business is growing all the time. As mentioned earlier, many shops and home-repair services once specializing in TV have now gone into home-video equipment repair as well.

But, just as in TV repair, you must be very careful when dealing with these firms. Some VCRs are packed with a sheet listing the factory service centers maintained by their brand. There's usually only one or two located in or near major cities.

If you don't see one that's convenient, use the toll-free telephone number that some VCR marketers offer to help you locate nearby authorized service centers. Your dealer should also be able to give you names of authorized repair places for a particular VCR brand.

Under federal law, as long as the store that sold the machine purchased it legally from a manufacturer, importer or distributor, and sold it to you legally, the manufacturer must honor the warranty. Of course, that's assuming that you registered purchase of the machine, if required. And you must provide reasonable care of the equipment as specified in the warranty instructions.

Federal law also states that you have the right to examine the warranty for an item before you buy it. Know your rights as a consumer. Don't be afraid to exercise them!

IS THE PRICE RIGHT?

We're sorry we can't make things easy for you by telling you the right price for a specific model or even category of VCR. It's impossible! Since VCRs and video cameras were introduced, prices have fluctuated tremendously.

On the average, prices vary according to the type of store you're dealing with. Also, you'll find lower prices in larger urban centers where there's more competition. Pick up a copy of the Sunday *New York Times, Los Angeles Times, Chicago Tribune, Washington Post* or a video magazine with advertising. Check video-equipment prices. Compare these to the ones advertised in your area. In many cases, big-city prices may be $50 to $150 lower.

You may have a good video-service outlet in your area. If you find a store in a place such as New York with a price you can't beat, you may want to shop by mail. We would suggest, however, finding a retailer in your area offering the same machine. Get a first-hand, close look at the VCR that interests you. And you have nothing to lose by asking if he'll match the mail-order price.

Be aware that prices are also seasonal. The video model year starts in the fall and runs through the summer. In many ways, the video-sales cycle resembles the one in the automobile industry.

In both auto and VCR shopping, buying in August—right before the arrival of the new models—may get you a bargain. Dealers are trying to clear out older models to make room for new ones. You may discover that a machine that was out of your price range during the peak of the selling season is affordable during the late fall and early winter.

A Final Word on Prices—They are subject to *bargaining* in some cases. Although department stores tend to have fixed prices, local discount stores and even some video-specialty shops may be more flexible. Some retailers even expect you to bargain!

How do you bargain? If a store runs an ad encouraging you to shop around to get the lowest price and they'll beat it, chances are you can make a deal. Check to see what optional accessories you might need, such as cases and extra batteries. And, find out if the retailer sells them. He may not lower the price of the VCR, but you might be able to get him to give you accessories at no extra charge.

We know from experience that the eyes of salespeople tend to light up when you mention that you're also interested in a camera, television set, or perhaps a projection TV. Use that to your advantage when shopping.

When making your VCR purchase decision, there are many things to consider, not the least of which are format (Beta or VHS), style (tabletop or portable) and sound capability (mono or stereo). Top right is Minolta portable T-770S VHS tuner that mates with the 5-head portable stereo VCR illustrated on page 24. Right is Sony SL-HF300 Beta Hi-Fi tabletop.

Chapter 3

All About Home Video Cameras

We've been talking about the videocassette recorder primarily as a device that can record off the air. But the VCR has another important and exciting capability. With the addition of another piece of equipment—a video camera—you can record live action!

In this chapter, we explain how the home-video camera operates. Then we talk about the range of features and how they work. Finally, we discuss what's important to have, and which functions you should consider as optional.

Down to Basics

Here's a simple way to explain how a video camera works: It's just the reverse of the way a TV-picture tube operates.

TV TUBE
A TV-picture tube is more accurately called a *cathode-ray tube (CRT)*. In it, a stream of electrons is guided across the tube's phosphored surface. The stream is controlled by circuits that

When you have a home-video camera and VCR, you can make your own "home movies" of any event. (Courtesy General Electric Video Products Division)

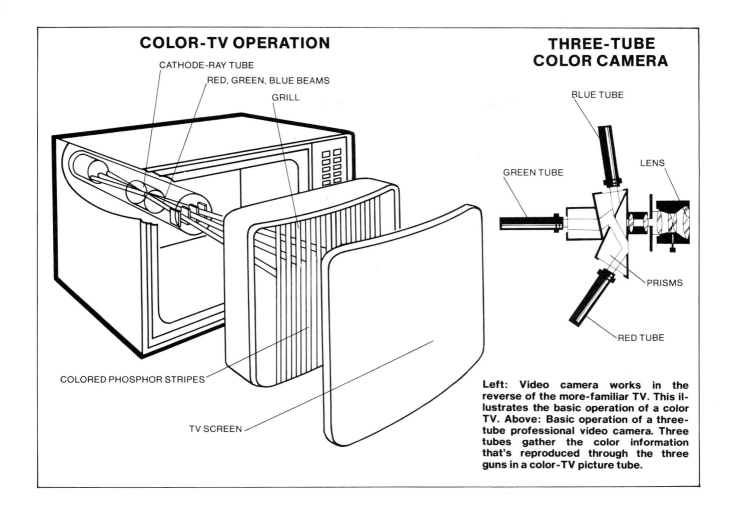

COLOR-TV OPERATION

CATHODE-RAY TUBE
RED, GREEN, BLUE BEAMS
GRILL

COLORED PHOSPHOR STRIPES

TV SCREEN

THREE-TUBE COLOR CAMERA

BLUE TUBE

GREEN TUBE

LENS

PRISMS

RED TUBE

Left: Video camera works in the reverse of the more-familiar TV. This illustrates the basic operation of a color TV. Above: Basic operation of a three-tube professional video camera. Three tubes gather the color information that's reproduced through the three guns in a color-TV picture tube.

determine the positioning of the electrons on the face, their intensity and when they start and stop.

A b&w TV has a single electron gun. When an electron hits the tube, a dark spot turns white. The picture is built up as a result of a lot of those strikes. The beam scans across the face of the tube to construct an image.

What About Color?—A color set uses three guns. There's one gun for each of the three primary colors: red, green and blue. When and where the beam falls determines the mix that provides the range of colors in the picture. Although there are single-gun color tubes, they're based on the same three-tube color principles.

CAMERA IMAGING

Camera imaging is almost the reverse of the way a CRT works. In a video camera, light collected by the lens is focused on the faceplate of an imaging device. This may be a camera tube or solid-state imaging device. More on those later.

An electron beam scans the face of the camera's imaging device. But rather than creating light by striking the surface, as in the case of a TV, the electrons detect the presence or absence

of light on the surface. The nature of the light entering the camera—its position and intensity—is read by an electron beam.

Color-Camera Imaging—A color camera operates similarly. But in this case, light collected by the lens is reflected onto a prism. In a professional broadcast camera, the prism breaks the light into the primary colors—red, green and blue. The light—now broken into its three components—is focused on three tubes inside the camera.

A three-tube professional camera as illustrated at top.

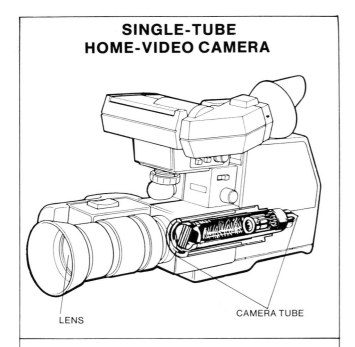

SINGLE-TUBE HOME-VIDEO CAMERA

LENS

CAMERA TUBE

INSIDE THE SINGLE TUBE

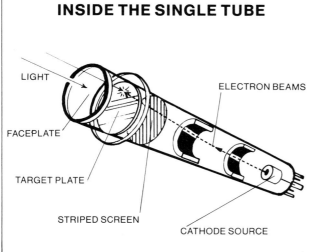

LIGHT

ELECTRON BEAMS

FACEPLATE

TARGET PLATE

STRIPED SCREEN

CATHODE SOURCE

Color home-video camera uses a single tube, located behind the lens. Filter inside the tube works with a scanning beam to produce the separate blue, green and red color signals. These are sent through the camera's cable to the VCR.

Home-video cameras work on a similar principle. But they contain a single tube and striped filter to help interpret colors. They work according to the methods already described.

The three signals are then combined in the video camera to create a color video signal that can be recorded on tape in the VCR. When you play back the videocassette through a TV, or show what your camera is shooting live on a TV set, the video signal is separated again to produce the color picture you see on the screen.

SINGLE-TUBE DESIGN

Most professional color-video cameras use

three tubes. They produce the highest-quality pictures. However, three tubes add cost and weight. For home-video cameras, engineers developed the single-tube color camera.

This tube has a striped filter on its face. The scanning beam inside the tube uses the information created by the stripes to produce the red, green and blue color signals. This is accomplished without the weight and expense of a three-tube system.

Of course, it's more complex than this brief explanation suggests. But this basic knowledge will help you understand how the home-video camera operates.

COLOR VS. B&W

Generally, b&w home-video cameras have been replaced by color models. People prefer shooting the world in color and don't mind paying the difference in price.

Some b&w home cameras may still be available. Or, you may be offered a low-end professional b&w camera or a 1/2-inch b&w reel-to-reel videotape (VTR) recorder. If so, here's some important information to keep in mind.

Let's consider what might occur if you mix color and b&w equipment—both cameras and VCRs. For example, you may have access to an old b&w recorder, even though b&w models are no longer made.

If you want a b&w video camera, look for a low-end professional model such as this Panasonic.

A color video camera produces a signal that can be viewed in color *and* b&w. But a b&w camera gives a picture in b&w only. When you connect a b&w camera to a modern home VCR, it will record images in b&w only. If you connect a color camera to a video recorder that records in b&w only, you'll record a good image—but it'll be b&w.

Remember that connecting a color camera to a b&w recorder won't magically give you color pictures. In addition, recording a movie originally shot in b&w won't deliver that movie in color, even though the VCR has the capability to record in color.

Here's something else to be aware of: Even though you may see b&w images in a color camera's *viewfinder,* you're still recording color images. When a color camera is connected to a home VCR and a b&w TV, the images you *record* will be in color. But you'll still *see* b&w images only on the TV screen.

An electronic viewfinder is a feature of Sony CCD-G5. Viewfinder has a 1-inch b&w picture tube.

VIEWFINDER

Whether you're shooting an image with a conventional photographic camera or a video camera, you need a way to view the subject through the camera. This is because your eye rarely has the same viewing perspective as the camera lens. And, you need a way to focus the lens. These requirements are met in a video camera much the same way they are in a photographic camera—with a *viewfinder.*

There are three basic types: *optical, through-the-lens reflex* and *electronic.*

Optical Viewfinder—Some inexpensive video cameras may have the simple optical sight once found on simple inexpensive film cameras.

Above: This Panasonic has an optical viewfinder. Such viewfinders are rare on home-video cameras today. Left: TTL reflex viewfinders, such as on this Elmo, are more common.

Most home-video cameras, such as this Minolta, feature an electronic viewfinder.

Electronic viewfinder on this home-video camera can be adjusted for left- or right-eye use, as illustrated below. You can adjust it other ways, too.

This viewfinder sits on the top of the camera. Its markings indicate the angle of view with different focal-length lenses. This means that it shows you the area that'll be imaged when you're shooting at a specific focal length.

The optical viewfinder offers the least amount of accuracy in judging how to frame your picture. It's the cheapest viewfinder to build into a camera. Because it doesn't use any power, it helps conserve the VCR's battery.

Although it's not common in home video, don't ignore this type. An optical finder might be just the right compromise if you don't have to see the image being sent to the VCR.

Through-the-Lens (TTL) Reflex Viewfinder—This type is more popular than the simpler optical variety. It's similar to a finder on a 35mm single-lens-reflex (SLR) still camera or most motion-picture cameras. It allows you to see the identical framing and magnification of the image through the lens, as it will look on the TV screen. For this reason, it's called *through-the-lens (TTL) reflex.*

The viewfinder is built into the camera and shows you a full-color image. It aids you in focusing and composition. It may incorporate LED indicators. These can indicate battery power, sufficient lighting, white balance and whether you're recording or not.

The reflex finder itself doesn't consume any power. However, a small amount of power is used by its LED indicators. It is relatively lightweight like its optical counterpart. Both types permit true color viewing because there's no electronic intervention when viewing the image.

Many people swear by the third type, the

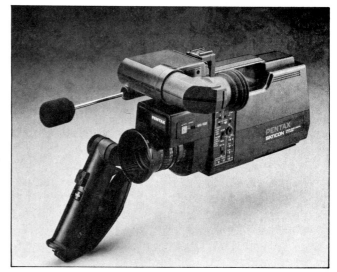

Left: Electronic viewfinder on this RCA home-video camera is built-in. Right: Electronic viewfinder on this Pentax camera can be oriented in different directions as required.

electronic viewfinder. But we believe that you should consider the virtues of the TTL reflex finder. It lets you view the picture in color as opposed to the b&w images typically presented with the electronic finder's tiny, built-in TV screen. In addition, you get a brighter picture for easier focusing with a TTL reflex finder than with an electronic finder.

However, the TTL reflex finder does share some of the optical finder's drawbacks. It may present pictures that appear bright enough for a good viewfinder image, even though there isn't enough light to produce quality recordings.

If you choose a TTL reflex finder, be sure that it's equipped with a *low-light-level warning light.* Some cameras with a TTL reflex finder also incorporate a jack that lets you add an accessory electronic finder.

Electronic Viewfinder—The most common home-video camera viewfinder is the electronic viewfinder. It's the top-of-the finder line. This option can be mounted externally or built into the top of the camera housing. It's actually a miniature TV that shows you camera output. Because it's also a TV, it can show the playback from your VCR as well. In other words, you can use the viewfinder like a built-in monitor.

As with the reflex viewfinder, you can look through the lens for focusing and composition.

This viewfinder indicates if there is enough light and power, even if your VCR is in the record mode. You may be disappointed to learn that most electronic finders show pictures only in b&w. *Don't be.* The $100,000-plus cameras used by TV networks don't offer color viewfinders! Although some super-deluxe home-video cameras

have a color finder, a b&w viewfinder image is more common. Color viewfinders are available. At the time of this writing, they're limited to super-deluxe cameras selling for about $2000.

If you're not sure you're producing good color pictures, you can connect the camera to the VCR and feed its output into a color TV. Then you can check the settings and system. Make sure all color, contrast and brightness settings on the TV are adjusted correctly. We explain this hookup in Chapter 7.

You can move electronic viewfinder mounted on this Hitachi VKC3400 camera, for left- or right-eye use. But what's more exciting is that the image you see in the 1.5-inch viewfinder is in color! Other features are a 2/3-inch MOS imaging device, *f*-1.2 6X power-zoom lens and character generator.

Some cameras have an electronic viewfinder called an *orientable finder*. This allows you to arrange the viewing screen for left- or right-eye use. To do this, manufacturers mount the viewfinder picture tube or its relay optics in a movable housing. In super-high-end cameras, the eyepiece can also be tilted up or down, depending on the particular shooting situation.

We explain more about TTL and electronic viewfinders, and viewfinder indicators in the next section, *Viewfinder Indicators*.

Which viewfinder type is best for your needs? You don't always have a choice. The finder type is usually dictated by the camera price range. You'll find TTL finders confined to leader-model cameras and a few in the high-end. Most video cameras above the leader-model level include an electronic finder whether you want one or not.

VIEWFINDER INDICATORS

When you've decided on a camera, you rarely have a choice of indicators. As when selecting a feature package for an automobile, you have to take what's available in the video camera's price category.

Some indicators are important enough to look for. But the inclusion of these warning lights might be enough to move you into another price range. It's important to be aware of which indicators you may find in TTL and electronic viewfinders.

As with any type of indicator, they tell you the status of a specific function. Typically light-emitting diodes (LEDs), they're connected to the circuits in either reflex or electronic

viewfinders. If the indicator is a warning light, the circuits make the LED glow when the condition reaches "danger" level.

In a through-the-lens reflex finder, the optical system takes some of the light from the optical axis—the line of sight of the lens. The system then relays the light to a focusing screen you view. One disadvantage of this finder is that you can't use it to view playback of images you've just shot.

As already mentioned, the electronic finder works like a TV. It shows the signal sent to it from the camera, or back from the VCR. The viewing screen has its own small optical system to direct the image from the tube in the direction you desire. Finder optics slightly magnify the image from the small tube. As a result, the image seems slightly larger than it actually is. This makes viewing easier, even when your eye isn't pressed against the rubber eyecup that usually surrounds the screen housing.

We'll explain more about controls related to some of these indicators, and how they work, later in this chapter, under *Operational Features*.

Recording Indicator—Have you ever been to a broadcast sporting event, or on the set of a TV show? If so, you're aware of how people know when the TV cameras aimed in their direction are actually recording. They see the glow of a red light, usually located above the lens. This recording indicator, also called a *tally light* or *mode indicator*, has been incorporated into the design of many home-video cameras.

When you've turned on the camera and set the VCR in the record mode to start recording with the camera, you press a trigger switch. This switch is usually on or near the camera grip handle. It also activates the recording indicators. One may be on the front of the camera. Another may be in the viewfinder.

The first, usually red—although we've seen green ones—tells your subjects that you're recording. The second light is typically red or green, although it could be some other color. It glows in the viewfinder, telling the camera operator that the camera is recording. Both internal and external lights are usually round.

In some cameras, the recording indicator is in the form of a white line superimposed on the viewfinder screen. The line blinks during recording.

The viewfinder tally light is a *must*. The one outside is nice to have. But it's not necessary unless you want to preserve some of the glamour of television for your subjects.

Waveform Display—This is perhaps the least-

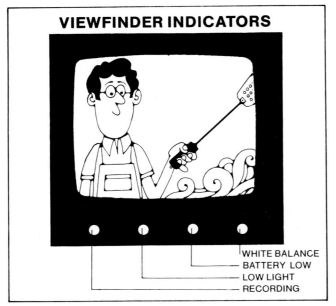

VIEWFINDER INDICATORS

WHITE BALANCE
BATTERY LOW
LOW LIGHT
RECORDING

Different camera models offer different viewfinder indicator displays. This is an example of a four-indicator display.

necessary indicator. It's found on some super-high-end cameras. Waveform display shows you—with a jagged line—exposure- or picture-quality levels as a graphic representation of the video signal produced by the camera. By sampling the circuits in the luminance—brightness—channel of the camera, you can have an oscilloscope-type display.

The line is superimposed over the image in the finder. The display certainly looks impressive. But there's almost nothing you can do to adjust the camera even if you take the time to learn how to read the display.

With a professional camera, you'd be able to adjust the camera's internal controls more extensively with special oscilloscopes. In home cameras equipped with waveform display, you can play video engineer by adding extra gain boost. This increases the camera's sensitivity.

Some models offering this waveform display also allow you to use the white line as an indication of correct focus. If you have difficulty focusing the electronic viewfinder image, this may be a feature worth considering.

Don't worry if your dream camera doesn't include a waveform display.

Low-Battery Indicator—In some video cameras, you'll find an indicator that shows if the battery is running out of power. It gives enough warning so you can change the VCR battery before the equipment goes dead. This indicator is not simply something nice to have. It's *essential*. Unlike some photographic cameras, video cameras don't have controls that will operate without battery power.

Low-Light Indicator—Why, you might ask, would you need this? You know when it's getting dark! But the video camera needs more light to "see" the subject than your eyes do. And, the video camera usually requires more light than a conventional photographic camera.

The low-light warning is calibrated to go on just as the light level drops to the minimum needed to record good images. It's a *must* feature.

Color-Control Setting—Often, you'll find a meter displaying the color-control setting. This can be toward either the blue or red end of the spectrum.

White-Balance Indicator—For some reason, some video cameras include an indicator that tells you when the white-balance circuitry is operating. We've always been puzzled by this. To activate these circuits, you've already made a conscious decision to push a button. It doesn't hurt to have a white-balance light. But we wouldn't suggest that you search the world just to have this feature.

Iris Scale—An iris scale lets you know lens-aperture setting. Iris-scale indicators are either electronic or electronically driven meter pointers similar to those found in some film cameras.

Counter Display—Another indicator that's more common with the increased use of electronic counters on portable VCRs is counter display. This gives a readout of the VCR's counter in the camera viewfinder. The indicator lets you know how long you've been taping. This in turn gives a measure of how much tape is left in the cassette.

Lens Focal-Length—Professional-studio video cameras usually have a meter or electronic scale to indicate the focal-length setting of the zoom lens. This may also be integrated into some home-video camera models.

LENSES AND IMAGING DEVICES

As with conventional photographic camera lenses, video lenses come in many varieties: interchangeable or permanent mount, single-focal-length or zoom (manual or power), manual or automatic exposure control, and manual or automatic focus.

Interchangeable Lenses—Some video cameras have interchangeable-lens capability. Unlike photographic cameras, home-video cameras are never sold without a lens. Interchangeability permits use of other lenses, such as a fixed-focal-length wide-angle or very long telephoto.

With some models you can change lenses. Pentax C-mount camera allows use of different video lenses and 16mm motion-picture lenses. And, if you own a Pentax 35mm SLR camera and accessory lenses, you can use all system lenses on your video camera with an adapter! Remember, though, that you lose some or all of the video camera's automatic features when a non-video lens is attached.

You can't tell what type or size of imaging device a video camera is using just by looking at it. For example, it's not obvious that the JVC GX-N4 at left uses a 1/2-inch tube and the Panasonic PK-410 above uses a 1/3-inch tube.

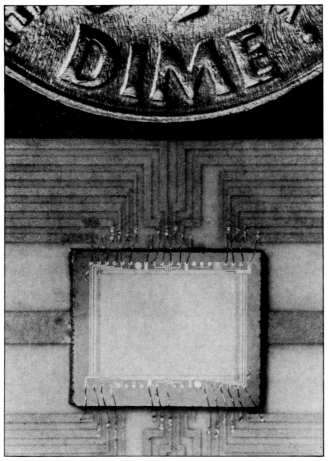

Miniature charge-coupled devices (CCDs) are used to replace the tube in some home-video cameras.

These lenses are rare and expensive. You can use 16mm motion-picture camera lenses. However, they are not a good match.

A striking difference between interchangeable video lenses and conventional camera lenses is that you won't know right away what type of video camera the video lens fits on. When you handle a film camera, you know immediately what film format you're dealing with: 35mm, 2-1/4 square, 110, super-8 or 16mm. You can usually tell by camera size and shape. Each format accepts a specific variety of lenses.

In addition, the "system" method of matched lenses common in 35mm SLR photography doesn't exist in consumer video. Although you *can* change lenses on some cameras, some automatic features don't work when a non-video lens is attached.

Because of the many variables involved in changing lenses on video cameras, most people shoot with only one lens. If you really want to try additional lenses, be sure they are compatible with the camera and its imaging system.

With a video camera, you can't be sure just by looking at the camera what type of imaging device is used to detect and process light. In addition, the diameter of the imaging device's target surface also determines the focal length of the lens you can use.

For example, some video cameras use a 1/2- or 2/3-inch tube. Others have a 1-inch tube. Some video cameras don't use a tube. Instead, they depend on a solid-state chip, such as a metal-oxide semiconductor (MOS) or charge-coupled device (CCD).

To find out what type of imaging device your camera has, refer to the owner's manual or remove the lens on cameras with this option. We *do not* recommend opening the camera.

Because both film- and video-camera lenses often use the standard *C-mount,* you may be able to attach a 16mm motion-picture camera lens to a home-video camera. The image size of the 16mm movie camera is similar to that produced by the 1-inch tube found in some video cameras. But, you can't necessarily switch lenses from one video camera to another because one may have a 2/3-inch tube and the other a 1-inch tube.

Don't be too surprised if a lens you have for a 16mm camera doesn't deliver good pictures when mounted on your video camera. Optical differences may cause *vignetting,* which is image cutoff in the corners. This occurs when the focused image is larger than the size of the video camera's imaging device. Although the mount may be the same on both cameras, the zoom and iris connections may be different. As a result, you may lose certain automatic capabilities with a non-video lens mounted.

For cameras that offer interchangeable-lens capability, you'll see an indication such as *Lens Mount: C mount* on the specification sheet.

Your best bet is to choose a video camera with the lens that suits your needs. For now, our advice is not to plan on being able to change the lens that the camera comes with.

Zoom Lens—A zoom lens enables you to change the focal length of the lens. By pushing a button or moving a lever on a zoom lens, you can make an object appear closer or farther away. In effect, the focal length of the lens increases. Or, you can fit more of the subject into the picture. The focal length decreases.

With one lens, you can get a wide-angle view, a normal shot or a telephoto perspective for closeups—and everything in between.

A zoom lens is described by its focal-length range. You'll find numbers such as 12—72mm, 14—84mm and 11—70mm on different lenses. To figure out the focal-length range, divide the smaller number into the larger one. Common ranges for video cameras are 3:1, 5:1, 6:1, 8:1 and 12:1, depending on the model and price. These numbers may also appear in specifications as 3X, 5X, 6X, 8X and 12X, respectively.

The greater the focal-length range, the more versatile the lens and the higher the price of the video camera. Low-end cameras may not offer more than a 2:1 or 3:1 range. High-end cameras

Hitachi's VK-C1000 was the first color home-video camera to use a CCD. Some newer models from Hitachi and other companies also use CCDs.

As with many models offering power zoom, you have a choice of manual or power lens movement with Hitachi VK-C830.

General Electric model offers a fast *f*-1.4 lens and 6X power zoom.

Canon VC-10A accepts an accessory 1.4X telephoto converter that extends the focal length of the camera's 11—70mm power zoom lens to 15—98mm. This increases focal length without decreasing lens speed—its sensitivity to light.

usually offer 5:1 or 6:1. Super-high-end models will give you up to 12:1.

Most cameras come with a permanently mounted lens. If you're looking for a certain range zoom, you have to take the camera you find it on. Then you have to accept the mix of other features that particular camera offers.

Power Zoom—Many cameras with a zoom lens allow you to change lens focal length with the push of a button. This is called *power zoom*. It operates much like the one you'll find on a super-8 camera. A small motor is activated by pushbuttons. It moves lens elements inside the lens barrel, changing focal length.

All cameras with power zoom also allow you to control the zoom manually. But some are easier to operate than others. The manual controls may be tighter, or harder to move, from one model to another. Check both power- and manual-zoom action on the camera you're considering. Be sure you're comfortable with the zoom operation.

Power zoom may offer one or two speeds. With the two-speed version, you must remember the location of both the switch that selects the speed, and the one that controls the actual zoom. You have to use all these controls without seeing them. While shooting, you're busy looking

JVC GX-N7 camera weighs 2.4 pounds and is small enough to fit in the palm of your hand. Its 1/2-inch Newvicon tube makes low-light shooting possible. With an adapter, the camera accepts 35mm SLR lenses.

ZOOM-LENS FUNCTION

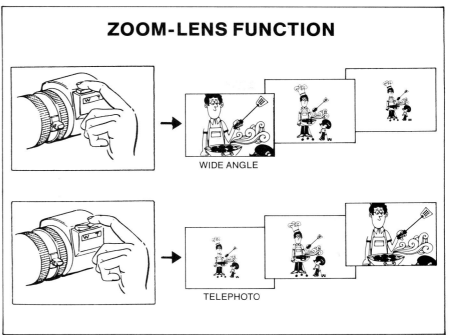

WIDE ANGLE

TELEPHOTO

With a zoom lens, you can get close-up images, wide-angle shots, or in-between views. When using a power zoom as illustrated here, all you do is push a button. The lens focal length changes automatically. In the illustration, the zoom control is located on the camera body. At left, control is on pistol grip, just below record button. For manual zoom, you change lens focal length by moving a lens ring.

through the finder. To many, this is a challenge they can live without. We suggest you try a model with two-speed power zoom before deciding.

Video zoom motors are designed so they don't produce electronic interference. Otherwise, the camera's electronic circuits carrying the picture might pick up interference called *noise*. You would record a visual and audio effect similar to what happens when you use a hair dryer or vacuum cleaner while watching television. The picture and sound become distorted.

Don't misunderstand us. Power zoom is not just a convenience feature. It can enhance the quality of your home-video productions. You avoid the jerky zoom movement that invariably occurs with manual zoom. To many, this feature seems about as important as power windows on a car. Although power windows are not a necessity, many people want them.

Despite all the challenges, we do suggest a power zoom. You'll find it on most high-end cameras.

Lens Speed—Some cameras require more light than others to produce a good image. Just as in conventional photography, the *speed* of the lens indicates its low-light capabilities. Lens speed is rated with an *f*-number. It's a measure of maximum aperture of the lens. A small *f*-number, such as *f*-1.2, signifies a large maximum aperture. It allows more light to pass through the lens.

When you're in low-light situations and there's no supplementary lighting, the camera with the fastest lens speed—smallest *f*-number—will give you a better chance for a good image.

Many experienced users of conventional film cameras often forget that they must give *special consideration* to the maximum aperture of the video-camera lens. Why? Because in conventional photography, you have other options to compensate for a slower lens.

In conventional photography, you can use more sensitive film when light is limited. In video, you don't have that choice. In the video camera, the equivalent of film speed is set by the characteristics of the camera's imaging device. You can't change it!

Similarly, in a video camera, there's no shutter speed to change. You can't compensate for poor lighting by making a longer exposure. The speed of the lens on your video camera is important. Consider this feature carefully.

Infrared automatic focus and 8X power-zoom lens with macro capability are features of Olympus VX-303.

JVC GX-N5 has two-speed power-zoom lens, electronic finder, auto iris, auto fade and auto white balance. Minimum illumination required is 10 lux (1 foot-candle).

In the video camera, lens characteristics are not the only elements that determine final image exposure. Size and type of imaging device are also related. We can't tell you which type of imaging device (Saticon, vidicon, CCD and so forth) or which lens aperture (*f*-1.2, for example) is best—or which combination would be the best choice!

Macro Capability—One feature that's almost standard on high-end cameras is the ability of the lens to focus closer than about 3.3 feet (1 meter).

If a lens can focus closer than 3.3 feet, it has close-up capability, sometimes called *macro capability.* Do you need it? If you plan to use your video camera to do nature studies or copy photographs and paintings, you probably do.

External Filter and Lens Adaptability—If you have experience with film cameras, you no doubt take for granted camera lenses with threads at the front of the lens barrel. The threads allow you to screw filters and lens accessories into the front of the lens. You can also use these threads to attach external close-up lenses. Video camera lenses often lack the threads.

If you think you want these threads, examine the lens. Read the specifications—and ask questions. If it's listed on the specifications sheet at all, you may find a notation such as *Filter Size: 52mm.* This means that the camera will accept 52mm filters with screw-in threads. These filters are available at video and camera shops.

In film cameras, you can color correct with external filters. It's accomplished in video by adjusting built-in electronic controls. But you may still want to use external filters for special coloration or other effects.

Auto-Iris or Electronic Exposure Control—In video cameras, two circuits control what is referred to in conventional photography as the *exposure level* of the picture. In video, the term is *white level,* or *gain.* The first circuit is a standard *automatic iris;* the second is an *electronic level control.*

Control over the iris in a video camera is much the same as it is in a film camera, with the corresponding influence on depth of field. For example, the smaller the aperture setting, the sharper the image will be from near to far. The video camera's iris opens and closes automatically, based on changing light levels. Auto-iris adjusts the camera's internal aperture. It lets the camera do some of the thinking for you. Then you can keep your mind on getting the shot instead of worrying about exposure.

The video camera doesn't have a control similar to the film-speed indicator on a conventional film camera. Although the electronic level control is similar, a boost in video gain in the video camera doesn't influence depth of field. With a film camera, you have the option of gaining a few exposure steps by using more sensitive film. The video equivalent of film speed is determined by the characteristics of the imaging device over which you have no control.

As mentioned earlier, the imager can be either a tube or solid-state device. You can't change the

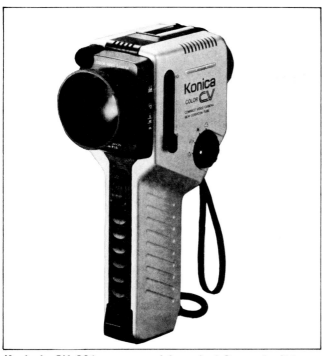

Konica's CV-301 camera weighs only 1.6 pounds. It has a TTL finder and Cosvicon pick-up tube.

High-end cameras, such as Panasonic PK-558, feature an electronic viewfinder, power 6X zoom lens and macro-focus capability.

imaging device that comes with your video camera. Each video-camera model is designed to house a specific size tube or solid-state device. Low-light sensitivity varies, depending on the type used. Some models with a Saticon tube rather than a vidicon tube generally do a better job of imaging in low light levels.

The second circuit is the *electronic level control,* which electronically measures the video camera's output level. It compares it to the way the circuit has been preprogrammed to know how the level *should* read. If the video level is too high, automatic adjustments are made.

If video-output level is too low—so low that a good picture may not be possible—a signal is sent to a low-light indicator. This is similar to indicators used in film-camera viewfinders.

Many video cameras with this feature include manual override. If you want a camera with manual override, check to see what kind of override—if any—is supplied.

On some models, the override takes the form of a two-position switch. On others, a dial allows you to open and close the aperture manually, using its motor. The dial gives you more control and is more precise.

If the camera you're considering doesn't offer a manual override you like, you might be better off with a camera that doesn't include auto-iris.

Auto-Focus—This is one of the latest additions to the lens and camera designer's bag of tricks. Auto-focus removes some of the picture-taking burden. Now you don't have to squint into the viewfinder, worrying if Aunt Mildred is in focus at the end of the table. The lens does all the work. Basically, all you have to worry about is composition.

Video-camera auto-focus is achieved in several ways: infrared sensors focused on mirrors that

This camera features infrared auto focus. One advantage over other systems, such as sonar auto focus, is that this type of camera can be used when shooting through glass. Other cameras use different focusing systems, such as sonar or video sampling using CCDs.

function as an automated split-image finder; solid-state charge-coupled device (CCD); ultrasonic (sonar) sensing system; video sensing system.

They all *attempt* to measure the distance from the camera to the object you're shooting. We say "attempt" because auto-focus is not foolproof.

If you have a problem focusing the lens on your film camera, the auto-focus feature is one you should consider in a video camera. Follow the owner's manual instructions carefully. As a result, you'll get a good image *most* of the time—especially after you discover the types of situations that can fool auto-focus.

Shooting through glass when using a sonar-focusing system is one example. This type of system would focus on the glass surface, not the subject on the other side. Infrared auto-focus isn't totally foolproof, either. But it'll work well when pointing the camera toward a subject behind a glass window or while operating in low-light situations.

Directing the camera at a subject some distance away with a nearby object within the range of the auto-focus sensor will cause a problem with most systems. Others, which compare light contrast by using mirrors and special circuitry, are often fooled by closely placed horizontal lines, backlighting or fine patterns that cover much of the picture area.

These situations may result in out-of-focus images unless you control focus manually or move the camera to another position. Automatic-focusing systems don't know which object in a scene is of greatest interest to you and must be in sharpest focus. Therefore, no matter which type of auto-focus system offered, the operator still has to make a judgment.

If you plan to do a lot of serious shooting, check to see how the manual override operates. Is manual focusing easy? Is it simple to go from auto-focus to manual? Or, do you have to move a switch or dial on the lens or camera body to go to manual operation? Manual override on a particular model may be inconvenient or difficult for you to use.

Are you planning to do a lot of action shooting at sporting events or other fast-moving activities? Check to see how the auto-focus system reacts when you pan or swing the camera quickly across a scene. Does it react fast enough for your needs?

Auto focus is featured on Minolta K-800S camera. Also included are power zoom, character generator, fade and VCR controls.

The different types of auto-focus mechanisms are a design choice. When researching cameras, don't be concerned with which type of auto-focus is integrated into your chosen camera. Although some systems work better in different situations, all are about equal in accuracy.

If you have a good eye and experience in conventional photography—especially motion-picture shooting—you may regard auto-focus on a video camera the way you would a similar feature on a photographic camera—for the amateur. You may want total control over focus, without the additional weight and bulk of this control.

To most home-video enthusiasts, auto-focus is a welcome arrival. However, you should examine the system on the camera you have in mind. See if it works in the real-life shooting situations you have planned.

So much for the basics of camera operation. As you see, there are many parallels between video and film cameras.

Camera Features

When compared to VCR features discussed in Chapter 2, home-video cameras are usually less complex. Some features are basic to the camera's operation. Others have been added for easier setup. Sometimes manufacturers include special functions to make their cameras more fun to use.

Today's lightweight home-video cameras de-veloped as a result of improvements in electronics. Thus, most of the features are electronic. There are no strictly mechanical features as in VCRs. Video cameras are electro-optical in nature, as opposed to electro-mechanical VCRs.

OPERATIONAL FEATURES

A video camera must perform many of the same functions as a film camera, but in video, it's often accomplished electronically. There are additional functions and features—both required and optional—that you see only with video cameras. Here's a look at some of them.

Power Supplies—A video camera needs power to operate. Usually, the power is supplied through a cable connected to a portable VCR. Video cameras are designed to operate on direct current (DC), the type of power supplied by batteries.

That's OK if you're using the camera with a portable VCR. But what if you want to connect your camera to an AC-powered tabletop?

In most cases, to use a camera with a tabletop, you need an auxiliary camera-power supply. Some cameras come with this power supply. It's an option with others. The camera-power supply converts household 110-volt AC voltage into the appropriate low-voltage DC needed to run the camera.

But the video camera-power supply also per-

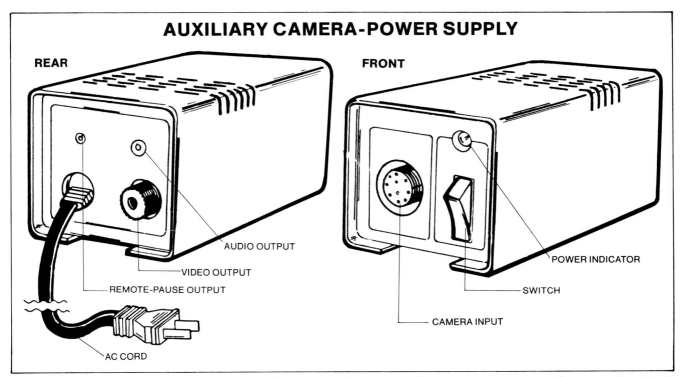

AUXILIARY CAMERA-POWER SUPPLY

REAR

FRONT

AUDIO OUTPUT

VIDEO OUTPUT

REMOTE-PAUSE OUTPUT

AC CORD

POWER INDICATOR

SWITCH

CAMERA INPUT

To use a home-video camera with most tabletop VCRs, you must have an auxiliary camera-power supply. It converts household AC voltage to DC, and provides separate video, audio and pause-control outputs for connecting the tabletop VCR and camera.

forms another important function. It provides separate connections for video and audio outputs, and pause control. With these separate connections, you can use your camera with a tabletop unit that doesn't have a 10- or 14-pin camera plug.

Canon VC-20A lets you produce smooth, even fades. Camera also offers automatic focus and allows adding titles in three colors to your video productions.

Power-Saver Switch—When a video camera is connected to most portable VCRs, it shares the recorder battery power. If the camera is on when you're not shooting, it drains the battery. However, if you keep turning the camera off, you have to wait for it to warm up each time you want to start shooting. In the meantime, you could miss an important shot.

To avoid this potential problem, buy a camera with a power-saver switch. This reduces the amount of power the camera uses when you're not actually shooting. It turns off the viewfinder while keeping the rest of the camera ready.

The power-saver switch is useful and worth considering.

Fade In/Fade Out—With motion-picture equipment, you can fade to black for a scene transition by stopping down the lens until the iris is completely closed. This doesn't allow any light to reach the film. If your camera lens allows, you can close the aperture until there's no light entering the camera. In video, there's another option: You can electronically fade the image to black.

The fade is performed by a circuit that gradually decreases the video signal. This doesn't affect timing pulses that drive the TV scanning system. As a result, the signal recorded on the VCR is "electronic" black. On the TV, this looks closer to a dark gray.

Fades add a nice touch. You may be new to video production, but you'll soon get better and

Videotaping a holiday event using a home-video camera and battery-powered VCR.

Right: Increasingly popular feature on cameras is a positive/negative switch, such as on Canon's VC-10A. With this, you can copy photographic negatives onto video as positives, or create unusual effects. To its left is a combination character generator on/off and power-saver switch. Far Right: To set white balance on Minolta K-2000S, switch white-balance display ON and point camera toward a white object. In viewfinder, you'll see a white pattern. Turn white-balance knob until you get largest white-pattern display. Switch white-balance display switch OFF. Below that is power-saver switch.

try to refine your skills. The fade feature is an example of a function that you might not consider important now, but one that will become more important or even essential later on.

An electronic feature like fade capability can't be added to the camera because it's not an accessory. Instead, it's integrated into the design of the particular video camera.

Many high-end cameras offer a fade switch that lets you create a controlled fade for smooth transitions from scene to scene. We recommend this feature. It's the best way technically to fade into or out of a scene to "black."

Positive/Negative Switch—If you want to copy photographic negatives on videotape, consider this feature. By mounting the negatives in an adapter, you can record a positive image on videotape if the camera has a negative/positive switch. You can't do this easily with motion-picture equipment. The adapter may come with the camera or be offered as an extra-cost accessory.

You can use this to keep a video record of what you have in your film files. Keep in mind, however, that some cameras require a special filter to eliminate the orange masking in color negatives. With other cameras, you use the built-in color-control without needing an additional lens accessory.

The positive/negative switch on a home-video camera also allows you to decide at any time if you want a resulting image in positive or negative. The camera's electronics reverse polarity—the positive/negative orientation—of colors comprising the video signal. This offers interesting creative possibilities. You can create strangely colored images of common scenes to add interest to your home-video productions.

This capability is becoming more common on video cameras. But many people don't know

their equipment has it. And others wouldn't know what to do with it if they did have it. Don't pay extra for this unless you know you'll use it.

White-Balance Control—The purpose of this control is to provide the camera with a reference for knowing the type of light it's shooting in. That way, you're certain that all the colors are adjusted properly.

In conventional photography, an 18% gray card is used as an exposure reference. In video, the camera's color circuits use *100% white* as a reference when they set themselves. A simple white-balance control has a two-position switch. An automatic control operates when you point the

One-touch automatic white-balance control in Sony HVC-2800 adjusts camera's built-in filters to changing light conditions. Camera uses an SMF (Saticon Mixed-Field) Trinicon tube, previously found only in Sony's professional cameras. This imaging device is known for its excellent resolution and color accuracy. This is another example of professional features being added to home-video equipment. Camera also has two microphones. One is built-in, above the base of the lens. The other is detachable and mounts on top. This extends the camera's audio-recording range.

camera at something white and press a button. With either, all the colors in the scene will be recorded correctly as long as the camera is used under similar lighting.

What you're doing is giving the video camera an allowance for variations in the red-green-blue balance (color temperature) of the lighting.

The most effective control is the automatic arrangement. All you do is point the camera at a white wall and press a button. Then you don't have to white balance again unless you move into a different type of lighting.

Color-Adjust Control—If you have the white-balance control, why would you need a color-adjust control, too? This feature permits fine tuning. It allows you to alter the color more toward red or blue, depending on your preference.

Artificial lighting—especially fluorescent light mixed with tungsten—may alter colors the camera's electronics pick up. This can happen even if the unit is white-balanced. The color-adjust control allows you to achieve closer to accurate, or at least more pleasing, color.

In photography, this function is accomplished in a variety of ways. You can use appropriate films or filtration. In video, you can also mount filters in front of the camera lens to alter or correct colors in the scene. These can be photographic-camera filters or those offered exclusively for video.

With your video camera, you can change the setting of the white-balance control. If you want additional creative control to change the color bal-

ance of a scene even more, you need a color-adjust control.

Manipulating the color-adjust control acts as an electronic filter, similar to adjusting a TV's tint controls. This changes the video image the way filters in a color-enlarger head alter the way photographic prints look. The video equivalent of the color-head enlarger is an accessory called an *outboard processor*.

Here's a note of caution: Be sure the TV you're using to view the image is adjusted correctly. Skin tone is the best subject to use for this adjustment. Depending on the TV in use, color is bound to look somewhat different, regardless of how carefully you set the controls on your own TV.

Backlight Switch—A standard rule of thumb for the amateur photographer used to be: "Keep the sun over your shoulder." Following this guideline would ensure enough light on the front of the subject. Perhaps his eyes were squinting, but you'd have adequate illumination on his face nonetheless. With modern films and photographic techniques, this dictum is no longer as important. But it is still a good, basic guideline.

In video, as in conventional photography, you won't always be able to follow this advice. Sometimes you'll shoot a backlit subject—with the light coming from behind. Some video cameras offer a solution to this type of lighting problem with a *backlight switch*. When activated, it overrides normal auto-iris operation by opening the diaphragm a bit more. It's a nice feature to have, but not a must.

Here's another reminder: *Never* point a video

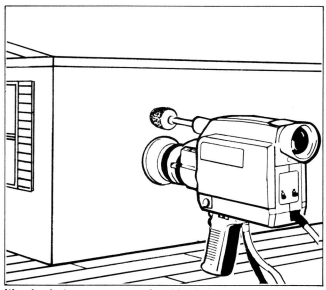

It's simple to use a camera's white-balance system. All you have to do is aim the camera at a white wall or other surface. Then adjust control according to owner's manual instructions. Remember to readjust this control each time you move to a different type of lighting.

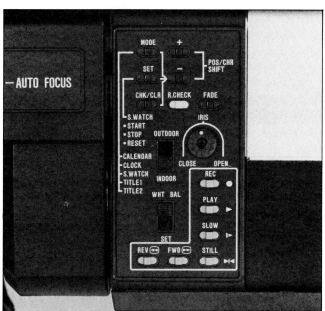

Side panel close-up of Minolta K-800S AF shows some of its features. RCA on next page has controls on camera body and on pistol grip.

camera directly at the sun or a bright light. It can cause *burn-in,* ruining the tube. Burn-in is the tendency for a bright image to be retained on the camera's phosphor imaging surface. This may result from aiming the camera at a brightly lit subject for a long period. This may cause permanent damage. Consult a repair service for more information.

It's a good idea to never point the camera toward such a subject, even if you have a CCD or MOS that supposedly is not susceptible to burn-in. You may not damage the solid-state pickup device, but the bright light may distort the image.

Watch for strong indirect light or reflections that may shine into the camera lens. Although this light probably won't destroy the pickup device, it may cause other problems such as poor exposure.

Sensitivity or Gain-Boost—Once again, electronics has given us a way to overcome a problem that's solved chemically with conventional photographic film.

Let's say you have poor lighting conditions when shooting with your SLR. To get good exposures, you may use faster film or ask the lab for push-processing. Professional cameras and more advanced home-video cameras accomplish much the same thing with *gain-boost.* The camera indicator may be marked **SENSITIVITY** or **GAIN-BOOST**.

As with using faster film or push-processing, the compensation afforded by gain-boost in video means sacrificing some picture quality. In film, it can register as a grainy look in the photos. In video, you'll find a lower signal-to-noise ratio. This shows up as poorer quality—"grainier-looking" pictures.

Those are the trade-offs. But if you think you'll find yourself shooting in low-light situations, gain-boost is a feature you want to consider seriously.

Character Generator—One of the most impressive features appearing on super-high-end home-video cameras is the *character generator,* or *CG.* It

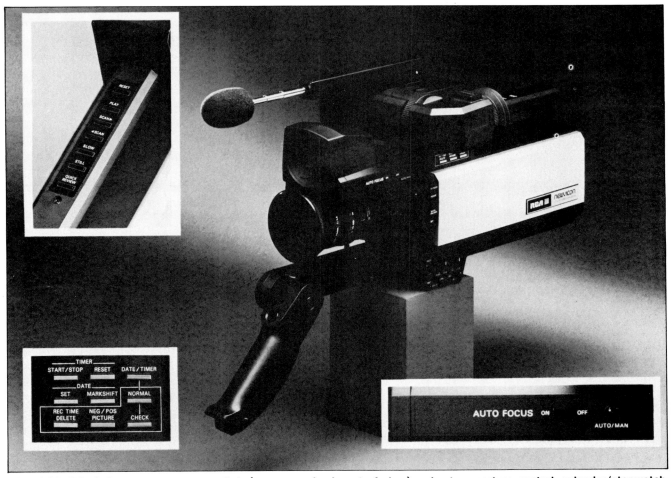

RCA CC015 includes a power-saver switch (on camera back, out of view), color-temperature control, calendar/stopwatch display, automatic focus and a range of remote VCR controls. On-camera remote controls allow you to review segments through the camera's viewfinder, and edit segments in the field.

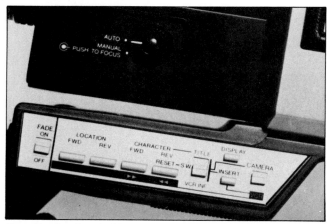

Top: Professional videographers use character generators such as this to add names and numbers to their productions. For example, they may want to identify individuals in an interview or sporting event. Center and Bottom: Using modern technology, manufacturers have reduced the large character generator to a size that can be incorporated into the home-video camera. Now, *you* can add titles to your home-video productions while you're shooting them.

allows you to put your own titles on an image, adding a nice touch to your videotaped segments. But, this handy little wonder takes some getting used to.

Electronic CGs have been around for some time in TV stations. For example, they're used to add the names of newsmakers and ballplayers' batting averages to the video image on the screen. In broadcasting, the CG is large, expensive and complicated. However, advances in integrated-circuit technology have made it possible to produce a small, relatively inexpensive CG. As a result, it can be used in home-video cameras.

With a professional television character generator, the information is entered using a standard-size typewriter-style keyboard. Obviously that's too large to be used on a portable camera. Design engineers worked out two approaches for entering the information when using a CG built into a portable camera.

On some models with the original design, you have to step through the alphabet, letter-by-letter, using one control. It operates like small plastic labelers. Instead of spinning a dial to choose the character, you push a button that makes letters flash on the screen. These are usually in alphabetical order. You just stop pressing when you reach the letter you want. It's then stored in the built-in temporary memory. You do this for each character.

Did you ever reach a high score on a video-arcade game and enter your initials with the fire button? The display is handled the same way here. The letters you've chosen are then mixed in with the camera's video output. They're super-imposed over the video image.

With other models, this process is simpler. There's one key for each letter and number. You no longer have to go through the full alphabet to indicate a Z, for example. This speeds up the titling process.

When you're ready to make your final purchasing decision, ask yourself how often you'll really use the CG. Is it just another status gadget you'll use once or twice and then forget about? Decide whether a camera with a CG is worth the extra cost.

Stopwatch Display—This works on the same principle as the electronic character generator. For a stopwatch display, a standard electronic timing circuit similar to a digital electronic stopwatch is used.

But the timing chip doesn't drive a digital display. It drives a character-generator circuit that changes the impulses representing the time display into video signals. These are superimposed over the picture. The new image is sent through the camera cable to the VCR while it's displayed in the camera's electronic viewfinder.

On-Screen Timer—A camera that offers a character generator often also includes a visual time display. As in the case with the letters for your titles from the CG, the timer's number display can be brought in and out of the picture as desired.

This on-screen timer can be used when you tape a sporting event such as a race. It's not the sort of thing that most people will be doing with their camera. Therefore, the on-screen timer may not be a feature you'll use often.

Auto Capping (Shutter Switch)—It would be nice if there were a super-programmable function to prevent you from losing your camera's lens cap. But that's not exactly the feature we're going to explain.

Don't confuse this with the fade-in/fade-out switch. This switch completely closes the opening into the camera. The shutter is positioned behind the lens but in front of the imaging device. An electronic circuit drops the shutter in front of the imaging tube or solid-state device. As a result, no light reaches it. This prevents damage to the device, should your camera be aimed accidentally at the sun or other bright light when you're not using it.

The shutter switch is a handy safety feature. It's especially valuable when it also includes a mechanism that automatically closes the shutter when the camera is not receiving any power.

Another way to protect the tube is by keeping a lens cap over the lens whenever you're not taping. The problem is that many people lose the cap, or forget to use it.

Remote Control—When shooting with a video camera, you're working with two important pieces of equipment—the camera and the VCR. But you don't want to keep pressing buttons on both the VCR and camera every time you start or stop shooting. Almost every video camera has a trigger-like start/stop switch that operates with a compatible VCR. This allows you to forget about the switches on the VCR while you concentrate on shooting.

The number of functions you can control from the camera depends on the video-camera model. Expensive cameras generally offer more remote-control functions than less-expensive models.

Commands are sent through the camera cable to the VCR, which is set up to record with the camera. In its simplest form, the video-camera remote control is nothing more than an extension

Pushing this I.R. (instant review) button on the pistol grip of some cameras automatically rewinds tape in the videocassette. It automatically plays in the viewfinder the last three seconds of tape you've just recorded. Also called *quick review* and other names.

JVC GZ-S5U VHS-C compact camera with optional CG-P50U character generator mounted on top. CG allows you to add titles, date and time in four different sizes to the recorded image. CG memory stores information for up to a year. Each time you enter new information in the memory, it erases the previous information.

of the VCR pause control. It's the trigger switch connected through the camera cable to the switch on the VCR.

Some cameras let you control the rewind of the videocassette on the VCR from the camera. You can then play back the segment you have just shot through the camera's viewfinder without touching the VCR.

But, we wouldn't advise putting this feature high on your priority list. When shooting, you won't be able to do much more than press the trigger while concentrating on your shots.

Some cameras even have a complete remote-control panel built into the camera. This can operate almost all VCR functions.

With the complete panel, not only can you start and stop the VCR from the camera, you can also rewind the VCR and put it on fast-forward. Or you can put it in the full-stop mode, as opposed to the pause mode in which the tape is stretched out against the heads.

Boom microphone mounts next to the viewfinder on this Sylvania model. You can extend the microphone toward the subject to reduce the amount of camera noises that are recorded.

Electronic viewfinder is built into the body of this Magnavox camera. As with most cameras, the viewfinder image is b&w. You can use the accessory shoe on top of the camera to attach an accessory microphone or a video light.

There's no denying that this extended range of remote-control functions at the camera end has its uses. This is especially true in playback through an electronic viewfinder.

One sophisticated control found on some cameras automatically backs up the tape in the VCR a bit each time you press the switch to stop recording. This gives an acceptable assemble edit on the tape with your camera. Assemble edits give clean transitions between segments recorded on the videocassette at different times.

Microphone—What good are pictures nowadays unless they're talkies? Most video cameras have a microphone. This allows you to record the sounds of the moment along with the images. There are several ways to mount the mike to the camera.

All mike types we discuss are part of the video-camera design. A *built-in* mike is the simplest design. This one is built into the front of the camera body.

The built-in mike often is hidden behind a grill or foam windscreen. This mike will do the job. But it won't be useful for picking up conversations more than a few feet away. It picks up too many sounds made by the camera operator—and even some camera-operating sounds.

That's why camera designers developed the *boom mike.* This is a microphone placed on an extending rod, or "boom." This moves the mike away from the camera, toward the subject.

Although this type of mike won't capture whispers 12 feet away, it's better than the simple built-in mike. It can pick up more sounds in front of the operator from farther away. And, it reduces recording of camera and operator sounds.

The third kind, a *zoom boom,* allows you the greatest flexibility in recording audio with your camera. It electronically alters the mike's pickup pattern. This gives the effect of moving the mike closer to, or farther from, camera position.

There's no clear-cut way to offer a breakdown for mike types by price range. That's because the kind of mike used with a particular camera is more a function of camera design rather than price.

The built-in mike design is OK. The boom is better. And the zoom boom is best. Now we've ranked the various camera-mike designs for you. But, when it comes right down to it, there isn't much difference in the sound-reproduction capabilities of the mikes—just the area they cover.

We strongly suggest a camera that features a jack for an *external mike.* Look for two jacks if you'll be shooting with a stereo VCR. Two jacks aren't common, however.

When you use an external mike plugged into the camera, you can stand farther from your subject while recording a conversation. And you won't pick up all the camera operating sounds or noises occurring right in front of the camera.

CAMERA STYLING

In addition to the feature list, you should also think about the style or basic design of the camera. Because of various viewfinder designs, there are two broad categories of styling.

We describe and illustrate both of them. However, this is clearly a case in which you have to pick up the cameras and "try them on for size" to decide the best one for you.

Super-8 Styling—The best way to describe the first of the two groups is to say that it most closely resembles the design of super-8 movie cameras. The viewfinder—optical, TTL or electronic—is built into the camera body. When using a video camera of this design, you hold the back of the camera up to your eye, with the camera in front of you. To aid in supporting the camera, a handgrip is usually mounted on the front of the camera.

With this type of camera, you'll tend to place one hand on the grip, with the other hand on the side or top to steady the camera body. Because your arm is stretched out during use, you may find that a camera featuring super-8 design is too tiring to use for long periods. If you're used to a movie camera, however, a video camera of this design shouldn't be any problem.

Professional ENG operator in action. He rests camera on his shoulder, places one hand in the grip and the other on lens for focusing.

If we removed the labels from these two cameras, would you be able to tell that one is a super-8 camera (left) and the other a video camera? Obviously, that's why we call one video camera design *super-8 styling*. (Courtesy Chinon USA Inc. and Aiwa America)

Make sure the handgrip is removable so you can place the camera on a tripod when the situation calls for it. Many handgrips include a tripod socket. It's best to mount your camera directly to the tripod, without the handgrip between them.

ENG Styling—We call it *ENG styling* because you hold this type of home-video camera similar to the way members of broadcast-TV Electronic-News-Gathering (ENG) camera crews hold theirs. The viewfinder extends out from the body of the camera. The eyepiece is arranged to bring the image closer to your eye.

Other than cosmetic differences, it's obvious that Sylvania VCC120 and JVC GX-N5 are built by same manufacturer—in this case, JVC. However, it's important to remember that Sylvania and other companies may not buy all of their camera models from only one OEM.

You'll only find ENG styling on units with an electronic viewfinder. Therefore, it's not common in the leader-model camera price range.

ENG-styled cameras are designed to be held with one hand on the grip while the camera body rests on your shoulder. If you develop your skill, you'll be able to plop the camera on your shoulder and shoot with only one hand on the grip. Even the pros usually place their other hand on the lens to steady the camera.

The ENG design may appear to be more comfortable while shooting. But, comfort is often in the "eye of the beholder." Not only does shooting position influence comfort, but you must also consider some other factors.

How much does the camera weigh? How is it balanced from front to rear? A light camera body with a heavy lens may cause discomfort. What's easiest for you? Find out by handling the equipment at your dealer.

When selecting a camera, try the different styles offered by several brands. Look at all the features and options. Do your homework and research beforehand. And use the checklist provided at the back of the book.

How to Buy a Camera

A color video camera will open up another new area of enjoyment for you. You'll be able to record your own home-video "movies" and play them back over and over. And, shooting video has at least two major advantages over motion-picture photography: You can see the images instantly. If you don't like the results, you can record something else on the same videocassette.

Here, we'll help you find out which is the best video camera for your needs. You should realize by now that there are very different factors to consider when purchasing a camera. But you'll also find a number of similarities.

As with VCRs, video cameras are sold under a variety of brand names. Actually, home-video cameras sold in North America are made in Japan by only a few companies. These are the OEMs. It's important to keep this in mind. You may be able to get a better deal on a camera sold by an unfamiliar brand than the same camera marketed by a brand you know.

CAMERA AND VCR OEMs AREN'T ALWAYS THE SAME

Although a brand is likely to buy its video cameras from the same company that makes its VCRs, this practice is by no means universal.

Some brands use different OEMs for their cam-

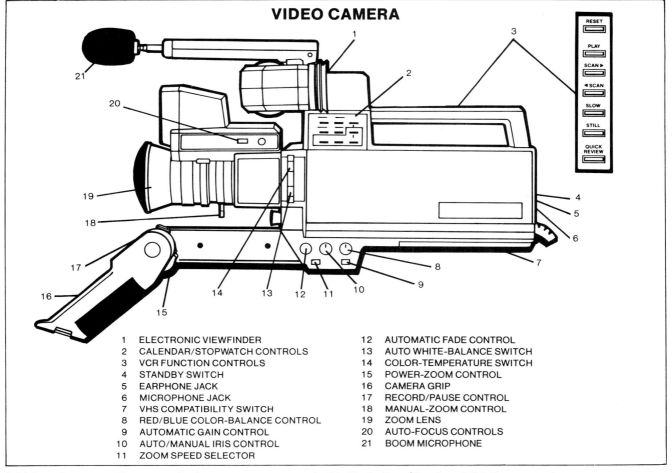

VIDEO CAMERA

1	ELECTRONIC VIEWFINDER	12	AUTOMATIC FADE CONTROL
2	CALENDAR/STOPWATCH CONTROLS	13	AUTO WHITE-BALANCE SWITCH
3	VCR FUNCTION CONTROLS	14	COLOR-TEMPERATURE SWITCH
4	STANDBY SWITCH	15	POWER-ZOOM CONTROL
5	EARPHONE JACK	16	CAMERA GRIP
6	MICROPHONE JACK	17	RECORD/PAUSE CONTROL
7	VHS COMPATIBILITY SWITCH	18	MANUAL-ZOOM CONTROL
8	RED/BLUE COLOR-BALANCE CONTROL	19	ZOOM LENS
9	AUTOMATIC GAIN CONTROL	20	AUTO-FOCUS CONTROLS
10	AUTO/MANUAL IRIS CONTROL	21	BOOM MICROPHONE
11	ZOOM SPEED SELECTOR		

A high-end camera offers many features, as you can see in this illustration. (Courtesy RCA Corporation)

eras than for their VCRs. Camera OEMs tend to change more often than do VCR OEMs. That's why it's impossible to give you a chart of camera OEMs by brand, as we did with VCRs. In addition, some brands will market the same basic camera as another brand, but use a different lens.

When comparing cameras, it's usually easier to spot similarities than with VCRs. There are fewer cosmetic variations in their design.

However, there's one factor that can sometimes make buying a camera very confusing. Although the camera may be the same as another brand, it may not use the same type of *connection* to attach to a VCR. We'll tell you more about the different types of connections later in this chapter.

Prices and Features

There are various prices and features to look for. You know that VCRs come in a variety of model classes, from leaders to step-ups to high-end units. This has developed differently with home-video cameras.

When home-video cameras first became

available, there were leader, middle and high-end models. Now, cameras fit into the leader, high- and super-high-end price categories. The middle range has all but disappeared. Here's a look at the price groups and what you'll find in cameras.

LEADER MODELS

The leader model, or low-end camera, is the least expensive. List price is generally less than $600. The low price doesn't mean inferior performance. Rather, it reflects fewer features offered.

Even so, today's low-end camera usually offers many of the same features found on mid-range cameras just a few years ago. Then, those mid-range units would have cost $200 to $300 more than you pay today for the leader-model camera.

Optical viewfinders aren't common today. Most leader-model cameras offer a TTL reflex viewfinder that allows you to view the same picture the camera's imaging device is seeing. Should you wish to add an electronic viewfinder later on, some low-end cameras allow this.

In the late 1970s, the first low-end home-video

Top: Toshiba IK-2200 high-end model has an electronic viewfinder, automatic focus and 6X power-zoom lens. Above: A super-deluxe model is the Magnavox 8280. This offers a Newvicon tube, character generator, stop-watch display, infrared automatic focus, among other features.

HIGH-END MODELS

If today's low-end camera has replaced yesterday's mid-range camera, where does the high-end unit fit into the price scheme? It's right where it has always been. List price is generally from $750 to $1200. However, the high-end camera is lower priced than the top-of-the-line unit of a few years back. And it offers more features.

As manufacturers develop a product, they not only make it better, they also can make it less expensive. We showed you how this has affected VCR prices. Again, if you consider inflation, a high-end camera actually costs less than it did a few years ago.

A typical high-end camera is equipped with a 6:1 power-zoom lens, electronic viewfinder, auto-white balance control and auto-iris. It also includes a full range of LED indicators in the finder, a built-in boom microphone and fade-in/fade-out control.

The list of features in this price range is getting even longer. The camera may be equipped with an auto-focus lens, built-in character generator and stopwatch timer for on-screen display.

Sometimes you'll also find full VCR remote controls built into the camera, instead of just the simple start/stop functions. Still other features may include a negative/positive switch, quick-review system and adjustable viewfinder.

SUPER-HIGH-END MODELS

If a high-end camera seems to have just about everything your heart desires, what's left for the super-high-end unit to offer? The super-high-end model may have a special lens, possibly with a zoom ratio of 8:1 or even 12:1! List prices are more than $1200.

Some replace the standard vidicon camera tube with the higher-quality Saticon or Newvicon tube. These tubes produce better pictures in dim light and are less susceptible to burn-in.

Others don't use a tube at all. Instead of a tube, they may have solid-state imaging circuitry, such as a CCD or MOS. As with a camera featuring a Saticon or Newvicon tube, one with a solid-state device is less susceptible to harmful burn-ins that can occur when the camera is aimed toward a strong light source.

A camera with a solid-state device or better tube can be panned from one lighting situation to another with less *lag*. Lag is the tendency of a camera's imaging device to retain a previous bright image for a short time. This is a function of the pickup device. Lag shows on the videotape as a momentary ghost of the previous image.

An important recent development has been

cameras had fixed-focal-length lenses. Today, the fixed-focal-length lens is almost as uncommon as the optical finder. Most leader models now have a zoom lens.

Although leader models lack fancy extras, they usually will do the job. In fact, their simplicity may even be a benefit to some users. Because they don't have extra features, the less-expensive cameras are lightweight and easy to use.

the addition of a color viewfinder to some super-deluxe camera models. These are very expensive. It may be some time before a color viewfinder will be on a camera selling for less than $1750.

The Cat's Meow—Video cameras with solid-state pickup devices are the cat's meow of the video-camera world. They're the lightest and least vulnerable to damage. They also produce quality pictures in the widest range of lighting situations. Although these cameras are in the super-high-end category now, look out! We predict that this will be the standard camera in the not-too-distant future.

WHICH FEATURES DO YOU NEED?

The best way to make an intelligent purchasing decision for a camera is to know the various features. This is the same approach you use when shopping for a VCR. You must decide which features you need. Then choose which you might be able to use but can live without. Use the checklist in the back of this book. Then search for the models that fill the bill.

With this information, you can compare the brands and models to see which come closest to meeting your needs. Then shop for the dealer with the best price and service combination.

Camera and VCR Compatibility

If all video cameras sold in North America have the same 1-volt NTSC video outputs, why are there problems in connecting one brand of camera to another company's VCR?

Given all the differences we've mentioned between the Beta and VHS formats, it should come as no surprise that you might not be able to use a camera from a Beta brand with a VHS recorder. But, in addition, sometimes you can't even plug one VHS brand camera into another's VHS VCR! The same may be true in Beta lines.

Within each format, different manufacturers use different connectors to attach their cameras to their VCRs. Some have 8 pins on the cable to

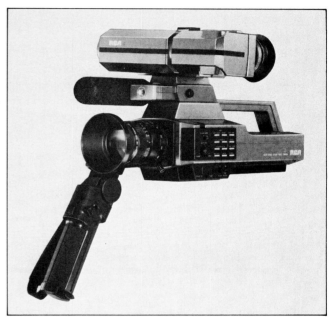

Listing for about $2000 is what many would consider the ultimate home-video camera. RCA CC030's electronic viewfinder displays the image in color. Camera also uses a solid-state MOS pickup device instead of a tube, and offers a character generator.

Panasonic PK-450 weighs 2.5 pounds. It offers a 6X power zoom, back-light compensator and automatic focus.

A camera such as this NEC TC-101E using a charge-coupled device for imaging is more resistant to burn-in than one with a tube. Regardless, *never* point any video camera toward a bright light!

When you build your video system, we suggest that you buy hardware of the same brand when possible. For example, Olympus camera, VCR, tuner/timer and AC adapter shown here are designed to be totally compatible. If you purchase another maker's camera, you may not be able to take advantage of features such as remote control. This is explained in the text.

the VCR. Others have 10, 14 or even 15 pins. Some manufacturers may use the same number of pins—but the pins themselves might be of different shapes and in different positions!

And, two manufacturers may use the same type of plug, for example. A 10-pin is the most common in VHS, and a 14-pin in Beta. However,

JVC GX-N80 camera has a switch (not shown) that permits you to use the camera and all of its standard features with many non-JVC VCRs. Read specification sheets of cameras offering this capability to find out which VCRs they will work with.

the plugs may not be wired the same way. For example, one brand's #6 pin might be a video feed; on another, pin #6 might be power.

There are also differences in the type of signal the VCR must receive from the camera to activate a function. For example, one manufacturer's VCR might need a positive signal to start and stop the VCR. Another could require a negative signal.

SOLVING THE PROBLEM

We wish we could give you a chart listing names of the various camera and VCR brands that could be interconnected. But things change too rapidly. Companies often switch OEMs for a certain model in their product line. The list would be out of date before you bought this book!

Some Tips—We can offer some tips to help you buy a camera compatible with your VCR. First, if you're buying a camera of a different brand from your VCR, be sure to bring that point up with the salesperson. Don't bring your VCR into the store. An unsuccessful test could damage your equipment.

There's an easy way to make sure the two are compatible. Have a knowledgeable technician check the schematic diagrams available in service departments for both VCR and camera. The diagrams indicate the correct number of pins and which ones provide which functions.

You May Be Able to Mix-and-Match—If your mind is set on a camera that doesn't seem compatible, take heart. There's still hope. Sometimes, incompatibility doesn't involve the amount of pins. Rather, it's in the VCR feed requirements.

Some model cameras have a *variable-setting switch* that allows its use with other brands and types of VCR. The owner's manual accompanying a camera with this switch will probably include a list of the brands and models it can work with.

If it's a question of pin numbers and their functions, there's other help available. Many accessory firms offer *in-line adapters*. These small boxes have jacks for the camera on one side and jacks for the VCR on the other.

The adapters make the appropriate changes in interconnection between one brand of camera and another brand of VCR. The adapter brochures tell which cameras can be hooked up to which VCRs with each adapter.

Another Option—If all else fails, there's still another option. You can employ the services of a competent technician or engineer to build a special adapter. We *don't recommend* this. However, if you're set on buying what appears to be an incompatible camera/VCR combination, you can usually find someone who will try to make it work—if you're willing to pay the price.

Reading Camera Spec Sheets

As with VCRs, you should examine specification sheets for various model cameras. Some of the listings include items that also appear in the VCR spec sheets already discussed. Some camera spec sheets are more detailed than others. Often you'll find superfluous information. We'll concentrate on the important categories.

SCANNING OR COLOR SYSTEM

It's unlikely that a dealer will try to sell you a camera for a system other than the one in use in your area. As mentioned earlier, for example, that standard is *NTSC* in the U.S., Canada and Mexico. You may also find some other wording on the spec sheet in the Scanning or Color-System category. For these areas, as long as you see NTSC listed, you can ignore any other indications in this listing.

PICKUP TUBE OR DEVICE

Here's your chance to find out what type of imaging device is used by the video camera. Actually, there are two pieces of information you learn: the *type of device* and *its diameter*.

Type of Pickup Device—If the camera uses a tube—as most do—the spec sheet will list a name such as vidicon, Trinicon, Saticon or Newvicon. The vidicon has been around for awhile. It offers basic, dependable technology.

The others are newer, more advanced tubes. They offer less lag or retention of the previous image, more resistance to burn-in and better picture quality at dimmer light levels. Much depends on the camera's circuitry. Therefore, a mere listing of the tube type is a hint, but not the total story about the camera's performance.

You may be considering a camera using a solid-state imaging device rather than a tube for capturing the image. This may be listed as *Pickup Device* rather than *Pickup Tube* on the spec sheet.

The abbreviation *CCD* on the sheet indicates that the camera uses a charge-coupled device as the imager. Most solid-state video cameras use CCDs. You might also see the words *MOS Sensor*. This tells you that the imaging device uses metal-oxide silicon technology.

Once you've analyzed spec sheets for several camera models, you'll better understand which cameras offer features you want, and can appreciate the sometimes subtle differences from camera to camera. Panasonic PK-975 offers a 12X power zoom, character generator, C-mount for lens interchangeability and low-light sensitivity.

Confused by all this terminology? Don't be. What the solid-state camera offers is reduced size, weight and power consumption. In addition, cameras with a solid-state imaging device are less bothered by vibration. They are not as susceptible to lag and require less warm-up time than their tube counterparts. Solid-state cameras are also more expensive.

Tube Diameter—Larger-diameter tubes were once considered better than smaller ones. But, with improvements in tube design, this is no longer true. A 2/3-inch tube is standard, but some are 1-inch diameter. And there are home-video cameras with 1/2-inch diameter tubes. The 1/2-inch tubes were first developed for portable broadcast-video cameras.

Tube size is important if you're planning to use lenses other than that provided by the manufacturer. If you hope to swap lenses with a friend, make sure his camera has the same-size tube. If not, his lens may not fit or operate well with your camera.

SYNCHRONIZATION SYSTEM

From this notation on the spec sheet, you'll find out if the camera has a built-in sync generator. A sync generator is the circuitry that makes the beams in a camera tube or scanning output of the CCD move in time with the beams in the gun of the TV's picture tube.

We don't know of any home-video camera that doesn't have a built-in sync generator. The sheet will always read *Internal* for this category.

If you happen to read the word *External* on a spec sheet for sync system, you're probably examining a brochure for a professional camera.

VIDEO SIGNAL-TO-NOISE

The higher the number, the better the picture. The number quoted on the spec sheet is for *luminance*. It was probably achieved under optimum lighting conditions. Therefore, don't expect the highest S/N when you use gain boost or if you shoot under less-than-perfect lighting

---

SAMPLE VIDEO-CAMERA SPECIFICATIONS

Pickup Device: 2/3-inch tri-electrode vidicon
Color System: EIA standard, NTSC color
Sync System: Internal
Video S/N Ratio: Better than 46dB (luminance signal f-1.4, 3200K 250lux)
Horizontal Resolution: Better than 250 TV lines
Vertical Resolution: Better than 450 TV lines
Minimum Illumination: 50 lux (f-1.4, 3200K S/N at 35dB)
Automatic Sensitivity: 75 lux, f-1.6, sensitivity switch at "high"
Lens: f-1.4, 6X zoom
Lens Mount: C mount
Color Temperature: 3000K to 6000K
Operating Temperature: 32F to 104F (0C to 40C)
Relative Humidity: 10% to 75%
Viewfinder: Electronic Viewfinder 1.5-inch b&w CRT (detachable, quick-start type)
Indicator & Alarm: 7-mode indication in viewfinder (iris, recording standby, recording, tape run, battery alarm, white balance, filter)
Auto Fade: Video/audio or video, white or black fade selectable
Remote Control: Capable of controlling all VCR functions from camera with optional remote-control unit (specified VCR models only)
Microphone: Non-directional electret condenser microphone

Video Output: 1V p-p 75-ohms (unbalanced)
Audio Output: −20dB low impedance
Video Input: 1V p-p 75-ohms (unbalanced)
External Microphone Input: −65dB high impedance
Audio Monitor: Magnetic earphone (8-ohms)
Power Requirement: 12V DC
Power Consumption: 7W (camera: 5.5W; electronic viewfinder: 1.5W, at 12V DC)
Dimensions: 2.8 x 9.6 x 13" incl. lens and handgrip; 2.8 x 5.7 x 13" exc. handgrip
Weight: Approx. 2.3 kg. (5.07 lbs.) including lens, hand grip and camera cable; AC adapter, 3.0 lbs.

Supplied Accessories:
Camera cable
Electronic viewfinder
Wrist strap
Lens cap
Lens hood
Eye cup

Optional Accessories:
Camera extension cable
Wide conversion lens
Teleconversion lens
Carrying case
Camera adapter (to be used when connected to a VCR not equipped with a camera connector)

Specifications are subject to change without notice for further improvement.

These are specifications compiled from spec sheets supplied by several brands and manufacturers. As with the VCR specs, this isn't meant to be complete. Again, we want to illustrate here the type of information you can expect to see. Some camera spec sheets are more detailed; others are more graphic. But they all give the minimum information required. It's up to you to check other brands and models to choose which features are most important and which you can do without.

conditions. Usually, there's just one figure in this category. A good norm is 45dB.

HORIZONTAL RESOLUTION
As in the case with VCRs, the higher the figure, the better.

VIDEO-OUTPUT SIGNAL
A 1-volt signal is standard.

AUDIO OUTPUT
In most cases, you'll see −20dB on the spec sheet. Make sure the camera's impedance level matches your VCR's input impedance.

MINIMUM ILLUMINATION
Usually measured in *lux,* this tells you the amount of light you need for an acceptable picture.

Lux is a measurement for illumination. It's the metric equivalent of the foot-candle standard. The wider the lux range, the greater the ability of the camera to produce acceptable pictures in varying lighting conditions.

When reading illumination figures, you may see a notation that the measurement was obtained with the gain-boost or sensitivity switch set at HIGH. Be careful with this one. There's nothing wrong with that information. Just make sure that all camera specification sheets are using the same criteria—the same speed lens, for example.

This is important when comparing two cameras or listening to a sales pitch. Don't fall into the trap of comparing apples with oranges.

LENS SPECIFICATIONS
Most spec sheets include information about the type of lens that comes with the camera. There are often several sets of numbers listed. That's how it should be because the lens is one of the most important parts of the camera.

You'll usually find the following items under the lens specs: *zoom ratio, zoom range* and *lens speed.* These are features we've already discussed.

You may see a spec-sheet indication that states *Standard Accessory* or *Built-in.* This tells you if the camera offers interchangeable-lens capability *(Standard Accessory)* or permanently mounted lens *(Built-in).*

Lens Interchangeability—If the camera can accept different lenses, you'll find a mention of the mount used. The most common type is the C mount. You should do more checking, however, to see if the lenses you hope to use will fit properly. C-mount 16mm motion-picture lenses,

for example, won't always give acceptable pictures when attached to a video camera. This is due to design differences between 16mm cameras and video cameras.

Some home-video cameras allow use of interchangeable camera lenses by fitting an adapter on the camera. You can use 16mm motion-picture lenses on some video cameras, but you can also use 35mm single-lens-reflex (SLR) lenses.

Cameras that allow this, typically have brand names from camera manufacturers, such as Minolta, Canon, Olympus and Pentax. But other video camera brands also offer this capability. You can get more specific information by inquiring at photo dealers and video-specialty shops, or writing those companies directly. Addresses are in the Source List at the back of the book.

When using non-video lenses mounted on your video camera, you may lose some or all of the video camera's automatic features.

POWER CONSUMPTION
Make sure the figures quoted include the power drawn by both the camera *and* any electronic viewfinder that may be attached. When comparing this spec for cameras, the less power drain the better.

CAMERA-POWER SUPPLY
Most cameras operate off the 12-volt DC power supplied by the host VCR. You should check, at this point, if an AC adapter is optional or included.

To use your camera with a portable VCR, you don't need an auxiliary camera-power supply. The camera uses the portable VCR's power source.

You may be comparing what appear to be identical cameras for the same price. Whether or not an auxiliary AC power supply is included can mean the important difference between the two units. If the camera you want doesn't include the auxiliary AC power supply, and you need one, use that as a bargaining point with the dealer. Suggest that the dealer include the power supply at no extra charge.

Connecting to a Tabletop—You may intend to connect the camera to an AC-powered tabletop. In that case, you must use an auxiliary camera-power supply that provides DC power to operate the camera. This also separates video and audio output for connecting to the tabletop VCR.

Don't confuse this with the AC adapter/battery charger used to power a portable VCR—and camera when it's connected to the VCR.

OPERATING-TEMPERATURE RANGE

Although these numbers appear a bit cryptic to many, they do tell an important story. They give you the temperature range—often in both Fahrenheit and Celsius—in which the camera will operate most effectively.

You probably won't be out shooting with your camera in temperatures higher than those recommended by the spec. But you may find yourself shooting outside in cold weather—especially if you're a winter-sports fan. Temperatures may fall below the range noted on the spec sheet, so be careful. At temperatures below freezing, battery operating time is reduced. Also, make sure you have checked the recommended temperature range for the VCR.

WEIGHT

When comparing weights for different cameras, be certain that they include the lens *and* viewfinder.

CABLE LENGTH

This tells you the length of the camera's supplied cable. On some cameras, one end is permanently attached. On others, you must plug one end of the cable into the camera. With all cameras, however, you must attach the other end to the VCR for recording.

Manufacturers supply at least enough camera cable so you can carry the VCR with a strap over your shoulder, or in a bag, while you're using the camera. But if you plan to place the VCR away from your shooting location, you'll have to purchase an accessory extension cable.

Going Shopping

In Chapter 2, we gave you many pointers for buying a VCR. You should follow that advice when shopping for a camera, too. We'll review some of the key points here.

Read the ads and test reports in video magazines. Collect and study brochures. Compare models. Ask people who own video cameras for their impressions of their equipment. Decide which features you must have, those that would be nice at the right price, and those you can live without.

VIDEO CAMERA CARE

● Don't point the camera at any *strong* illumination, such as the sun or other bright light.

● Avoid accidents and injuries. Be sure all camera and VCR cables are out of the way.

● Keep the cap over the lens when the camera is not in use. This will protect the camera's pickup device from accidental burn-in.

● Store the camera in a horizontal position by laying it on its side. Never rest the camera on its lens end.

● Clean the front surface of the lens only with compressed air or special lens cleaner recommended by the manufacturer. *Never* use pressure when wiping the lens surface.

● If you have any problems, ask your dealer or authorized service representative.

ASK QUESTIONS

When you're at the store, ask questions. After all this preparation, if you aren't really sure what to buy, you'll probably get more help at a video-specialty store, photo or audio/video dealer than at a discount outlet. Full-service stores generally have well-trained sales personnel.

If you're concerned about service, consider buying your camera from a dealer that also has a repair department. But not all stores do repairs. Make sure there's an authorized repair outlet nearby for your camera brand. Know your warranty rights.

Bargain—Don't be afraid to shop at a discount store or by mail if you know what you want. When it comes down to settling on a price, don't hesitate to bargain, especially at stores that have made a name for themselves as discounters.

And when you bargain, use optional accessories or other video products as bargaining points. You might even get the salesperson to throw in a couple of videocassettes at no charge.

Chapter 4

All About Videocassettes

Up to now, we've talked about where the video signal comes from. The source can be a camera, an off-air tuner or a prerecorded program. We've also discussed the machine that does the recording and playing, the VCR. But there's one final ingredient in the video stew—the videocassette.

When you own a VCR and camera, you'll be buying blank videocassettes. Over a three-year period, a true videophile may spend as much on videocassettes as he invested in the hardware! It's important to remember that the type you buy can affect recorder life and maintenance.

In our opinion, videocassettes are not given enough attention in discussions of home-video recording systems. They're often overlooked in many video-equipment manuals, too. The videocassette is mistreated, blamed for problems it

didn't cause. It's tossed about carelessly and many times totally misunderstood.

What Is Videotape?

Simply, videotape is the magnetic recording medium inside a plastic housing known as a *cassette.* As mentioned in Chapter 1, today's video-recording technology evolved from developments in audio. As the materials used to make audiotape have changed over the years, so similar improvements have taken place in video. These changes have affected the materials used to make both the tape base and tape coating.

Videotape shares many characteristics with audiotape. To comprehend the differences, you first have to understand the nature of magnetic tape.

Left: A few of the many brands and types of tape. There are different lengths in VHS and Beta, and standard and high-grade tapes. (H.P. Madden Photography)

All licensed videocassettes will display one of these logos prominently. Don't buy a videocassette that doesn't! When the logo appears, it means the manufacturer has produced the tape and cassettes to specifications that ensure correct operation with specific equipment.

You can see from this display of Konica tape products that audiocassettes are smaller than both Beta and VHS videocassettes. That's because audiotape in these cassettes is about 1/8-inch wide. Videotape for VHS and Beta is 1/2-inch wide. VHS-C cassette, not pictured here, is a little bigger than an audiocassette. But because it uses 1/2-inch-wide videotape rather than 1/8-inch wide audiotape, it's thicker than an audiocassette.

Magnetic tape is a thin, plastic film base coated with a fine powder that can hold or react to a magnetic field. Glue, called the *binder,* holds the particles to the plastic film. If you put it all in a case—and you can see here where the word comes from—you have a *videotape cassette,* or *videocassette.*

CASSETTE VS. CARTRIDGE

It's called a *cassette* rather than a *cartridge* because the tape is in two spools sitting side by side. A cartridge configuration has the two reels sitting on top of each other with the tape feeding out from one reel and taken up by the other.

Typically, cartridges don't work well in the fast-forward mode and are impossible to reverse.

VIDEOCASSETTE CONSTRUCTION

UPPER SIDE SHELL

LEADER

TAPE

LOWER SIDE SHELL

TAPE GUIDES

Disassembled cassette reveals two tape reels, top and bottom of the housing and other parts required for precision operation in the VCR.

They don't work reliably. These are some reasons why VCR designers don't use them.

AUDIOCASSETTE VS. VIDEOCASSETTE

There are several differences between these two cassette types. They include tape width and cassette design. Videocassettes for the major home-video recording formats—Beta and VHS—use 1/2-inch-wide tape. Audiocassettes use 1/8-inch-wide tape.

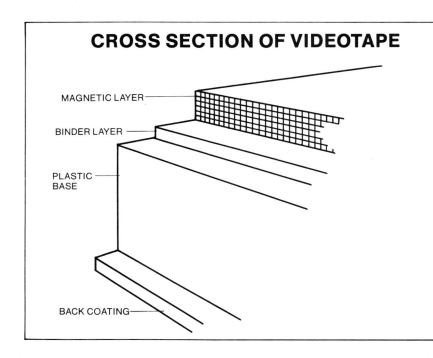

CROSS SECTION OF VIDEOTAPE

MAGNETIC LAYER

BINDER LAYER

PLASTIC BASE

BACK COATING

Cross section of tape found in both Beta and VHS videocassettes gives you a basic idea of the complexity of videotape. There are four layers. Top layer is about 5.0 microns (0.198 mil) thick and contains magnetic oxides. Binding layer, also called the *under-coating layer,* is about 0.3 microns (0.012 mil) thick. Plastic layer is also called the *base layer.* It's about 14.0 microns (0.552 mil) thick. Back coating, about 0.7 microns (0.028 mil) thick, is found on most high-grade and some standard-grade tapes.

A videocassette is designed with a door to protect the tape when the cassette is not in the VCR. The door is opened by a series of levers and springs. This happens when the videocassette is placed into the VCR and a function, such as PLAY, RECORD, REWIND or FAST FORWARD is keyed in. Audiotape needs less protection, so there is no need for a door.

Another difference is that with an audiocassette, on the first pass you record on half the tape. Then, you turn the cassette over to record on the other half. Videocassettes record the full width of the tape in only one pass.

Audiotape and videotape also have different mechanical specifications for operating in their respective recording devices. As a result, audiotape and videotape vary in strength and thickness.

There's a difference in the nature of the magnetic materials used, too. In audiotape, the magnetic particles may be ferric oxide, chromium dioxide, pure-metal particles or cobalt-doped ferric oxides. Each has a different requirement that the audio recorder must match. This requires a special setting on some audio recorders. Some audio units can't use the newer tapes.

Beta and VHS recorders use similar tape, though the magnetic material may be either a doped oxide or chromium dioxide. There's no need for a tape-adjustment switch on the VCR.

A third format, 8mm, uses metal-particle or metal-evaporated tape. More on 8mm videocassettes in Chapter 8.

A more important difference between audiotape and videotape is in the orientation of the magnetic particles on the tape. During a crucial step in tape manufacture, the particles are lined up in a certain direction. They're oriented so they can meet the technical requirements of the recording system they'll be used with.

For example, in audio, information is recorded parallel to the edge of the tape. Recalling our earlier explanation of the VCR, you'll remember that the VCR's helical-scan approach records the video signal diagonally. For video use, the particles must be lined up differently from those for audio recording.

Don't "Byte" on Computer "Videotape"—If someone tries to sell you cheap videocassettes loaded with computer tape, pass up the bargain. Even if it's the best computer tape—which it probably isn't—it has different particle orientation and magnetic properties!

How Videocassettes Are Made

Let's look inside a videocassette-manufacturing

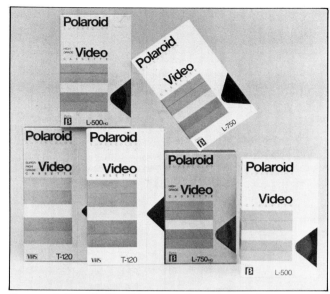

You can tell easily if a videocassette was made by a company authorized to use the Beta or VHS patents. It's also obvious which format each of these videocassettes works with.

Eastman Kodak offers many types and formats of videotape for home and professional use.

plant to see how cassettes and tape are made.

MAKING TAPE

Tape starts out as clear plastic film in wide rolls. The coating begins as magnetic oxides, ground into microscopically fine powder. The particles are mixed with the binder and other additives. They're then blended into a soupy mixture.

The tape is coated with the mixture on the front. After coating, the particles are given their "orientation orders" as they pass through a magnetic field. This is done while the tape is drying and the coating smoothed.

Remember that the VCR heads move over the tape at a high speed. If the tape surface isn't perfectly smooth, it can damage the heads. Not only must the coating be smooth, it has to be evenly applied over the entire tape surface. If a spot isn't properly coated, or if the binder doesn't hold the magnetic coating, you won't be able to record any information at that point on the tape.

Above: Here's how 3M Company stores rolls of clear plastic film until they're needed for use as the base for videotape. Top Left: Cassette housings being fitted with their parts in Sony manufacturing plant. Left: Loaded videocassettes are now ready for packaging at TDK plant.

Instead, you'll have what is known as *dropout.* That name literally comes from coating imperfections dropping off the tape. When you play back a videocassette with dropouts, you see white dots on the TV screen.

An interim manufacturing step for some tapes is the application of a coating on the back of the tape. This doesn't face the heads. It aids the passage of the tape across the VCR guides without sticking to them.

When the tape has dried and has been polished, the large rolls are precision slit to the required width. Then the tape is wound onto large, open-top reels called *pancakes.*

CREATING CASSETTES

Meanwhile, the cassette shells are being molded. They are created from styrene plastic called *ABS,* and are made from precision master molds approved by Sony or JVC. These companies license manufacture of Beta and VHS videocassettes.

The molds can cost up to $500,000. They are what separate the real thing from cheap, non-licensed videocassettes that you may find from time to time. If a videocassette doesn't have the VHS or Beta trademark, it's a sure giveaway that the mold used to produce it was not approved. It also means that the videocassette was produced without the proper license.

This is more important than you might think.

The VCR's tolerance for variations in the operation of the videocassette is slim. If the cassette is not manufactured precisely, it could jam. This may damage your VCR.

After the cassette housings are trimmed, they're fitted with their parts. Now it's time to load the tape into the cassette.

LOADING THE CASSETTE

The tape may be placed into the cassette housing in one of two ways. Some companies draw off a piece of tape from the pancake. Then they splice leader to the front, clip the leader to the reel hub and wind the tape onto the reel. Leader is then attached to the end of the allotted length of tape. Next, the reel is placed into the cassette along with an empty reel. The end leader is clipped to the empty reel. The top is added and secured with screws.

Other manufacturers attach a single piece of leader to both of the reel hubs. When the cassette is screwed closed, a machine takes the leader out of the cassette and cuts it. The correct length of tape is wound onto one reel. When all is done, the machine splices tape and leader together.

It's an Art and Science—As you can conclude from the description, tape manufacture is somewhat of an art as well as a science. You can understand why working with tape outside the cassette is not something we recommend you do yourself.

There are many parts that must be placed carefully inside the cassette. You can't see some of these parts even if you open the door in the front of the videocassette.

We recommend that you *never open up a videocassette* or attempt to make splices. You could accidentally lose some valuable parts of the cassette. And, splices could damage the delicate heads on your VCR.

If you really like to see how things look inside, take apart and inspect an old videocassette that you don't plan to use again. Then throw it away.

AN IMPORTANT NOTE ABOUT THE TAB

Examine the outside of a videocassette. You'll find a small tab on the narrow side of the cassette that faces you when you place the cassette in the VCR (VHS), or on the cassette bottom (Beta). When the tab is removed, your machine will not record on the tape.

Many people remove the tab to prevent accidentally recording over a program they want to save. That's why the tab is relatively easy to remove. When the tab is gone, if you push the record button on your VCR with that tape inserted, the machine won't go into the record mode.

If you change your mind later and decide you want to reuse the tape, all is not lost. You can reuse a tape with the tab missing. It's simple. Place a piece of any type of cellophane tape over the tab area. The recorder will think the tab is there. You can then record over the original audio and video.

Differences Between Brands and Grades

There are more similarities between each of the videocassette brands than there are differences. But those variations can be important. Manufacturers use different components and materials for both the tape and cassette.

Because the specifications for the basic product are set by Sony and JVC, you can be certain that all approved and licensed videocassettes—those carrying the trademarks mentioned earlier—will work in the appropriate VCR.

Licensed manufacturers use extensive testing procedures for all aspects of the tape-making process. They reject bad batches of tape. But the inherent inconsistency of the process means that sometimes you might buy a bad videocassette that has somehow slipped through quality control.

WHAT TO DO
WITH A BAD VIDEOCASSETTE

What do you do if you think you have a bad videocassette? First, be sure it's the videocassette, not your machine. One way to check is to play a videocassette you know has given good images on your VCR. If that cassette produces poor pictures, something is probably wrong with the equipment, not the videocassette.

If the equipment is OK and a videocassette is either jamming or producing white specks on the TV screen, it's usually the videocassette causing the problem.

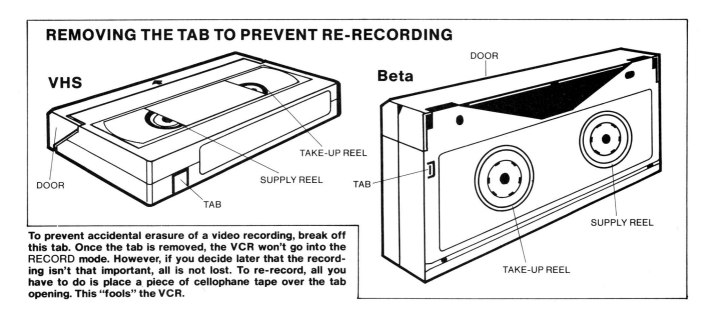

REMOVING THE TAB TO PREVENT RE-RECORDING

VHS — DOOR, TAKE-UP REEL, SUPPLY REEL, TAB

Beta — DOOR, TAB, SUPPLY REEL, TAKE-UP REEL

To prevent accidental erasure of a video recording, break off this tab. Once the tab is removed, the VCR won't go into the RECORD mode. However, if you decide later that the recording isn't that important, all is not lost. To re-record, all you have to do is place a piece of cellophane tape over the tab opening. This "fools" the VCR.

TDK manufactures *all* of the components in their Extra High Grade videocassettes. Several companies buy complete videocassettes from other firms. Magnavox is one of them.

Don't hesitate to return a defective videocassette to your dealer.

You might not know the name of the actual tape manufacturer. As with VCRs and cameras, videocassettes often carry brand names of companies that only distribute the tape. This is called *private labeling*.

Who Makes Videocassettes?

It's not difficult to find out what firm manufactures which VCRs and cameras. Simply compare outward appearance, features and "family traits." More detective work is required with videocassettes.

Earlier, we explained that the Beta cassette is noticeably smaller than its VHS counterpart. Each format has design constraints. As a result, all licensed videocassette brands within each format must look reasonably alike once the packaging and labels are stripped away. And they do.

Videocassettes are sold under more than two dozen brand names. Some companies produce their own videotape but buy the plastic housings. Others do the opposite: They make the housings and buy the videotape. To further complicate matters, there are firms that buy both housings and tape. They just load the cassettes!

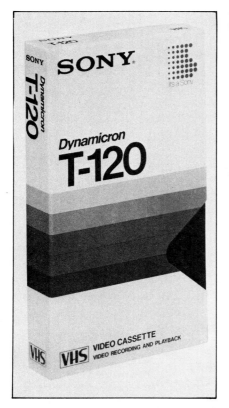

Sony offers a full line of Beta videocassettes under the Dynamicron name. The company also manufactures videocassettes for use in VHS equipment.

If you're still following this, there's still another way. Some companies buy the entire videocassette and put their own label on it.

Of course, some companies simplify matters. They produce the entire videocassette—tape and housing. They sell it under their own label.

Selecting a Brand

One of the prime rules in buying videocassettes is to stay with a brand offering a product manufactured under license from a recognized patent holder. When a videocassette has a VHS or Beta logo, you can be reasonably sure you're buying the real thing.

If you find a package that says *Beta Compatible,* or something similar, and you don't see a logo, beware! Pass it by, regardless of how good a bargain it may seem to be. The tape or housing—or both—may not be up to standard. This may damage your VCR's heads or cause other problems, such as jamming.

Beyond this, it's difficult to judge videocassettes. Again, stay with brand names you know. No reputable manufacturer will put its name on a substandard product.

TAPE BRANDS VS.
HARDWARE MANUFACTURERS' BRANDS
Some people think that it's best to stick with a videocassette sold under the same brand name as their VCR. Others prefer to stay with the major tape brands they know from audio or other magnetic-media product lines.

In one sense, both approaches are correct. You can't go wrong by staying with such brand-name tape marketers as TDK, Fuji, Maxell, Memorex, BASF or Scotch, for example.

As to brands sold by the hardware companies, you're still safe. For example, JVC makes its own housings and tape. Remember, JVC owns the VHS patents. Similarly, Sony owns the Beta patents and is a major tape manufacturer.

Other hardware marketers also have more than a passing interest in the tape sold under their brand names. It doesn't matter if they have anything to do with manufacture of the tape.

Here are some examples. Panasonic and Quasar are both owned by Matsushita of Japan. Matsushita manufactures tape and housings. Hitachi may not sound like a big videocassette brand name—or audiotape name for that matter. But guess what company Hitachi owns? Maxell. Guess who makes Hitachi-brand videocassettes?

Other VCR brand names also sell videocassettes. Most of this tape comes from the Japanese tape manufacturers. You can rest assured that it'll be as good as the standard-brand lines from TDK or Fuji, for example.

What Are the Differences?

There are both seen and unseen differences between videocassettes. Here's how the brands distinguish themselves.

PACKAGING
In the store, you probably notice videocassette packaging. You may compare the packaging of one brand to another.

Cassettes for use with VHS-C cameras and VideoMovie camcorders are marked with VHS-C logo.

Most videocassettes are sold in cardboard slip cartons. These are inexpensive and easy to mass produce. However, pieces flake off the cardboard. This is often carried into the VCR with the cassette. Along with dust, this is the enemy of good video pictures and long head life.

Some brands set themselves apart by packaging their videocassettes in plastic slip cases. Others sell the videocassettes in book-like plastic cases. These reduce the dust and flaking problem.

You may decide to purchase plastic cases later, so you might want to buy videocassettes that are supplied with this type of packaging. Of course, that's something to consider only after you've decided that the tape is satisfactory for your needs.

Fuji packages its videocassettes in a plastic slipcase. Standard cardboard slipcases tend to flake. The resulting dust particles may then be carried into the VCR when you insert the cassette. This could cause damage to the tape and/or VCR.

Memorex sets its high-grade series apart by packaging videocassettes in plastic see-through cases. When such cases are supplied at the time of purchase, you don't have to buy accessory cases later.

Other packaging differences may be of interest. This depends on your needs. You may, for example, prefer the type of labels supplied by one brand. Or, you might like the paper time-counter or color-coded dots supplied with another.

THE SPECS

There are technical differences among brands. But it's generally hard to find out at the store what they are. Most retailers don't have spec sheets for videocassettes. Instead, they prefer to sell videocassettes as a price-oriented item.

Highest S/N and Frequency-Response Range— Look for cassettes with the *highest signal-to-noise ratio,* for both video and chrominance. Tapes with high numbers produce recordings that are less "grainy," with the best color reproduction. Also important is the widest range of frequency-response figures. These tapes will give you sharper images. Generally, these two specifications track together: A cassette with high S/N will also provide a wide frequency-response figure.

DROPOUTS

Beyond examining specs, there's another way to judge the quality of a particular videocassette. You can record on the tape. When you play it back, look for *dropouts.* These are flaws in the tape where the magnetic coating has fallen off. They appear on the TV screen as white spots or sometimes white lines. The fewer and smaller the dropouts, the better the videocassette.

TAPE COATING

You'll also find different types of coating on videotape. Most videotapes are covered with ferric oxide or cobalt-doped oxides. Some manufacturers use chromium dioxide.

As with audio tape, there's a never-ending debate in video circles about which coating type is better. We can tell you only that they're all about equal when used with the best of today's VCRs.

TAPE LENGTH

Most modern VCRs offer at least two recording speeds. Some have a third one for both record and playback, or playback only. When you consider that fact in terms of the various tape lengths available in videocassettes, there's bound to be some confusion. After you read this section, you'll understand how tape length and machine speed relate.

For a given length of tape, the number of minutes of material that can be recorded is determined by the speed of the tape passing over the heads at the time the recording is made.

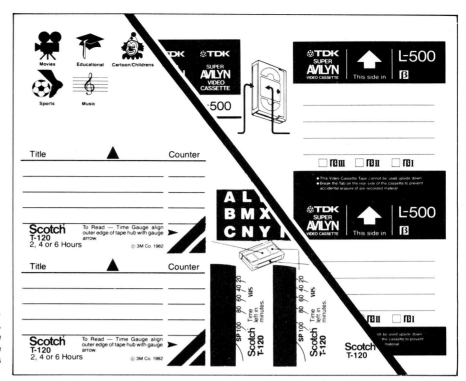

Most companies include a sheet containing labels with their videocassettes. These can help you organize your tape files. TDK gives you labels for the cassette and outside case. 3M includes picturegrams and tape counters.

For example, you can fill a VHS T-120 cassette by recording a two-hour program at the fastest speed, SP. If you set the VCR for the middle speed, LP, that same T-120 tape can record a four-hour program. Or, you can record a six-hour show on the T-120 if the VCR is set at the slowest, EP, speed. Several companies offer even longer videocassettes in the VHS format. These allow up to eight hours of programming by using thinner-base tapes.

Although we've used a VHS cassette in this example, the same principle applies with Beta cassettes. The accompanying table details by format how long videocassettes of different lengths will record at each speed.

Manufacturers offer different-length tapes in their videocassettes. Typically, you'll want as long a tape as possible when recording broadcasts. You may prefer shorter lengths when shooting with a camera or for other projects.

With all the recording speeds and tape lengths, you have many options. Use the chart as a guide for your particular shooting situations and needs.

TAPE THICKNESS

Videocassettes that record for a longer period of time contain more tape. To do this, manufacturers load thinner tape in the cassettes. Because cassette size is fixed, using thinner tape is the only way they can squeeze more recording time into the cassette without changing recording speeds.

HUB SIZE

Another difference is that shorter-length cassettes usually include larger hubs on the reels. Various mechanisms ensure that the tape moves through the VCR correctly and at the right tension. The same care must be taken to move

VIDEOCASSETTE RECORDING TIME (in minutes)

VHS

	Cassette Recording Speeds		
	SP	LP	EP
T-30	30	60	90
T-60	60	120	180
T-90	90	180	270
T-120	120	240	360
T-160	160	320	480

BETA

	Cassette Recording Speeds		
	X1*	X2	X3
L-125	15	30	45
L-250	30	60	90
L-500	60	120	180
L-750	90	180	270
L-830	**	200	300

* X1 speed was original Beta consumer recording speed. It's available today as a recording speed only on professional Beta VCRs. X1 speed is available on some home VCRs as a playback speed only.

** You shouldn't record at X1 speed with L-830.

Eastman Kodak is one of many videocassette marketers offering high-grade videocassettes.

the tape out of the cassette when it's threaded into the machine. Without the increased hub size, there would be too much stress on the tape in shorter-length cassettes. This could cause defective recordings, a break in the tape, or both.

Standard vs. High Grade

Other than the differences among brands, there are now differences in the types, or grades, of tape sold by the same manufacturer. You now can buy premium videocassettes, called *high-grade*. Just because premium tapes are available, it doesn't mean that standard-grade cassettes are bad. It's just that the more expensive lines are a bit better.

When both VCR manufacturers and tape marketers started selling videocassettes, they recognized that something other than packaging was needed to set their brands apart. They also understood that most people won't study spec sheets to find out how one brand is better than another. So, the videocassette marketers brought out *High Grade,* or *HG,* products.

High-grade tape manufacture involves even stricter quality-control procedures to ensure the best product. And, these videocassettes may be packaged in the dust-free plastic cases mentioned earlier.

Tape in high-grade videocassettes may also be smoother. This makes it easier for the tape to pass over the VCR's heads. All high-grade tapes are back-coated. Some regular-grade tapes are back-coated, too. Some high-grade tapes have a better back-coating than others. A better coating permits the tape in a cassette to function at a higher performance level at the slower recording speeds offered by most VCRs.

The film used as a base for high-grade tapes may also be stronger than that found in a standard videocassette. A stronger base prevents the tape from stretching as much. When combined with better binders, this stronger tape gives you better recordings at the slow speeds and better still frames. This is because tape is more prone to stretching at the greater tensions that occur when recording at the slower speeds or during still-frame scanning.

Finally, the coating in high-grade tape may hold more information. As a result, it delivers higher video and audio signal-to-noise (S/N)

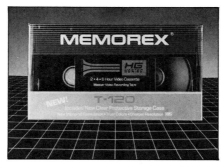

You can record a maximum of six hours of material on a VHS T-120 videocassette at the slowest recording speed. With a T-160 videocassette, you can record up to *eight* hours! Again, this depends on recording speed. The T-160 videocassette is no larger than the T-120. Manufacturers use thinner tape to fit it into the same-size housing. BASF, Eastman Kodak and other companies offer 8mm video cassettes for camcorders. They record up to 90 minutes. These videocassettes probably will cost more than Beta and VHS because 8mm uses new, metal-based formulations.

ratios. Improved S/N ratios are especially important when recording at slower speeds.

Compared with standard-, or regular-grade videocassettes, HG products are the premium of the videotape world.

WHEN TO CHOOSE HG TAPE

If you're looking for the best, HG cassettes usually are it. But they're more expensive. Consider using a HG cassette when shooting footage you plan to edit or duplicate with another VCR. Because HG tape has better binders, the tape usually has fewer dropouts. It follows that if your original tape has fewer dropouts, you'll be able to make better copies.

For example, tape is stretched slightly as it moves back and forth in the VCR while you're looking for the beginning point of an edit. When you set the VCR in the still-frame mode, the tape is also stretched slightly. Because HG cassettes have stronger binders, they're better to use under these circumstances.

Some people use HG tape when shooting with a camera. This ensures that the footage they're shooting of memorable, one-time events is on top-quality tape that will withstand the test of time and usage.

When you're taping broadcasts, you'll probably use standard-grade videocassettes. After all, many programs are broadcast more than once. You may be able to re-record the show if you wear out the tape.

Going Shopping

You may be ready to write us a nasty letter because we haven't told you a sure way of knowing which videocassette brand you should purchase. Here's why we haven't told you: *There is no sure way to tell which is the best brand of videocassette!*

From our discussion, you should realize that there are many variables. Not the least of these are your judgment and budget. Manufacturing videocassettes is an art and science. Sometimes there are problems with a specific batch of tape. You may also find that a brand's T-120 may appear to work better for you than the same company's T-60. This situation can often be traced to variables in your VCR's design.

GREMLINS

When evaluating brands and grades, remember that the videocassette is often blamed for problems not related to its manufacture. You may be able to attribute the video-production "gremlins" to other reasons. These can include poorly maintained or broken equipment, improper operating procedures, or poor lighting conditions when you shoot.

In addition, the tape you've been using may be defective—but not because of manufacturing faults. Dropouts and other defects may be caused by storing the cassette in too hot or too damp a place. So don't be too quick to blame the manufacturer.

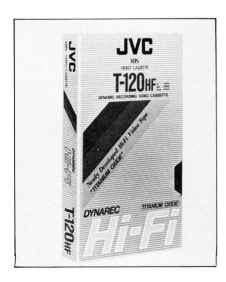

Left: JVC offers a series of Dynarec tapes for use with VHS Hi-Fi VCRs. The Hi-Fi cassettes use a new magnetic coating. Right: Three other grades of JVC line: standard, high-grade and super-high-grade.

The best advice we can give is to choose a brand of tape based on specifications, recommendations from friends and your own experience. Then shop for the best price. When you find a brand that gives you good pictures and fewest dropouts, stay with it. If a brand gives you trouble—and you're sure after testing that it's not your fault or the VCR's—change brands.

Check local newspapers for special sales. Buy enough videocassettes to last until the next sale.

If you follow this suggestion, you'll always have enough cassettes on hand when you want to make a tape recording.

We've run out of tape here—couldn't avoid using that one. By now you have a good idea of how all the elements in the home-video recording system work.

One other aspect of the *complete* home-video setup is accessories. Many are available for the VCR, camera and videocassette.

VIDEOCASSETTE CARE AND USE

● Store in an upright, vertical position to prevent tape sag around the internal hub.

● Replace manufacturers' cardboard slip cases with a plastic case to keep out dust. Cardboard cases flake. Less dust contamination prevents potential damage to expensive video heads.

● Keep cassette away from excess heat. Don't store in direct sun, a hot car or glove box, for example.

● Don't store near strong magnetic fields, such as electrical equipment or motors. Such magnetic fields may erase the electronic signals. Don't place cassettes on or near electronic equipment such as a TV.

● Don't store tape partially wound. After recording, let the tape run to the end. This maintains even tension. It's better to rewind the tape just before next playback.

● Use cassettes at room temperature only.

● Don't expose cassettes to smoke, dust or moisture.

● Don't touch the tape inside the cassette.

● If you're having trouble recording, check all equipment, connections, wires and indicators. If everything is OK, the tape may be faulty. Check this by testing the system with another cassette that you have used previously. If this tape works, return the other tape to the dealer.

● Don't overuse the VCR's pause control. Leaving the equipment in this mode too long may damage both the tape and the recording heads. Use a maximum of five minutes as a guide.

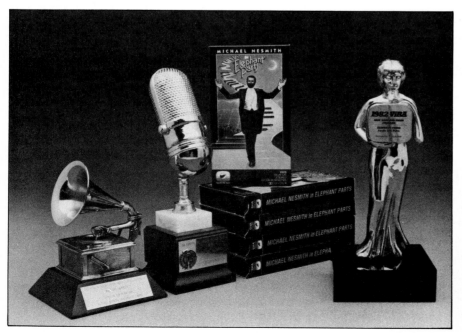

Don't think we've neglected prerecorded tapes in this chapter. It's just that if you want to rent or buy a movie or other program, you typically don't have any choice as to the type of tape it's recorded on—only the format, either VHS or Beta. However, if you have stereo video equipment, you may want to search for that information. Here, it's on the bottom of the box, just above the Dolby NR logo. The *Michael Nesmith in Elephant Parts* videocassette received the first Grammy Award for the Best Video of the Year.

Chapter 5

Accessories

Home video is exciting! The equipment is easy to use and the results are a lot of fun to watch. Once you've gotten used to video, however, you might want to expand your basic system's capabilities.

The complete basic home-video system consists of a tabletop VCR or portable VCR, tuner/timer and battery charger, and camera. But you needn't stop there! As with conventional photography, there's a wide range of accessory

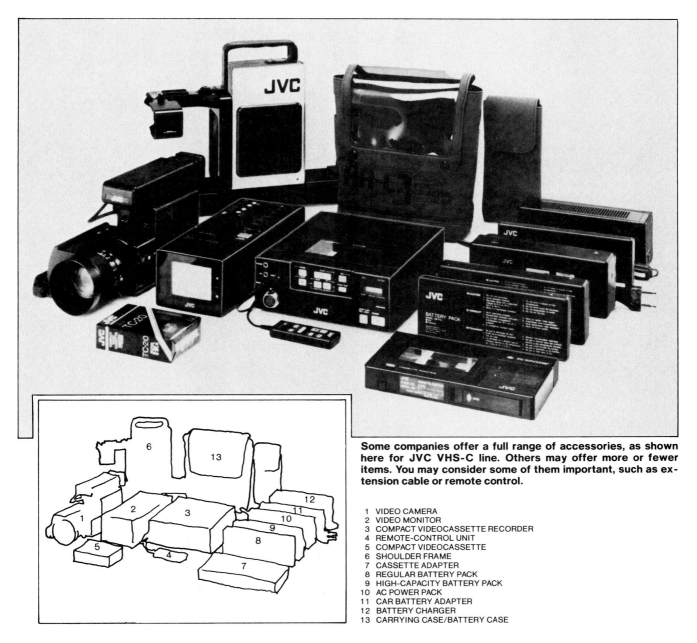

Some companies offer a full range of accessories, as shown here for JVC VHS-C line. Others may offer more or fewer items. You may consider some of them important, such as extension cable or remote control.

1 VIDEO CAMERA
2 VIDEO MONITOR
3 COMPACT VIDEOCASSETTE RECORDER
4 REMOTE-CONTROL UNIT
5 COMPACT VIDEOCASSETTE
6 SHOULDER FRAME
7 CASSETTE ADAPTER
8 REGULAR BATTERY PACK
9 HIGH-CAPACITY BATTERY PACK
10 AC POWER PACK
11 CAR BATTERY ADAPTER
12 BATTERY CHARGER
13 CARRYING CASE/BATTERY CASE

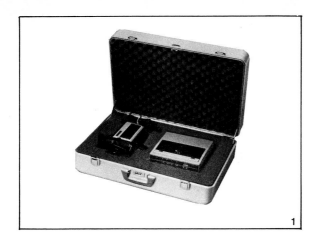

items that can make your home-video experience even more exciting. Do you have a conventional photographic camera? If so, you probably have bought accessories such as filters and a tripod, for example. Some of these can be used with your video equipment!

There are also many specialized video items that you can use on, over or around the video equipment. You can attach some items to the top of the camera, in front of the lens or instead of the lens if your camera has interchangeable-lens capability. Some cameras allow for accessory electronic viewfinders and microphones, for example. And with some, you can add a character generator, too.

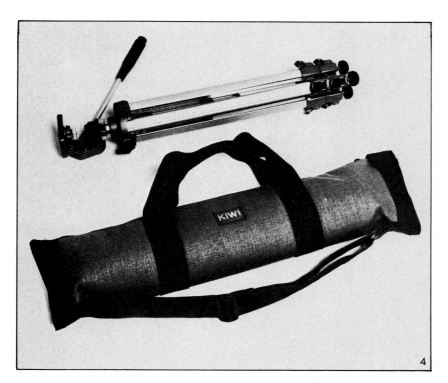

Several of these accessories are mentioned in Chapters 2, 3 and 4. Here, we illustrate some of those, and offer other accessories that don't fit into the discussions in those chapters. We should note here that any listing of accessories may be out of date. As we write this, manufacturers are dreaming up new ideas for ways to expand the utility and fun of your equipment.

To keep up to date, read video magazines and ask your retailer for information about new items he may currently stock or can order for you. It's also important to note here that, although we may be illustrating one particular brand's accessory, a similar item is often available under another name.

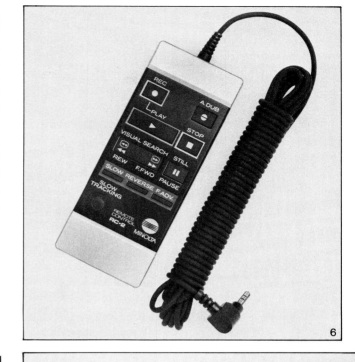

1. Zero Halliburton case protects VCR and camera during transport. With replaceable foam inserts, you can customize its interior.

2, 3. Comprehensive Video Supply Corp. and other companies offer soft or hard VCR dust covers.

4. Even accessories can have accessories! Here's a carrying case for your tripod.

5. Because you must carry the portable VCR with you when using a camera, you need a carrying case for it. Many different kinds are available, such as this Minolta model.

6. This may be standard or optional, extra-cost accessory. With some portable video setups, both VCR and tuner/timer have separate remote controls. Sometimes these remotes offered as standard items. Only one of the remotes may be included. Typically, when only one is offered as standard, you'll receive wireless remote control for tuner/timer. Wired remote control for VCR may be extra-cost accessory.

7. You can purchase extra batteries for portable VCR to allow longer remote recording. Many standard batteries offer only 30 minutes' of recording time. On right side is an accessory battery charger.

8. When mobility is not important, use AC adapter. This replaces battery in VCR. With this, you must have access to an AC wall outlet. Some AC adapters also charge batteries.

9. To play a VHS-C cassette in a standard VHS VCR, you must use this C-P1U cassette adapter.

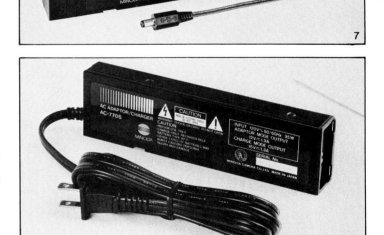

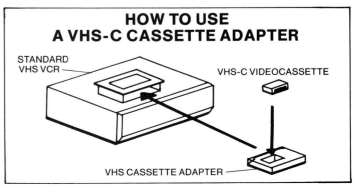

HOW TO USE A VHS-C CASSETTE ADAPTER

STANDARD VHS VCR

VHS-C VIDEOCASSETTE

VHS CASSETTE ADAPTER

As with all such equipment, check around for the best prices and service.

VCR ACCESSORIES

Your VCR should come with all the parts you need to record broadcast signals and play them back. However, when you have cable hookups, a video camera, another VCR or other electronic accessories, you may have to purchase additional cables, connectors, splitters and related items.

You may also want to purchase a wired or infrared remote control, if one doesn't come as standard equipment.

A dust jacket will protect your tabletop or portable unit when it isn't being used. This is important. You must prevent dust, moisture, smoke and other materials from getting inside the VCR. And, a carrying case makes it easier to carry the VCR when making video movies.

A battery is an important item if you plan to use your portable VCR away from household AC

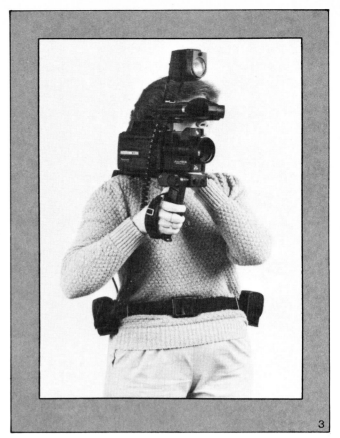

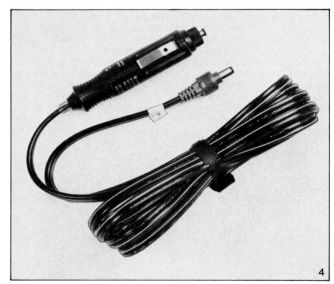

1. Another type of rechargeable battery, Saft America's Again & Again models operate up to five hours on a charge.
2. If you don't want to have to carry the VCR with you while shooting, you'll need an extension cable. This connects between camera plug and VCR Camera Input, allowing you to move away from the VCR.
3. Battery belt distributes weight of accessory batteries evenly. Ambico battery belt powers camera and VCR for up to 10 hours, depending on wattage required. Or, it can power a 100-watt video light for up to one hour.
4. To operate your video camera and VCR while traveling without extra batteries, use the battery in your automobile. Plug this car-battery cord into the cigarette-lighter socket.

power. A portable VCR generally comes with one as a standard item. However, many batteries offer only about 30 minutes of power on a charge. And it may take as long as 14 hours to recharge! You can see the benefit of having a second battery as a backup. You can purchase a longer-lasting battery, or a different style, such as a battery belt.

Another power accessory is the car adapter. This allows you to operate equipment with power from your car's battery, generally through a connection to the cigarette-lighter socket.

A longer camera-connecting cable makes it possible for you to operate your camera without carrying the VCR on your shoulder. Typically, about 25 feet is as far as you should go without boosting the signal. Plug in the extension and

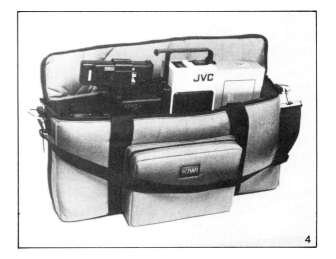

1. Hervic case enables you to carry camera and accessories in one package, and protects them during transport.
2. When you want to rewind or rewind and erase the contents of a videocassette, use a rewinder/bulk eraser.
3. When total mobility isn't important, use a video tripod to support the camera. Tripods, such as these Slik video models, are built to handle weight of video equipment. Special pan heads, for smooth, even movement, are also available. To move the camera smoothly during a shooting session, mount the tripod to a video dolly (foreground).
4. There are many different types of camera cases and bags, some from camera manufacturers, others from independent companies. Among other styles, Kiwi offers a bag made exclusively for VHS-C system.

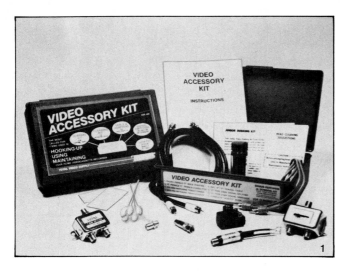

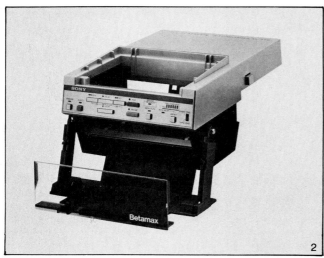

leave the VCR in one place. As a result, you don't have that extra weight to carry around.

If you do a lot of copying of tapes, or reuse many tapes, you can purchase a bulk tape eraser.

Another item that might be considered as an "accessory" is a second VCR! This could be used for duplicating your favorite tapes to send to friends. For example, you want to show a tape of your child's first steps to people living hundreds of miles away. Rather than giving up your copy—and taking a chance of losing or damaging the original in shipment—you could make a copy to send off. And you can personalize it by adding a message. What a great gift! A second VCR also makes it easier to edit tapes.

If you own a Sony Beta VCR, an interesting accessory is the Betastack Autochanger. This allows up to 20 consecutive hours of recording.

To integrate your video equipment into the room decor, you may want to buy furniture designed for use with video components. Many such pieces are available.

Maintenance Accessories—One area that we haven't dealt with in detail is equipment maintenance. There are many types of head cleaners, demagnetizers and related items, but we don't recommend using them. Some of these products could damage your equipment if not used correctly.

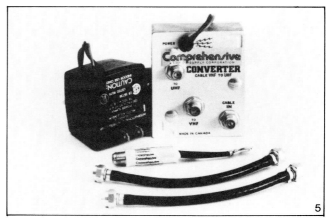

1. Video accessory kits, such as Total Video Supply kit, include items that may not be included with your VCR. This one includes cable, adapters, splitter, switcher, head-cleaning kit, a dubbing kit for interconnecting two recorders to copy tapes, and storage box.
2. Sony's Betastack Autochanger allows up to 20 consecutive hours of recording with Beta recorder.
3. Ambico also has kit with lens attachments for rainbow, starburst and multi-image effects.
4. Create different video effects by adding accessories to the front of a video-camera lens. Ambico fisheye attachment more than doubles camera lens' field of view. Close-up/wide-view lens allows lens to focus as close as six inches.
5. Block converter allows use of all programming and remote-control capabilities of your VCR and TV when a cable-converter box is required.

For example, abrasive head-cleaning tapes can scratch the video-recording heads. Although most products sold for maintenance—such as head-cleaning tapes—*shouldn't* damage equipment, many people don't follow the instructions. For example, if you're supposed to use a head-cleaning tape for 30 seconds, 30 seconds is the maximum! An extra 15 seconds "for good measure" may cause scratches on the heads. This could result in a costly trip to a repair shop.

Although typically low-maintenance, video equipment does need servicing. Owner's manuals should indicate if this is required, and how to recognize problems. However, you don't want that to be any more often than absolutely necessary.

You don't want to pay for service or repairs that aren't necessary. Some books about video may tell you to use head cleaners. Others tell you how to use cotton swabs to clean the video heads. Remember: If you don't follow manufacturer's maintenance instructions, you may *void* the warranty. Don't take chances with expensive equipment. Preventive maintenance is the best approach—if you follow instructions to the letter.

If you think you have a problem, contact your retailer, a qualified repair outlet or the distributor of your equipment. They should be able to tell you what type of maintenance you can do, and how often.

VIDEO-CAMERA ACCESSORIES

As with the VCR, there are many accessories for use with video cameras. Some are repackaged conventional photographic items, such as filters and lens-cleaning kits. Others are designed specifically for video use.

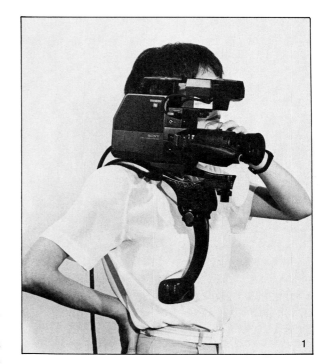

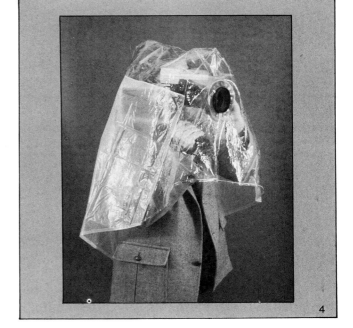

1. Ideal Shoulder Support may be the answer for more support and freedom for your hands. It allows you to hold the camera without using both hands.
2. Do you want to copy 8mm movies and slides onto video? Tele-cine converter, such as this one from Ambico, allows you to control duplication process. Later, you can add a soundtrack.
3. Vivitar has adapters and a teleconverter for video equipment. 1.5X teleconverter (top) allows you to extend video camera's lens focal length 1-1/2 times. Video C-Mount adapter (bottom) allows mounting of Canon, Nikon, Minolta, Pentax or Olympus 35mm SLR camera lenses to same brand's video camera.
4. Just in case, Comprehensive Video Supply offers a video camera raincoat.

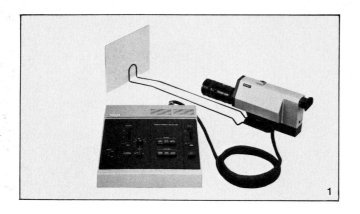

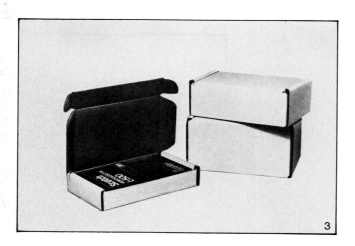

As with photographic cameras, when possible, you should protect the front element of the camera's lens from dirt, fingerprints or other damage. The simplest solution is to screw a clear-glass, skylight or UV filter into the camera lens filter threads.

When traveling with your video equipment on a long trip, use a hard carrying case. Going outdoors for a day's shooting, try a soft carrying case. It's lighter than a hard case, yet still protects the equipment from scratches and the elements.

You may want to distribute the weight of the camera more than the ENG or super-8 design allows—a shoulder brace might be the answer.

When you'll be doing a lot of shooting, or if you want smooth, controlled movement, use a tripod. Although you can use your photographic tripod for video, remember that a video camera is heavier than a photographic camera. And the weight is distributed differently. The tripod could tip over if not correctly balanced. You can buy a special fluid head for the tripod. This provides smooth movement for the camera, such as when panning.

A related item is a dolly. Professionals use dollies when they need smooth movement while the camera follows the subjects through a scene. You can achieve similar quality with a video dolly.

Often—especially when shooting indoors—you need additional light. Many types of video lights are available. Typically, these have their own batteries, or can operate with accessory batteries used for the video camera.

As we mentioned earlier, there are many lens accessories. These can be filters to change the color of the light entering the camera's imaging device to ones used for star or other special effects. You can also take advantage of photographic filters, which may screw into the video lens or mount onto the front. There's almost no limit to the type of effects you can create. Examples include starburst, multiple images and frames, such as a heart or other shape.

1. Another Sony accessory. Special-Effects Kit allows for superimposing images, altering colors, b&w reversal and remote-control of VCR functions.
2. Need additional light? Mount one of Ideal's Unomat video lights on your camera.
3. Comprehensive offers different types of videocassette shippers and mailers. Cardboard mailer can be used for shipping tapes.
4. Plastic case is a good replacement for cardboard slipcases or for storage.

A tele-cine converter allows you to copy your 8mm movies or 35mm slides onto video. Then you don't have to bring out the projectors and screen when you want to show off your travels. And, once you've copied your slides and motion pictures onto tape, it's simple to add a soundtrack. Make a copy of your final production and you've got a great gift!

Some accessories allow you to take your equipment out into the rain, or even under water!

VIDEOCASSETTE ACCESSORIES

You'll even find accessories for that maltreated and unappreciated—yet vital—part of your video system: the videocassette.

We mentioned earlier that you should store videocassettes in plastic cases. If you replace the cardboard slipcases that are standard with many brands of tape, you won't have to worry about paper particles flaking off and ending up in the VCR. This could cause damage to the very sensitive heads. With plastic cases, you'll be preventing dust contamination, too.

There are different types of accessory cases. You can use some for storage only. Want to send a video holiday greeting? Or a duplicate of a wedding you shot? Send the tape in a special shipping case.

When you have a lot of tapes, you'll need a place to store them. There are several storage alternatives, too. You can use vertical racks designed to keep the tapes upright when not in use.

Or, you can integrate videocassette storage into the decor of your room. Some companies have designed furniture to fulfill just such a need.

These accessories are just the "tip of the iceberg." As you can see, there's no end to the fun you can have buying accessories for your electronic habit!

1. Operate your VCR and camera for up to five hours on a charge with Red Line Research 12-volt, 6 amp battery belt. It weighs 5 pounds, 10 ounces and converts to a shoulder pack.
2. With O'Sullivan Industries cabinet, you can store valuable recordings under lock and key.
3. Once you have a large library of videocassettes, you may want to store them within easy reach of your VCR. Gusdorf VCR/cassette library cabinet makes it easy.

Chapter 6

Buy or Rent?

By now you should have a good idea of what equipment you want, and the features you need. Perhaps your biggest question at this point is whether you should wait to purchase video-recording equipment or buy now. Many people want to wait. You may have heard that prices will continue to fall, and additional features will appear on future models.

In this chapter, we'll tell you about some home-video recording hardware on the horizon. But first we'll discuss another option if you're not ready to buy.

Renting Video Equipment

Suppose you want to videotape an important family event such as a wedding. But you're not ready, for whatever reason, to buy the necessary equipment. If you plan to use video equipment for a short time, consider renting it. For long-term use, however, you have to weigh carefully the arguments in the rental-vs.-purchase dilemma.

SHORT-TERM RENTAL

Take a tip from professional TV producers regarding short-term rental. The cost of buying the latest equipment for a particular project is often too high, even for them. They typically rent their equipment on a short-term basis. This gives them access to the most modern hardware. And they don't have to worry about whether they've bought something that will soon be out-of-date.

Just as you can rent a new car for a weekend to try it before you buy, you can also rent home-video equipment. If your local home-video dealer doesn't offer rentals, ask who does. Or, you might contact a professional audiovisual equipment-rental firm. Usually, they can get what you want. Look in the Yellow Pages under *Audiovisual.*

Rentals Aren't Cheap—Sometimes these rentals aren't cheap. But, you get exactly what you need, and only for as long as you need it. Using a rental can help you decide if home-video recording is something you really enjoy.

One way to "get your feet wet" in video is to take advantage of short-term rental. Rent a videocassette *player* and some prerecorded tapes for a few days. Companies like Portavideo have play-only units available for rental at local video stores, shopping malls and grocery stores in some areas. PortaVideo VHS player is housed in a rugged case with a handle, and comes with all necessary cables and connectors. For more information, check your local retailer. Otherwise, contact Portavideo Entertainment, 3325 W. Catalina Drive, Phoenix AZ 85017.

Be sure you know how to operate the equipment before you leave the store. It's no fun paying for equipment and then later finding out you can't use it because you don't understand how it works. A reputable rental firm will answer any questions you may have.

Check It Out First—Before you leave the dealer, make sure the equipment is working. You don't want to be charged for damage you didn't cause. And you don't want to be stuck far away from the store with equipment that doesn't work. When renting battery-powered equipment, make sure the batteries are charged.

Be certain that you receive all the accessories listed on the rental bill. You'll have to pay for any items listed on the receipt that aren't returned. Read the rental agreement *very carefully*. Be sure all the necessary information has been filled out. Just as important is to be sure there are no blanks that can be filled in after you leave the store.

Insurance—Do you have insurance to cover lost or stolen equipment? Make sure your homeowner's policy covers this. If not, ask the rental dealer if he offers a low-cost, short-term policy to cover the equipment while you have it.

Cost—Rental prices aren't usually subject to deals and bargaining as in sales. However, if you're renting a full package of equipment for a long period, ask for a discount. You have nothing to lose.

Unless you've made arrangements in advance, your rental fee may not be deductible from the purchase price, should you decide to buy. We suggest that you get any such arrangements in writing.

LONG-TERM RENTAL

Renting TV sets has never been popular in the U.S. But the practice is widespread in England. There, more than 50% of the sets are rented, most on a long-term basis.

With the rapid changes in home-video technology, several companies—some British, to no surprise—have set up long-term video-equipment rental/service franchises in the U.S.

Here are some reasons why people think that long-term rental is the solution to the rental-vs.-purchase dilemma:

• Rates are lower than short-term rental prices.

• You can use the equipment before buying, to see if you like it.

• Long-term rental is the answer if you're afraid that the equipment might soon be outmoded if you buy now.

Protection From Repair Costs—Another reason some choose this option is to avoid potential repair costs. Before you sign a rental contract, make sure you know what the service policy covers. Is it for parts only, or does it also include labor? Does it give you free service *and* free equipment loan while yours is being fixed? Are there hidden charges?

Professionals often rent equipment instead of buying. Labels on this camera indicate that a sports network rented the camera from a company that bought it from RCA.

British-based Granada TV Rental, and similar companies, offer long-term rentals on home-video equipment.

SELECTION

A company renting video equipment on a long-term basis may not offer a lot of brands and models. Nonetheless, you'll probably find a unit with most of the features you need.

Here's a guideline to help you decide the rental question. Divide the purchase price of the model you plan to rent by the number of months you plan to keep the machine.

• If the resulting figure is lower than the monthly rental fee, it makes sense to buy.

• But, if the cost is higher than the monthly rental fee, renting makes more sense. Your decision will also depend on whether you can spend the total cost of the equipment in one lump sum.

THE CHOICE IS YOURS

Remember that at the end of the rental, you own nothing. The rental fee usually doesn't accrue toward purchase price—unless a prior agreement has been made.

Renting equipment can be an attractive alternative if you want to try a machine or experiment with home-video recording. Rental is also good if you want the latest video equipment every year. For others who might use this equipment for business, there may be tax advantages with long-term rental. Discuss this with your tax accountant.

Hardware on the Horizon

Before we explain how to connect the equipment you've bought or rented, we'll tell you about some video products that you may soon see at your dealer.

Many people are anxious to find out what new types of VCRs and cameras will be available in coming months and the next few years. This is similar to the curiosity that existed for years as everyone awaited the arrival of new car lines each fall. People *are* following video-equipment developments these days.

You may want to find out about the future of video for more practical reasons. If you don't own video hardware, perhaps you want to know if you should wait. Should you buy something promised for the near future that meets your needs better than today's equipment?

And, of course, other people who own equipment might buy something newer if they like it and can afford it.

PRICE TRENDS

The trend seems to be that prices will continue to drop for both cameras and VCRs. More retail establishments are selling video equipment. As a result, there's more competition. Manufacturers are making VCRs and cameras more efficiently. And, more features will be offered than are currently available. We've already discussed most of these.

For these reasons, you'll probably get more for your money next year than you will today. *But,* if you've been reading closely, you'll know that today's VCRs and cameras offer all the features most people need.

If you check the advertised prices for equipment, you'll see that you can buy a VCR for less than $400, and a camera for well under $800. Don't expect those prices to come down as much as they have in the past.

If everyone waits for the ultimate machine, nobody will ever buy anything. And the video industry would collapse before the great units reach the market. Yes, technology is on the march. And no, we don't expect you to treat the video manufacturers as you would your favorite charity.

But as more people shop for cameras and more dealers offer them, increased competition could help lower prices. At the same time, manufacturers may lower wholesale prices because they'll be making more cameras. This often results in even lower retail prices.

FEATURE TRENDS

Many features available only on the more expensive VCRs and cameras now will become part

Compare the features offered on current VCR models like the Sharp VC-481U above with the first VCRs for home use. Today's purchase buys a lot more. But that "wait-for-more-features" attitude doesn't work any more with VCRs. Tomorrow's equipment won't offer much more than you'll get today—unless you want super-sophisticated equipment. Camera prices haven't dropped as dramatically as VCR prices, but today's models give you more for your money. Hitachi camera at right features auto focus, instant review and a character generator.

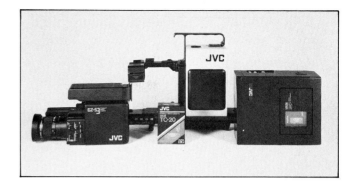

of the lower-priced leader and mid-range models. And these lines will sell for less than they do today, even with the addition of new features.

VCRs—It's difficult to think of many features that can be added to the super-high-end VCRs. Most of the capabilities that *we* could have wished for in a VCR just a few years ago are now included in many machines.

Some former VCR "dream features" include cable-readiness, frequency-synthesized tuning, wireless remote-control and stereo sound with noise reduction. Near-digital audio is available now in video with the Beta and VHS Hi-Fi models. You can expect all these to become more commonplace, along with running-time indicators, front-loading and more than two video heads.

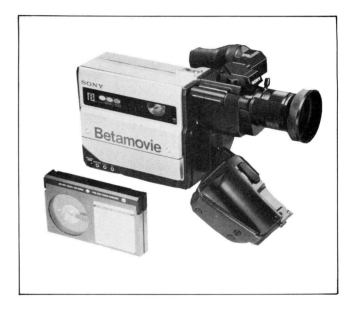

Cameras—There's a similar trend here. However, the overall price of cameras hasn't fallen as much. This is partly because fewer cameras than VCRs have been manufactured and sold. As a result, competition isn't as great. This trend continues.

Some built-in camera features that you'll find more frequently are character generators, solid-state imaging and auto-focus.

THE FUTURE OF BETA AND VHS

Many people are concerned about whether the Beta and VHS formats will still be the main home-video recording formats in the future. You've no doubt read about the newer, smaller, less-expensive systems that supposedly will replace today's two major formats. Before we get to the formats promised for the future, let's address these fears about Beta and VHS.

Don't Worry!—With almost 10 million VHS and Beta machines in the U.S.—and an equal number in other countries around the world—VHS and Beta won't be disappearing. In addition, most pre-recorded videocassettes for rental or purchase are either Beta or VHS.

Top: Home-video enthusiasts have had the opportunity to use a "one-piece" unit since 1982, when JVC introduced VHS-C. But this isn't a true "one-piece" setup. Center: Sony's Betamovie is the first one-piece camera/VCR to reach North America. It complements the existing Beta system. Above: VHS one-piece VideoMovie records on VHS-C cassettes.

Any new format *could* replace Beta and VHS. But this could occur *only* if the machines could record off the air for extensive time shifting and if the manufacturer could convince marketers of pre-recorded tapes, called *software,* that the public would buy vast numbers of these new machines, called *hardware.*

Manufacturers of VCRs and cameras—even those promising new formats—have a stake in the public's confidence in the future of Beta and VHS. Manufacturers and the brands they serve don't want to alienate the public by making their equipment obsolete overnight.

Yes, the companies that make VCRs and cameras are developing new products. But, as you will see in Chapter 8, new hardware has been designed—and its marketing planned—to complement, rather than replace the two major existing home-video recording formats.

The Choice Is Yours

In this chapter, we've given you many things to consider as you decide whether to buy or rent. We suggest that you decide *when* to buy the same way you decide *what* to buy.

Decide what you want in a home-video recording system. Then check for equipment that'll do the job. If there's a VCR or camera at the right price, buy it now.

If you wait for prices to fall, and new features and formats to appear, you'll miss out on the immediate enjoyment of home-video recording.

Regardless of whether you decide to buy or rent equipment, once you have it, you'll be anxious to use it.

Chapter 7

How to Connect and Operate Your Equipment

Now that you've made the decision to join the home-video revolution, you'll want to start using your equipment as soon as possible.

If you're like most people, you won't read the instruction manuals from cover to cover when you first bring home your video equipment. But you're reading this book, so please follow our recommendations. Equipment manuals contain valuable information about the VCR, camera or camcorder you've just bought or rented. Read them thoroughly!

After you read the manual once, *reread* the section on connecting the equipment! Do this before you start unpacking everything.

Many manuals omit important information. As a result, people often become frustrated and confused when the time comes to connect the equipment. In this chapter, we supplement even the best of those manuals. Read this chapter carefully. We know it'll save you a lot of potential grief.

But first, we'll help you unpack the equipment.

Each piece of video equipment you buy or rent will have an owner's manual. Don't throw this aside. Read it completely through, at least once before unpacking and installing your equipment. As much information as we give you in this book, we can't be *model-specific*. You'll have to depend on publications like these for details about your particular model.

This might sound too basic, but we think you'll see how helpful this can be when you're finished reading the next section of this book.

Unpacking

Before you can connect and use your machine, you have to remove it from its packing materials. Don't approach this like a child on Christmas morning. Care now will save you from crying later.

First, carefully cut through any tape sealing the top or sides of the carton. Be careful not to cut too deeply. Sometimes, manufacturers pack manuals, instruction sheets or warranty papers directly below the top of the carton. You don't want to slice into them.

Next, pull the carton flaps up to open the carton. Be careful not to cut yourself with any large staples securing the flaps.

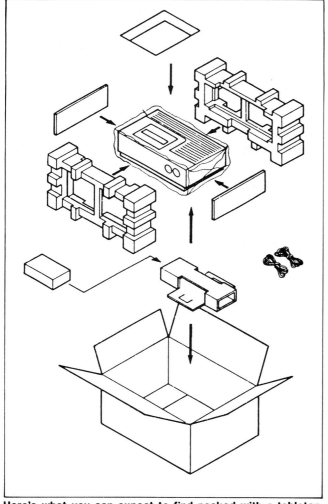

Here's what you can expect to find packed with a tabletop VCR. Aside from the VCR itself, you'll see foam and cardboard packing materials, plastic or other wrap protecting the VCR, accessories such as connectors and cables, videocassette, power cord, and booklets containing instructions and warranty. Keep track of each item in case you have to return the machine for any reason.

NOW YOU SEE IT

There it is. Your new piece of video equipment. It's waiting for you to take it out and give it "life."

Check to see if there are any accessories on top. If so, remove them and put them aside. Then, look at how the machine is secured in the carton. You'll most likely find the equipment's right and left sides nestled in hard, white foam inserts. These protect the equipment from shocks during shipping.

If your machine is packed this way, have someone hold the carton firmly while you gently slide the equipment out. Carefully set the machine down on a flat surface. Remove the foam and unwrap the equipment. It's probably covered with a plastic sheet to keep out dust.

VCR—Examine the carton to see if you left anything behind. There will probably be some accessories. Most VCRs are packed with a blank videocassette, connecting cables, 75-ohm-to-300-ohm and 300-ohm-to-75-ohm transformers, and the remote control—if the machine includes one. You may even find a cover for the equipment.

Camera—A camera comes with fewer accessories. It's often disassembled. The camera body, viewfinder, shoulder brace, microphone—and sometimes the lens—are separate parts. Find the list of standard accessories that come with the unit. Make certain everything is there. If anything is missing, contact your dealer *immediately*. Also, make sure you have a warranty card. In many cases, it's packed with the instruction manual.

Connections

We cover more information than you'll find in the owner's manual. Nonetheless, you should consult it. There are some aspects of connecting equipment that are specific to your particular machine. This includes channel tuning and the location and specific names of controls and connectors.

Familiarize yourself with your specific model. Then you'll be able to use the additional information we provide to its greatest advantage.

Although we detail several different ways to connect your equipment here, we can't cover *every* possibility. Conditions change. So do equipment and cable hookups. Try our suggestions. If you can't find any that work the way you want, talk to people at electronics or video outlets. Or contact the local cable company for information.

WHY DO YOU NEED CONNECTIONS?

This may seem like a silly question. But some

people don't understand that a VCR can only operate and perform properly if it's connected to a *power source, signal source* and *outputs.*

For example, if you want power—and you're not using a battery-powered portable—you must plug the VCR into household AC current. This is your power source. When you want to record broadcasts, you have to attach the VCR to a signal source—an antenna or cable system. And, if you want to play back what you've recorded, or a prerecorded videocassette, you must attach the VCR—through its outputs—to a TV.

Depending on the type of VCR and the kind of signal inputs available, the hookup will differ. We give you the information you need to make these connections. But first, let's locate the plugs, switches and connectors used for hookups on your machine.

CONNECTION POINTS AND SWITCHES

The connection points are found on the back of most VCRs. On others, these will be divided between the front and back. With the book open to this section, try to match up our descriptions with your equipment. Remember, not every recorder has all of these connections. And, some of the names may vary slightly.

AC-Power Cord—On tabletops and tuner/timers used with portables, one end of the AC cord is permanently attached. For house current, plug the other end into a 110-volt AC wall socket.

VHF Input—Through this connection, signals are sent from your television antenna or cable system into the VCR. It's a female 75-ohm F-connector. This is a small round, silver-colored jack that you may also find on newer TVs. We tell you later how to connect your equipment if you don't have a female F-connector on your TV.

VHF Output—The RF signal leaves the VCR through this output. It's always a female F-connector.

UHF Input—This is for reception of UHF channels. It's two wire lead posts. You usually attach 300-ohm flat twin-lead wire to these posts.

UHF Output—UHF signals leave the VCR through the UHF Output. This is another pair of wire lead posts. With flat twin-lead wire, you connect these posts to the TV's UHF Input.

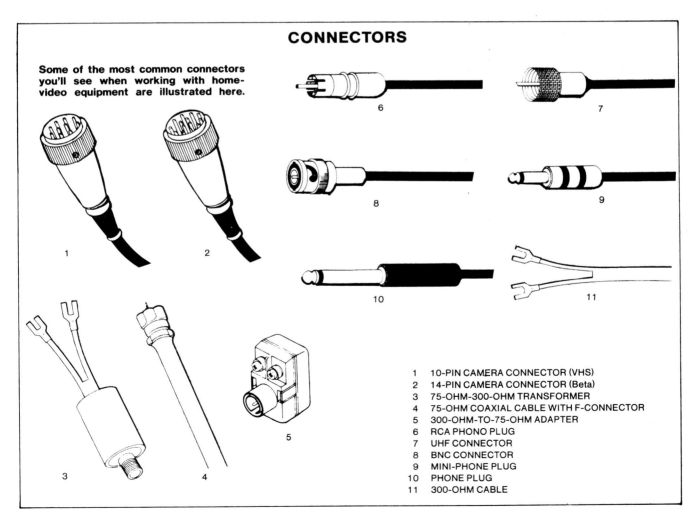

CONNECTORS

Some of the most common connectors you'll see when working with home-video equipment are illustrated here.

1   10-PIN CAMERA CONNECTOR (VHS)
2   14-PIN CAMERA CONNECTOR (Beta)
3   75-OHM-300-OHM TRANSFORMER
4   75-OHM COAXIAL CABLE WITH F-CONNECTOR
5   300-OHM-TO-75-OHM ADAPTER
6   RCA PHONO PLUG
7   UHF CONNECTOR
8   BNC CONNECTOR
9   MINI-PHONE PLUG
10   PHONE PLUG
11   300-OHM CABLE

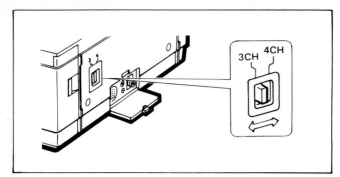

RF converter changes video and audio signals from the signal source to standard TV-broadcast signal on channel 3 or 4. Set the RF converter selector switch to the broadcast channel not used in your area, either 3 or 4. Switch may be located on the side, back or bottom of the VCR.

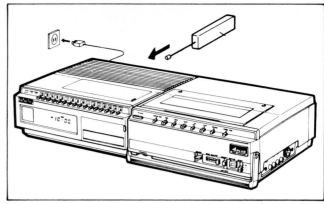

There are several ways to charge the batteries in a portable VCR. The instruction manual will tell you the best approach.

Audio Input—You may want to feed an audio signal to the VCR from an outside source. This can be from another VCR, an audio receiver, tuner or pre-amp. You plug the signal source in here. It's usually a female RCA phono jack. It can also be a mini-jack.

Audio Output—This is generally another female RCA phono jack or female mini-jack. You'll use this connection if you want to connect your VCR to play back sound through a stereo receiver. You can also send the VCR's audio signal directly to another VCR or a TV equipped with an Audio Input through this output.

Video Input—Use this connection when you want the VCR to receive a video signal directly from another VCR—for example, to copy a tape. When using a tabletop VCR to record with a camera, you usually need an auxiliary camera-power supply. Plug the video cable from this unit into the Video Input.

On all VHS and some Beta machines, the Video-Input connection is a female RCA phono jack. Other Beta models use a female mini-jack.

Video Output—This sends the video signal from the VCR directly to another VCR or to a TV equipped with a Video Input. Depending on the format and brand of your VCR, this female jack will be a phono, mini- or BNC-type connector.

Output Channel Selector—This small but *important* switch has two positions—3 and 4. Set the switch to the channel not used in your area. Don't be confused if your cable system offers both channels 3 *and* 4. Set the switch for the *broadcast* channel not used for over-the-air transmission.

PCM Switch—Some machines have a switch that should be turned on when the VCR is connected to a PCM audio adapter. Otherwise, be sure the switch is turned off. We discussed the PCM feature in Chapter 2.

Changer Control—Some Beta VCRs may be used with an external videocassette changer that can extend the length of unattended recording time. If you have a machine with this capability, this is where you plug in the external control cable. That connects the changer to the VCR.

CATV Switch—A cable-ready tabletop VCR or portable tuner/timer may have one or two switches not found on other VCRs.

If your VCR is connected to a cable-TV wire, and the video machine includes a CATV switch, make sure that the CATV/Normal switch is set to the **CATV** position.

Some VCRs have a second switch labeled CATV/IRC/HRC. This allows you to set your tuner to the delivery systems used by some cable companies. If the signal seems to need more tuning, moving the switch to the HRC (harmonically related carrier) or IRC (inter-related carrier) position may help. Your local cable system's customer-service representative should be able to tell you if the cable system uses one of these transmission methods.

FOR PORTABLES ONLY

Depending on the brand, format and model of your portable, you may have some or all of the following connection points in addition to those already mentioned.

Tuner/Power Connector—Audio, video and power are brought into the recorder section from the AC-powered tuner/timer unit through this female multi-pin jack.

Camera Connector—This is where you attach the camera to the portable recorder. As mentioned in Chapter 3, these connections vary in the number of pins they can accommodate and the type of information or function each pin carries.

On some portable recorders, the Camera Connector doubles as the Tuner/Timer Input. On these models, you'll also find a separate DC-Power Input so you can use the AC-to-DC power-conversion capability of the tuner/timer while shooting with a camera. That way, you can use AC house current to power the VCR and camera.

POWERING UP

After you have identified all the connection points, the next step is to supply the VCR with power. Tabletops, portable tuner/timers and stand-alone power adapter/battery chargers have a two-prong, *polarized* AC plug at the end of the power cord.

The plug is different from standard 110-volt AC plugs because the prongs are different sizes. The plug won't go into the outlet the wrong way. If you have difficulty, turn the plug around. It should fit.

Some extension cords and outlets in older homes won't accept polarized plugs. Don't force the plug. Instead, buy the correct type of cord or adapter at a hardware store.

For Portables Only—If you have a portable VCR and want to use battery power, be sure to read the owner's manual. It'll tell you how to charge the battery. You may have to charge the battery longer the first time you use it.

GETTING RF

Found everything? Good. It's time to get going on the actual hookups. Remember, video and audio signals generally will enter your VCR from an antenna or cable-TV wire. Both audio and video are combined in a *radio frequency* (RF) signal. The tuner and its circuits in the VCR then separate the audio and video signals so each can be recorded on different parts of the tape.

Now you can see that, to record off the air, you must connect the VCR to your RF source.

Conventional and Cable-TV Hookups

As explained in the accompanying box, there are several options for connecting your television and VCR together. The options depend on the type of VCR and TV you have—cable-ready or not, or electronic or mechanical tuning, for example. Figures 1 through 3E cover most situations you'll experience.

FIGURE 1

This is the simplest hookup. Use it when you don't have cable-TV or you have a cable service offering only 12 channels (2-13), none of them pay.

CONNECTING YOUR EQUIPMENT

The best way to help you figure this out is with diagrams and accompanying text descriptions. Look at the selection of situations described here. Find the one that most closely matches your home setup. Follow the detailed instructions in the text while following the guidelines in the appropriate diagram.

No doubt some of the terms in this list will be unfamiliar. We'll explain each of them as we go along.

Here's a list of the situations we describe and illustrate.

Figure 1—VHF off-air recording using antenna or 12-channel cable system.

Figure 2—VHF and UHF off-air recording using antenna.

Figures 3A-3E—These are for cable systems offering more than 12 channels:

Figure 3A shows connections for non-cable-ready VCR connected to record only channels 2-13; or a cable-ready VCR for recording all non-scrambled channels. This approach allows viewing of all non-scrambled channels on either VCR.

Figure 3B allows recording of all channels, but without the ability to record one channel while watching another.

Figure 3C is for hookup of non-cable-ready VCR using two cable converter boxes.

Figure 3D illustrates use of an external block converter to restore programmability with non-cable-ready VCR.

Figure 3E shows hookup with cable-ready VCR and pay-cable channels.

Figure 4—This is for hookup to an STV system.

Figures 5A-5D—There are two basic ways to connect a video camera to a VCR.

Figure 5A illustrates connecting the camera to a compatible portable VCR. This is the most common approach.

Figure 5B indicates how to connect a camera to a non-compatible portable VCR, using an accessory in-line adapter.

Figure 5C shows how to connect a camera to most tabletop VCRs that don't provide for direct camera hookup. This requires using a separate camera-power supply.

Figure 5D indicates how simple it is to connect a home-video camera to a tabletop VCR that provides a direct camera input on the front panel.

Connect the antenna leads or cable-TV wire to the VCR's VHF Input. Some antennas use 300-ohm flat twin-lead wire. If this is the case, attach the 300-ohm-to-75-ohm transformer supplied with the VCR to the VCR's 75-ohm F-connector. This is the VHF Input.

Use the supplied coaxial cable to connect the VHF Output—another F-connector—to the VHF Input of your TV.

If the TV has a 75-ohm F-connection, you can make the hookup easily. The coaxial cable has F-connector plugs on both ends. But if your TV is an older model with only screw terminals for the VHF Input, you'll need a 75-ohm-to-300-ohm transformer. This important transformer comes packed with most VCRs—but not always.

Check the list of standard accessories that comes with your VCR before you buy one. The transformer is available wherever electronic accessories are sold.

Two Ways to View TV—You can use this setup two different ways to watch any channel on your TV. One way is use the TV's tuner to select the channel you want to watch when the VCR/TV Switch on the VCR is in the **TV** position.

Or, you can use the VCR's tuner. Set the tuner's VCR/TV switch to **VCR**. Set the TV to the output channel you've selected—3 or 4. Using the VCR's tuner, choose the channel you want to watch.

With this approach, to play back tapes, you must tune the TV to the correct output channel—3 or 4.

Channel-selection settings are easier to make on a VCR with a mechanical tuner than on one with an electronic tuner. Essentially, with a mechanical tuner, you don't have any setting to do! You physically turn a dial to the proper station.

Although VCRs with electronic tuners usually come pre-set from the factory for VHF channels 2 through 13, you must set UHF and cable channels. If you don't need all the pre-set channels, you can retune them as needed. You can repeat a favorite channel at two settings if you have an electronic tuner.

FIGURE 2

You'll need more wire for this one. Connect the UHF antenna wire to the screw-terminal UHF Input on your VCR. With a piece of flat twin-lead wire, connect the VCR's UHF Output to the UHF terminals of the TV. This wire is usually supplied with the VCR.

Next, connect the VHF antenna wire to the

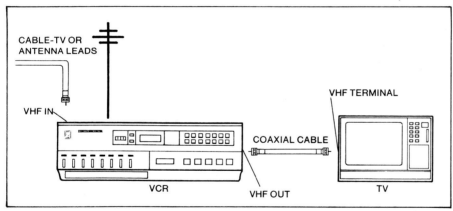

Figure 1

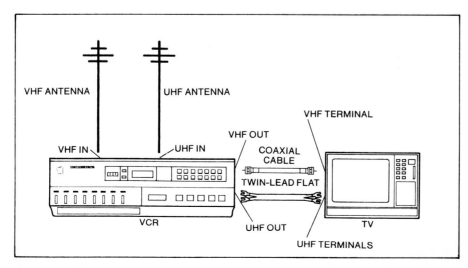

Figure 2

VCR's VHF Input. Use the supplied coaxial cable to attach the VCR's VHF Output to the TV's VHF terminal. You may need the 75-ohm-to-300-ohm transformer if the TV uses screw terminals instead of an F-connector.

With this setup, you can view VHF and UHF channels. To view a channel selected by the VCR's tuner, regardless of whether it's VHF or UHF, remember to tune the TV to the output channel, either 3 or 4.

FIGURES 3A to 3E

Use these with cable TV. Find the setup that best suits your needs, the cable system in your area, and the capabilities offered by your VCR.

FIGURE 3A

If your cable system offers more than 12 channels, this is one of your options. The additional stations are those other than the standard VHF channels 2-13. If your VCR is cable-ready, the hookup is relatively easy.

Connect the cable-TV wire to the VCR's VHF Input. Attach one end of the supplied coaxial cable to the VCR's VHF Output. Connect the other end to the input of the cable-converter box supplied by the cable company. The wire from

the converter box goes to the TV's VHF Input.

With this setup and a cable-ready VCR, you can record any nonscrambled channel while watching any channel, scrambled or not. Keep the TV tuned to the output channel you've selected, either 3 or 4.

If the VCR isn't cable-ready, you'll be able to record channels 2-13 while simultaneously watching any other channel with this connection.

To view a videocassette or watch a channel selected on the VCR's tuner, you'll have to tune both converter box *and* TV to channel 3 or 4. To view the TV when not using the VCR, simply tune the converter box to the channel you want to watch, with the TV set to channel 3 or 4.

Even if the VCR isn't cable-ready, you may still be able to tune in some of the mid-band cable channels *if the VCR features electronic tuning.* Try setting one of the VCR's channel-selector switches in the **7-13** position. Turn the thumbwheel toward channel 7—but don't stop. Keep turning until you hear a click. You may discover that your VCR *may* be able to tune in some or all of the mid-band cable-system channels.

FIGURE 3B

Use this setup if you have more than 12 cable

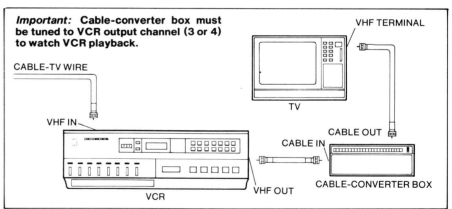

Figure 3A

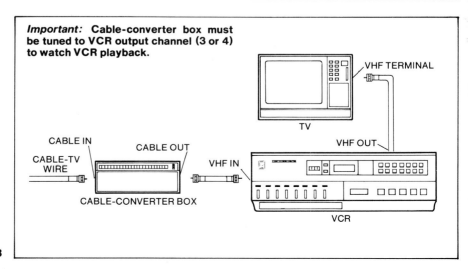

Figure 3B

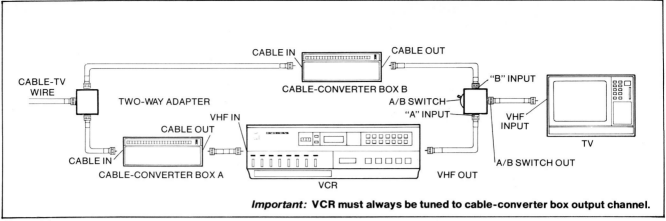

Important: VCR must always be tuned to cable-converter box output channel.

Figure 3C

channels and a VCR with a mechanical tuner. You can also follow this hookup if the VCR has an electronic tuner. This setup allows recording of all channels without incurring additional cable-TV installation costs.

Connect the cable-TV wire to the converter-box input. Next, attach the box's output wire to the VCR's VHF Input. Then, using the coaxial cable usually supplied with the VCR—or one you can purchase separately—connect the VHF Output of the VCR to the TV's VHF terminal.

With this hookup, the converter box selects everything. Tune both VCR *and* TV to channel 3 or 4. This allows you to record every channel the cable system provides, including any pay channel you subscribe to, such as HBO or Showtime.

Drawbacks—But there are some drawbacks with this setup. You can record from only one channel when you're not at home, even if you have an electronic VCR with multi-channel programming capability. That's because the converter box can't change channels by itself.

And, because the VCR can pass only the single channel it's receiving from the converter box through to your TV, you won't be able to watch one channel while recording another.

FIGURE 3C

This is a modification of 3A. But with this procedure, you can watch any channel while recording another. What makes it different from 3A is that you lose the VCR's multi-event programming function, if the machine offers that feature. And, you must have more accessories.

Here are the extras you'll need: a second cable-converter box, a two-way adapter and an A/B switch. The two-way adapter allows for two output RF sources from a single RF input. The A/B switch allows you to choose from two signal sources. Many video dealers now sell these devices that help you make cable hookups.

You can't buy a converter box, however. To obtain a second converter box, contact your local cable company. Some cable companies will do the complete installation of TV and VCR for you. If they do it, you'll probably be charged for both the second box and the installation.

Follow these instructions carefully if you decide to do the installation yourself.

The cable-TV wire goes into the two-way splitter. Connect one wire from the splitter to one of the converter boxes. We'll call this *Box A*. The output of Box A goes into the the VCR's VHF Input. Next, attach a wire from the VCR's VHF Output to the A side of the A/B switch.

Moving back to the splitter: Connect the other wire to the second converter box, *Box B*. The wire from Box B goes directly to the B side of the A/B switch. To complete the hookup, attach the single wire from the A/B switch to the TV's VHF Input.

Using the Equipment—To watch TV only, set the A/B switch to B. You then use converter Box B to tune in the channel you want to watch.

When you want to record with the VCR, select the desired channel on Box A. To view a channel you're recording or watch a prerecorded cassette, turn the A/B switch to A. Make sure your VCR is tuned to the output channel of Box A—3 or 4.

A Drawback—You can *watch* any channel while recording any other. But there's a drawback with this hookup. You lose the ability to change channels in unattended recording if your VCR features an electronic tuner and multi-event programming.

FIGURE 3D

This setup requires more accessories than the preceding ones. With it, you can receive all channels on both TV *and* VCR, even if your equipment isn't cable-ready. It also allows you to record most pay-cable channels on your cable

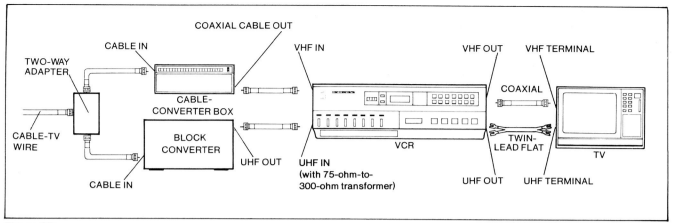

Figure 3D

system—scrambled or not. And, you can use the VCR's programming function to change channels for unattended multi-event recording.

The key to this hookup is a *block converter*. This converts mid-band and super-band cable channels, as well as the standard VHF broadcast channels, into standard UHF frequencies. The block converter won't work with the hyper-band channels on 55-channel cable systems.

Many video dealers and electronic stores sell block converters. Some cable systems carry channels outside the block converter's frequency range. As a result, you can't receive these channels using a block converter.

Setting Up—Connect the cable-TV wire to the two-way adapter. Run one wire from the adapter to the block-converter input. The other wire from the adapter goes to the cable-converter-box input.

Attach the block converter's UHF Output to the VCR's UHF Input. To do this, you need a 75-ohm-to-300-ohm transformer. With flat twin-lead antenna wire, connect the VCR's UHF Output to the TV's UHF Input.

AN IMPORTANT WORD ON PAY CHANNELS

We can't tell you which is the correct cable-hookup procedure for your system. This is because different cable companies use different techniques to control pay channels, such as HBO and Showtime. Justifiably, they use various methods—usually electronic—to keep you from receiving these channels unless you pay for them.

Scrambling—There are two major techniques for controlling access to pay channels. The first is called *scrambling*. If you don't pay for a channel offered by your system, you can tell if it's scrambled by tuning it in with the cable-converter box. When your system uses a scrambling technique, you usually hear the sound of the channel but see a distorted picture. When you order a pay service that's scrambled, the cable company provides a special converter box with a descrambling feature.

To complicate matters further, not all cable systems use the same scrambling system. But, in general, regardless of the system, your hookup will be more complicated if the cable operator scrambles to control access to pay services.

If your cable system scrambles a signal you're paying for, you want to integrate the converter box's descrambling capability with the VCR's programmable tuner. Remember, a scrambled signal cannot be unscrambled even with a cable-ready VCR. The hookups described with Figure 3D or 3E give you

procedures you can follow so your VCR can receive those signals that you're paying for.

Traps—A second popular method used by cable companies to control pay channels is the use of *traps*. Traps completely filter out, or trap, the signal from the pay channel. This prevents them from entering your home. When you subscribe to the pay channel, the cable system removes the trap.

To know whether your cable operator uses the trap technique, tune your converter box to a pay channel you're not paying for. If you see only snow without any picture at all, the cable system probably is using a trap.

There's an advantage if the company uses traps. Once the trap is removed, the channel can be picked up by a cable-ready VCR without the use of a special descrambling converter box. If your VCR isn't cable-ready, you can accomplish the same thing by using a block converter, available at video-specialty stores.

WARNING

If you connect your VCR to receive pay channels you're not paying for, that's called *theft of service*. It's illegal in many states.

Don't take chances. By all means, hook up your home-video system in the most economical and convenient way possible. But, don't do anything that might subject you to a fine or other penalty.

Next, connect coaxial cable from the cable-converter box to the VCR's VHF Input. Finally, attach coaxial cable between the VCR's VHF Output and the TV's VHF terminal.

Tune one of the VCR's channel-selection positions to the cable-converter box's output channel, either 3 or 4. Then tune the remaining channels on the VCR to the UHF equivalents of the stations you want to watch. A conversion chart included with the block converter will tell you how to do this.

When not using the VCR, you can watch any channel available from your cable system. Select it on the cable-converter box. You can also record any non-scrambled cable channel. Select it on the VCR for recording while you use the cable-converter box to select the channel you want to watch on TV.

Problem and Solution—The only problem with this hookup is that when you record a pay channel that comes through the cable-converter box, you can't watch any other channel tuned with your TV's VHF selector.

The way around this is to attach one end of a piece of twin-lead 300-ohm wire to the UHF Output of the VCR. The other end should be attached to the UHF terminals of your TV.

To watch a non-scrambled channel while recording a scrambled channel, tune the TV to the UHF equivalent of the over-the-air or non-scrambled cable channel you want to view. Use the block-converter conversion chart to find the correct number.

FIGURE 3E

If your cable system uses traps and you have a cable-ready VCR and cable-ready TV, you should follow the instructions accompanying Figure 3A. Some cable systems use a scrambled signal for their pay channels. If yours does, and you want to use the VCR's programming function, you'll need a more complicated hookup than Figure 3D.

Required Accessories—You must incorporate an external cable-converter/descrambler box with a cable-ready TV. For this hookup, you need a two-way adapter, a two-way hybrid splitter and a channel trap. The hybrid splitter is sometimes called a *signal mixer*. The channel trap, also called a *notch filter,* completely filters out a single channel.

These devices are available at video-specialty stores. They mix the output of the cable-converter/descrambler box with the signals coming from the cable-TV wire. They filter out the signal from the cable-TV wire that's the *same*

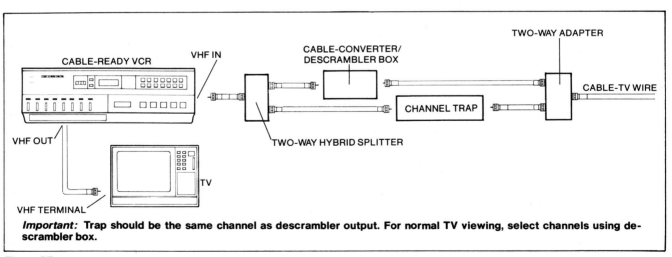

Important: **Trap should be the same channel as descrambler output. For normal TV viewing, select channels using descrambler box.**

Figure 3E

as the output of the cable-converter/descrambler box.

This special hybrid splitter can also act as a combiner. Be careful when choosing a splitter. Not all of them can perform the combiner function—which is actually the opposite of what a splitter accomplishes.

The trap should be the same channel as the output of the descrambler box. With this setup, when you just want to watch TV, use the cable-converter/descrambler box to select the channel you want.

The best way to select the accessories to meet your specific needs is to talk to a local video dealer familiar with your cable system.

Setting Up—Study Figure 3E. As you can see, the cable-TV wire goes to the two-way splitter input. One coax wire from the two-way splitter goes to the cable-converter/descrambler box. Then connect the descrambler to the two-way hybrid splitter. The other two-way adapter output is connected to the channel trap. The channel-trap output goes to the second input on the two-way hybrid splitter.

The two-way hybrid splitter has only one output. This goes to the VHF Input on the cable-ready VCR. Connect the VCR's VHF Output to the VHF Input on your TV.

Be sure to set the CATV/Normal or CATV/IRC/HRC switch to its proper position.

STV Hookups

STV is the industry abbreviation for *over-the-air subscription television.* You may know it by trade names such as WHT, ON-TV and Selec-TV. These services transmit a scrambled signal using a standard UHF television station's signal. You use an antenna to receive the STV signal, not a special wire as is the case with cable TV.

To unscramble the signal, you need a *decoder box.* This is similar to the requirement for scrambled pay-TV channels on cable. With STV, there's usually only one channel, so you don't have to worry about many of the things we discussed involving hookups for cable TV.

FIGURE 4

This setup will accommodate most STV hookups.

To take full advantage of the STV service and your VCR's programming function, you have to mix the output of the STV box and standard VHF signals. For this, you need a two-way hybrid splitter, as used in Figure 3E.

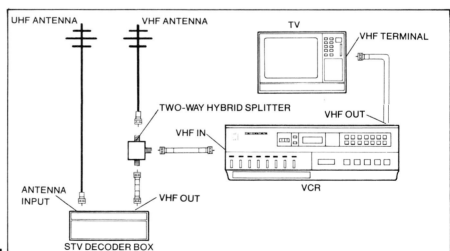

Figure 4

In this hookup, the mixing device doesn't have to trap out a similar channel. Although this approach works, it isn't the best way because some interference may leak in from channels adjacent to the STV box's output.

Following the wiring diagram, you see that the UHF-antenna wire goes to the STV decoder box's inputs. The decoder's output is connected to one input on the two-way hybrid splitter. Connect the VHF antenna to the other two-way hybrid-splitter input. Output from the splitter goes to the VCR's VHF Input. VHF Output from the VCR goes to the TV's VHF terminal.

If you don't want to use the do-it-yourself approach just described, you can buy an *accessory device.* This will replace the two-way hybrid splitter in the hookup of Figure 4. The box combines the signals, usually with some switches and a fine-tuner. Consult your local video dealer or a service person. He can tell you what to buy that will match the STV box to your VCR.

Some STV stations use a descrambler box that feeds only a picture with the RF cable. The audio comes through a speaker built into the STV box. To get around this setup, you have to buy an audio cable with the correct male plugs on both ends. Connect one end to the Audio Output of the STV box and the other to the VCR's Audio Input.

Most VCRs are designed to sense when something is plugged in. The VCR will automatically record the external audio along with the picture coming in on the RF wire.

About Switches and Settings

When you operate your VCR with or without a camera, you'll always have switches to flip and

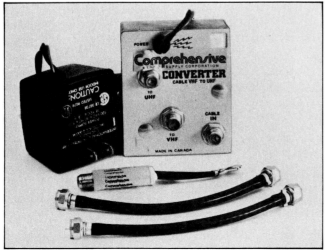

A block converter, such as this Comprehensive Video Supply unit, converts cable channels into UHF signals. See the text for more information.

buttons to press. Most cameras have switches, too. Make sure you've turned on all the necessary switches and pressed all the proper power and function buttons before you start recording.

Check the owner's manuals to find out which buttons and switches you must use to activate a particular function. Because of differences among cameras and VCRs, the individual manuals packed with the equipment are the best place to find this information.

ADVICE

We've been using home-video equipment for years. And we've been answering questions from people who can't master the controls even after reading the owner's manuals. Based on that experience, here are some additional pointers.

● When you're ready to set up the VCR, rent or borrow a prerecorded videocassette. Often, the tape that's packed with the VCR is blank.

● The first connection you should make is the one for playback. This connects the VCR and TV. Then plug in the AC-power cord. Turn on both television and VCR.

● Make sure the VCR's Output Channel Selector is set for the correct channel for your area, either 3 or 4. *This is very important!* If your VCR is connected to a cable-TV system that uses both channels, choose the one that's not used by a *local* broadcast station.

● Set the TV to the output channel of the VCR, either 3 or 4.

● Insert the prerecorded videocassette into the VCR. Push the **PLAY** control. The machine will automatically thread the tape and start playback. If picture and sound aren't clear, fine-tune the TV. If you see white horizontal breakup on the screen, you may have to adjust the VCR's *tracking control.* See *Tracking Control,* page 137.

By playing the prerecorded cassette at the beginning of your hookup procedure, you see if the VCR is operating in the playback mode. You'll also find out if you've chosen the correct Output Channel.

Correct Connections—Remember this: If the VCR is not correctly connected to the TV, you won't be certain that the other hookup to your antenna or cable-TV wire was made correctly. Why? Because you won't be able to play back an off-air recording. Take our advice. First make sure you've made the correct VCR-to-TV hookup before you start the others.

While we're on the subject of playback, be certain that the VCR-TV control is set to **VCR.** This switch or button is on all tabletops. It's on the portable system's tuner/timer unit.

• If you use your tabletop with a camera and auxiliary camera-power supply, make sure you set the VCR's Camera/Tuner Selector to **CAMERA**. Leave it set to the **TUNER** position at all other times.

• If you're using a hookup for cable-TV or STV, make sure you've made all the appropriate settings on the TV channel selector, cable-converter or STV box, and VCR.

Camera Hookups

Connecting a camera to your VCR is much easier than most of the hookup procedures just explained. In Chapter 3, we discussed the problem of camera and VCR compatibility. Here, we review the key points.

Working with a home-video camera and portable VCR is simple. Although using a camera with a tabletop VCR is a little more complex—unless the unit provides for direct camera input—it's still relatively easy.

Once again, *consult the owner's manuals* for specific VCR and camera requirements. The following information should supplement those procedures.

Each portable VCR includes a Camera Input. The multi-pin plug at the end of the camera cable goes into the VCR's Camera Input. Most cameras use a 10-pin plug. But others may use 8, 12, 14 or even 15 pins. These plugs aren't always interchangeable. Sometimes plugs with the *same*

number of pins will use the individual pins to perform *different* functions.

Let's assume you have a camera with the correct pin configuration for your VCR. When operating on battery, the VCR will supply power to the camera through the camera cable. The tuner/timer's power supply or the AC-power supply powers both camera and VCR.

If you're shooting outdoors or moving around indoors, you'll no doubt be using the VCR's battery power. When planning a lot of shooting indoors in one room, for example, you may decide to use house current.

Regardless of location or power source, the camera will be sending images and sounds it's receiving through the camera cable to the VCR. The simple camera remote-pause switch that lets you stop or start recording from the camera-end also sends its signal through the camera cable.

Some cameras feature controls for operating VCR functions from the camera. These commands are also sent through the camera cable.

When you play back a videocassette through a camera with an electronic viewfinder, the signal is sent from the VCR through the camera cable to the camera.

Be sure you connect the camera correctly and securely to the VCR. You can't make a half-hearted effort. Every pin must fit. And the locking sleeve must be screwed on tight if the VCR and camera are to work together.

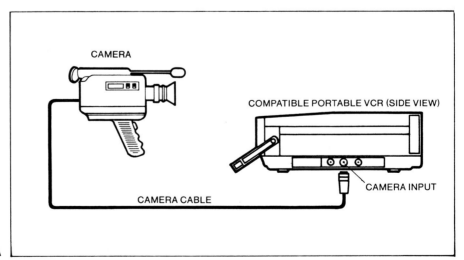

Figure 5A

Note: Once you have separated a camera's audio and video outputs using a breakout box or power supply, any VCR format or camera brand can be used.

FIGURE 5A

To connect the camera to a portable VCR, simply locate the VCR's Camera Input. Align the pins on the camera's multi-pin plug with the VCR's Camera Input and plug it in. Turn the locking sleeve to ensure a good connection.

If the camera isn't the same brand as the VCR, you may have to reset the camera's Variable-Setting Switch in order to use all of the camera's remote controls. Again, check owner's manuals for specifics. If this simple solution isn't possible, use the approach in Figure 5B.

FIGURE 5B

When using a camera that's a different brand from the VCR, an accessory *in-line adapter* may be required. This is available at your video supplier. The adapter's multi-pin connectors on each end are designed for mating a specific camera model to a specific VCR. It eliminates the need for additional cables and hookups.

FIGURE 5C

To use a camera with a tabletop VCR, you usually need the camera-power supply discussed in Chapter 3. This power supply performs two functions.

First, it converts AC power into the DC power required to operate the camera. Second, it pro-

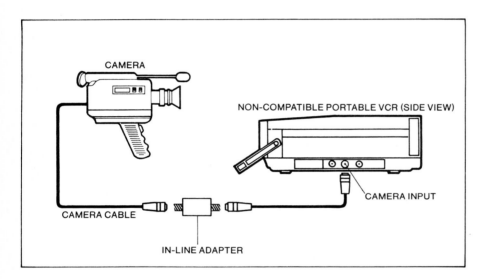

Figure 5B

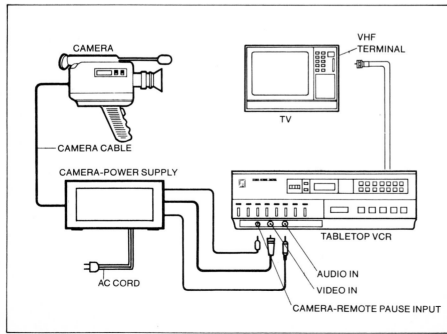

Figure 5C

vides a way to transmit signals from the camera to the tabletop unit. These signals include the video, audio and remote-pause command. They are combined in the camera's multi-pin plug. The remote-pause command is used to start and stop recording from the camera.

How to Connect—Plug the camera's multi-pin plug into the Camera Input on the camera-power supply. Connect the cables from the camera-power supply's separate Video, Audio and Remote-Pause Outputs to the tabletop's Video, Audio and Remote-Pause Inputs. You'll find these on the back or front of the VCR. Sometimes they're behind a panel. This should give you use of camera functions and indicators.

Be sure all connections are secure. Plug in the camera-power supply's AC cord. And keep the VCR plugged into the wall outlet, too. Now the equipment is all hooked up!

FIGURE 5D

Hookup to a tabletop is simple if your VCR has a multi-pin camera plug. Locate the Camera Input on the front panel. Align the pins on the camera's multi-pin plug and insert it into the Camera Input. Tighten the sleeve to ensure a good connection. Camera functions should be operational.

MONITORING LIVE IMAGES

It's simple to watch on your TV what you'll be recording. You can use this setup as a test without actually taping. Or you can monitor images and sound during recording. As with other video techniques, it's impossible for us to tell you exactly how to do this with your equipment. However, there are generally two ways to set up for live monitoring.

Connect the camera to the VCR and the VCR and tuner/timer to the TV as you would

normally. With a portable, this should be all you need to do. Turn everything on, remove the lens cap from the camera and you should see a live image on the TV screen.

For some portables and most tabletops, you'll need to be sure the Camera/Tuner switch is set to **Camera**. Set the VCR's VCR/TV switch to **VCR**. Turn on the camera and press the VCR's Record control. You're now viewing a live image!

Disc, Computer and Earth-Station Hookups

The world of video also includes a growing number of devices that compete with the VCR for your TV's screen. These include videodisc players, home computers, video games and satellite earth stations.

Because all of these devices produce an image, you may want to record the output with your VCR. That's no problem. All you have to do is decide how you want to transmit the video and audio signals from the device to your VCR.

FIRST OPTION

One option is to input them as an RF signal. This transmits the video and audio with one wire. Another choice is to use separate wires to plug in the audio and video as individual signals. The RF method requires fewer cables. But separate video and audio connections give better-quality pictures and sound.

If you choose the RF method, you'll have to buy a *switcher*. Different models are available at most video specialty stores. We can't make a recommendation because there are so many, and different needs may require a different model switcher.

Plug all the wires from the devices *and* the antenna or cable-TV wire into the switcher. Make

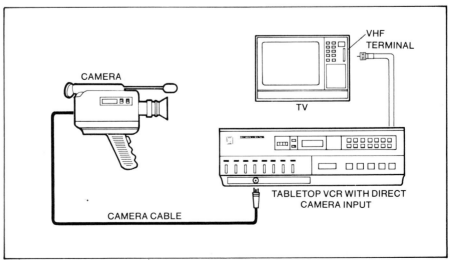

CAMERA

VHF TERMINAL

TV

TABLETOP VCR WITH DIRECT CAMERA INPUT

CAMERA CABLE

Figure 5D

sure all the inputs are set for the same channel—3 or 4. Then connect the switcher to the VCR's VHF Input.

Don't forget: When you've set the VCR for unattended recording, you must select the antenna or cable-TV feed setting on the switcher.

ANOTHER OPTION

We mentioned that there is a second way to connect other electronic devices to your VCR. You can use separate wires to attach the video and audio outputs of the other equipment to the corresponding VCR inputs. Although this method provides a better picture and audio for recording, it has drawbacks.

● Many electronic devices don't have separate video and audio outputs.

● The hookup is more complicated because you have more wires.

● You have to buy a more expensive switcher, often called a *combination box*. This has to accommodate all the individual audio and video wires.

Your cable company will supply a descrambling box when you subscribe to special channels like HBO or Showtime. This Jerrold descrambler is a remote-control unit. With other models, you must operate the channel selector manually.

You can even record the output of your video game with your VCR.

If you want to connect video games and other devices to your VCR, we suggest the RF method.

POSSIBLE INTERFERENCE

Here's another important point to keep in mind. Although videodisc players, video games and computers may also use channel 3, their channel 3 is not always precise. As a result, there might be some slight variation among the output frequencies even if everything is tuned to the same channel. To compensate, you may have to fine-tune your TV or VCR when switching from one signal source to another.

It's worth noting that all these devices have their own *modulators*. A modulator is a miniature TV transmitter that combines the separate audio and video signals into an RF signal. If the modulators are located close to each other, interference may result.

The cable-converter box may be affected by modulators in these other devices. Their signals may interfere with the cable channels in the box's tuner.

A Solution—The solution may sound silly, but try it. Wrap the cable-converter box in aluminum foil! Be sure the foil doesn't block or enter any vent holes, or touch any metal surface on the box, connectors or cable. The foil acts as a shield to keep out unwanted signals.

Making Settings

When you've connected the VCR, you'll want to use it for a variety of functions. To prepare the VCR for its first off-air recording, you have to set the tuner/timer. If you have an electronic timer, you must deal with the channel-selector panel, too.

OWNER'S MANUALS ARE GOOD, BUT . . .

Most VCR owner's manuals explain in great detail the procedure for making necessary settings. Sometimes, however, these publications fail to emphasize certain aspects. We'll point out some general guidelines.

Remember that these procedures vary from machine to machine. As a result, you may have to adapt this information for your particular equipment.

Clock—The clock setting is the one you'll probably make first. That's because when you plug in most VCRs, you see a number flashing, usually 12:00. It can drive you crazy!

You have to set the clock if you want to do unattended off-air recording at the correct time. The clock is part of the VCR's timer. It tells the

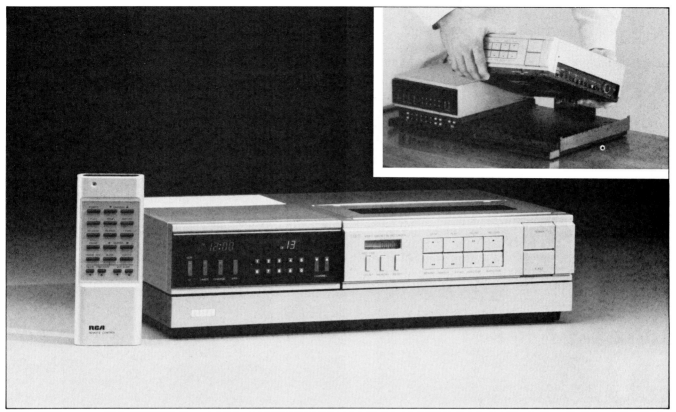

With RCA's convertible VJP900, the portable recorder attaches to a frame containing the tuner/timer. You don't have to attach separate connecting wires to use these together.

VCR when to switch on and off. Follow the instructions in the owner's manual.

Channel Settings—If your VCR has a mechanical tuner, you don't have to set any channels. You're limited to those on the channel-change dial. Just turn the click-stop dial to the channel you want to view.

With an electronic tuner, you have more versatility. Many VCR channel-selectors are pre-set at the factory for channels 2-13. Other VCRs aren't pre-set. With these, you have to follow the instructions in the manual. If you have an electronic tuner—factory pre-set or not—you can vary the position on the channel-selection unit where a channel is tuned in.

If the VCR is cable-ready and your home is wired for cable, you may have to make even more settings. The extent to which you can use the many features of the VCR's electronic tuner depends on which of the hookups you've used. For example, some connections won't allow use of the multi-event programming function.

Timer—You have to set this each time you want to make an unattended off-air recording. Be sure the clock is set to the correct time. If it isn't, the timer can't tell the VCR to record the program you want at the correct time.

When taking the signal from a TV antenna, be sure all the channels are tuned in. When using cable, make sure you've connected your equipment according to one of the setups allowing unattended recording of the channel you want. Those setups were explained and illustrated earlier in this chapter.

We suggest that you do some "dry runs" with the timer after reading the manual. Practice! Don't use the timer for the first time when an important show is on TV. Familiarize yourself with the timer's controls. Know how to make settings to record more than one event, if your VCR offers this capability.

When you're finally ready to record off the air, remember to:
- Insert a videocassette into the recorder.
- Be sure the cassette has enough tape to record the event.
- Check to see that you're recording at the speed you want, such as SP on VHS or X2 on Beta. Remember that the amount of tape you use depends both on program length *and* VCR recording speed.

Tracking Control—This knob adjusts the VCR's playback circuitry to accommodate electronic differences from machine to machine. You should not have to use this control very often. Leave the Tracking Control in its normal position.

When playing back a prerecorded videocassette, if you notice distortion in the picture—such as a snowy horizontal line—adjust the Tracking Control by turning the knob to the left or right until the distortion disappears. If it doesn't disappear, the fault may be with the tape, your machine or the machine that recorded it.

If you have to use the Tracking Control on *all* videocassette tapes recorded on other machines and if tapes made on your machine play back acceptably, this is an indication that your machine may need servicing.

Connecting a Portable VCR

To record off-the-air with most portable VCRs, you need a separate tuner/timer. As explained earlier, this tuner/timer also converts AC house voltage to the DC voltage required to power the portable VCR. The tuner/timer charges the portable's battery, too.

If you simply want to power the portable VCR and charge its battery, all you need is a stand-alone power adapter.

Remember, to record off the air with a portable, you must supply it with an RF signal through a tuner/timer. This signal can be from an antenna or cable-TV wire. Follow the diagram and explanation earlier in this chapter for the connection procedure that best meets your needs. When using a portable with a tuner/timer, the hookup is the same as if you were using a tabletop unit.

Read the VCR's owner's manual for correct hookup of the portable and tuner/timer or stand-alone power adapter. Again, we can't be specific because the connecting procedure varies from model to model.

"Wireless" Portables—On some new-model portables, you don't have to attach any wires at all between VCR and tuner/timer! A single terminal on the VCR plugs into a wired metal base unit that also holds the tuner/timer in one neat package. It's designed to be simple, and looks like a tabletop when the VCR is mounted.

READY TO GO

There you have it. You've got a basic understanding of how to connect your video equipment. Now it's time to play back videocassettes of your favorite movies, record off the air or shoot with your camera.

We've made some references to the future of video, but couldn't be too specific. That's because companies marketing home-video equipment often can't be pinned down to introduction dates, specifications or format. They work with what their engineers are developing in the lab and what the public wants. And they often keep that information secret until the last possible moment.

But there's something we *can* see in the future: Once you get into home-video, you'll wonder how you ever lived without it!

The recorder in Panasonic VHS Hi-Fi snaps into place on the tuner in a unique vertical design. It also offers one-touch recording and 17-function wireless remote control. The quartz synthesized tuner can access 139 channels.

Once you have all your equipment hooked up and operating correctly, you can sit back, relax and enjoy it. You can view a happy event immediately, and save it to watch over and over.

Chapter 8

All About Camcorders

You already know that there are three major uses for home-video equipment: recording off-the-air or from cable, playing back prerecorded cassettes and creating home movies. The first two weren't possible for the average person before the development of home-video equipment. But making home movies is a hobby that's been around for years.

For people with 16mm, 8mm or super-8 moviemaking experience, video recording with a separate camera and VCR may seem bulky and inconvenient. Many consider the video camera and VCR combination too heavy to carry around. Although relatively lightweight equipment is available, there are still objections. For example, the separate VCR and camera require a connecting wire. With conventional filmmaking, you work with a simple, lightweight camera containing the film. A new generation of video equipment has changed that!

Technology Marches On

Engineers and scientists, working with designers, developed new electronic devices to make both camera and VCR even lighter and more compact. They combined them into a one-piece, integrated unit called a *camcorder*—video *cam*era and videocassette re*corder*.

Development of the camcorder evolved along with other technological breakthroughs that affected camera, VCR and videotape products. Just as cameras and VCRs have become smaller and lighter, research in the tape industry has led to new tape formulations. These developments play an important role in some camcorder systems.

Camcorders are more portable and easier to use than separate camera and VCR units. Once again, camcorder development for the home has followed in the footsteps of developments in the professional video world.

With a camcorder such as this 8mm Kodavision model, camera and VCR functions are combined in one lightweight unit. And there are no wires to get in your way!

Introduced in 1983, home camcorders are available in several formats and designs. For the home-movie enthusiast, they remove a major barrier to shooting with video—lack of portability. They also offer advantages of shooting on videotape, such as instant playback.

In this chapter, we tell you how camcorders work, how they differ from each other, and how they differ from standard Beta and VHS recorders. We explain how to shop for a camcorder and how to use one. We also share our opinions about the benefits and drawbacks of each system, and what to expect in the future.

BETAMOVIE

Betamovie was the first home camcorder. It was introduced in 1983 by Sony, inventor of the Beta format. Betamovie uses any standard Beta cassette.

This format records in X2 speed only. This means that when you shoot with an L-830 cassette, the longest-running Beta type, you can record for almost 3-1/2 hours before changing it.

To get recording and camera functions in one small package, Sony uses a slightly modified version of its U-loading system. Even so, cassettes recorded with Betamovie work with standard Beta VCRs.

At present, Betamovie can only record. There is no playback capability. Nor is there rewind or fast-forward capability. To play back a cassette recorded with Betamovie, you must use a standard tabletop or portable Beta VCR. You don't need any adapters to play a Betamovie cassette in a Beta VCR.

Current Betamovie models have a through-the-lens (TTL) finder, discussed in Chapter 3. Because Betamovie can't play back tapes, there's little need to include an electronic viewfinder, which would add weight.

Betamovie camcorders weigh less than six pounds. Toshiba, Sanyo, NEC and Sony currently sell Betamovie camcorders listing for about $1500.

VHS VIDEOMOVIE

The VHS format entered the camcorder race in 1984 with the introduction of JVC-developed VideoMovie. This camcorder weighs less than five pounds—lighter than Betamovie. VideoMovie evolved from the VHS-C recorder, discussed in Chapter 1. Both use compact VHS-C cassettes.

With VideoMovie, you can record up to 20 minutes on one T-20 videocassette. VideoMovie currently records only in the VHS SP speed. This camcorder has an electronic viewfinder and play-

Betamovie, the first camcorder for the home, records using a standard Beta cassette. No special adapter is required for playback in a home Beta VCR.

back circuits so you can view the recording instantly through the viewfinder eyepiece. With VideoMovie's playback function and video and audio outputs, you can connect the unit to a monitor to view tapes. An optional RF adapter is required to view tapes on a standard TV.

As you would expect, VHS VideoMovie cassettes are incompatible with those recorded with Betamovie. And, although you can play back VideoMovie cassettes in a VHS-C VCR, you must use an adapter when using VideoMovie's VHS-C cassette in a standard VHS-format machine.

VideoMovie, initially offered by JVC and Zenith, is about the same price as Betamovie, about $1500.

8mm VIDEO

Throughout this book, we mention the arrival of a third video recording format called *8mm video*. This long-awaited format was introduced in 1984. Some people consider it the video replacement for 8mm motion-picture film.

Not only is 8mm tape much narrower than standard 1/2-inch-wide tape used in Beta and VHS machines, but it's also a new type—either *metal particle* or *metal evaporated*. A combination of improvements on existing video-recording technology coupled with the new, smaller 8mm cassette allow for the compact size of 8mm camcorders.

JVC's VideoMovie debuted in 1984. It weighs under 5 pounds and records on VHS-C cassettes. To play back with a standard VHS VCR, you must insert the cassette into an adapter.

This is General Electric's planned entry into the 8mm video camcorder market.

Enter Eastman Kodak—You'll be seeing and hearing a lot about 8mm camcorders. Perhaps the major force behind the fanfare will be Eastman Kodak Company, a name you'll recognize from conventional photography. The company has entered the home-video field with the Kodavision 8mm camcorder.

Kodak has bypassed both Beta and VHS hardware in favor of the 8mm system. Indications are that Kodak—along with General Electric and RCA—will be among the first delivering 8mm camcorders to dealers.

Kodak isn't building its 8mm system. Matsushita in Japan is producing this equipment. Japanese companies are expected to be the OEM for 8mm systems for other American marketers, such as General Electric and RCA. Kodak-brand 8mm tape, along with the Beta and VHS videocassettes the company is marketing, is also from Japan, made by TDK.

Kodavision, including the top-of-the-line autofocus camera, cradle and tuner/timer, lists for about $2400.

CASSETTE-SIZE COMPARISON

8mm Video	= 95x62.5x15 mm
VHS-C	= 92x59x23 mm
Beta	= 156x96x25 mm
VHS	= 188x104x25 mm

Although 8mm uses tape that is narrower than Beta, VHS and VHS-C, its actual size is rivaled by VHS-C.

8mm: PROS AND CONS

Before we explain how camcorder systems operate, let's briefly discuss advantages and disadvantages of the new 8mm system.

One advantage is that 8mm camcorders probably will be the easiest to use of any one-piece systems. They may be just right for the home-movie enthusiast ready to move into video.

However, as this book went to press, 8mm video was limited to a 90-minute recording time. Tapes will never be compatible with VHS or Beta. And, although 8mm cassettes are much smaller than VHS or Beta, they will probably be more expensive.

Included in the 8mm system—as an extra-cost option—is a cradle, or adapter, that allows playback of your home video movies through a TV, and a tuner/timer for off-air recording. However, the 90-minute cassette limits 8mm's potential use for time shifting. Additionally, the 90-minute length and the expected higher cost would make it difficult for release of many motion pictures on the 8mm format. Record time may be increased with longer-running thinner-base tapes and a second, slower, recording speed.

As originally announced by Eastman Kodak, the Kodavision 8mm system requires that you place the camcorder in a cradle to play back tapes or time shift. More on that later.

How Camcorders Work

Camcorders are the result of ongoing research efforts and market needs. New techniques and designs have made the one-piece video systems possible.

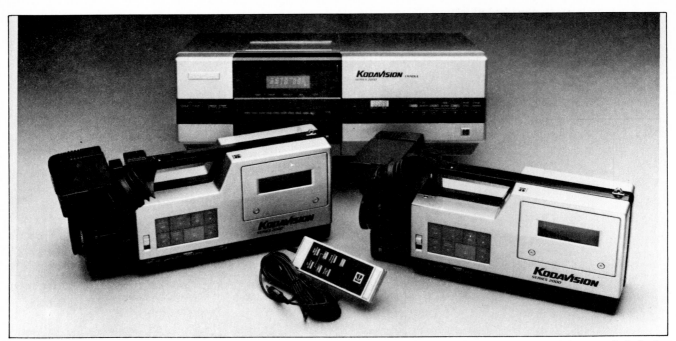

Eastman Kodak joined the video revolution in 1984 with an 8mm system that includes two camcorder models, a cradle/adapter and a tuner/timer.

BETAMOVIE AND VIDEOMOVIE

In Chapter 2, we explained that specifications for Beta and VHS formats are set by license and patent agreements. For different-brand VHS machines or different-brand Beta machines to be compatible with each other, it's obvious that manufacturers must build VCRs that follow established specifications.

How They Did It—You may be wondering how engineers can make Betamovie and VideoMovie equipment so small. And you may be curious about how camcorders can be so small and still be compatible with their "parent" formats.

Reduction in camera size was accomplished by using smaller imaging devices. Many standard color cameras for the home use 2/3-inch tubes or solid-state imaging devices. This is explained in Chapter 3. Betamovie and VideoMovie cameras have 1/2-inch tubes. To make future systems even more compact, Betamovie and VideoMovie could use the 1/3-inch tube developed for 8mm systems, discussed later. Or, the Beta and VHS camcorders could eventually use solid-state imaging devices.

To save space and weight, the viewfinder on these camcorders is also different from the type used in most conventional home-video cameras. Betamovie includes an optical TTL finder, which is lighter than an electronic viewfinder.

The VHS VideoMovie, which permits playback of cassettes in the camcorder, has an electronic viewfinder. But this finder offers only a 1/2-inch-diagonal b&w picture instead of the 1-inch or 1-1/2-inch image commonly found in finders of conventional home-video cameras.

The major reason Betamovie and VideoMovie can be made so small is miniaturization of the VCR's head-drum/scanner recording mechanism and loading system. The challenge was to maintain compatibility with standard-size VCRs of the same format.

Camcorders of both formats include drum/scanners up to 40% smaller in diameter than their predecessors. To maintain compatibility with the parent formats while including smaller scanners, Betamovie and VideoMovie use video heads that rotate at a faster speed. This increase in *writing speed* offsets the scanner's size reduction. The result is compatibility between Betamovie and Beta VCRs, and VideoMovie and VHS VCRs. What's impressive is how Sony and JVC, inventors of the Beta and VHS systems and developers of Betamovie and VideoMovie, ingeniously reduced the scanner's size and increased writing speed.

Sony's Betamovie—Sony reduced the scanner diameter by using a new type of double-azimuth video head. As discussed in Chapter 2, with conventional home VCRs, each video head is set at a specific azimuth angle dictated by the format. You need at least one pair of video heads to record a signal with one head recording at a + angle while the other is at a − angle.

However, a single video head is used in Betamovie that records both the + and − azimuth signals. With this technique, the tape can be

TAPE-EFFICIENCY CHART

To find out the most tape-efficient format and recording speed, figure out the number of square feet of tape required to record for one hour. Multiply the number of feet of tape used, by the width of the format.

You'll notice that broadcast formats use a lot of tape. Also, you'll see that one-hour recording with 8mm uses a longer piece of tape but less total tape area than VHS recorded at EP speed or Beta recorded at X3, the most efficient 1/2-inch recording speeds. That's because of the increased packing density of 8mm's metal tape, explained in the text.

FORMAT	SPEED (ips)	TAPE WIDTH	LENGTH OF HOUR REEL (feet)	SQUARE FEET PER HOUR
8mm Video	0.56	8mm (approx.)	168	4.5
VHS EP	0.44	1/2-inch	132	5.5
Beta X3	0.53	1/2-inch	159	6.6
VHS LP	0.66	1/2-inch	198	8.3
Beta X2	0.79	1/2-inch	237	9.9
VHS SP	1.31	1/2-inch	393	16.4
Beta X1	1.57	1/2-inch	471	19.4
3/4-inch U-Matic*	3.75	3/4-inch	1125	70.3
1/2-inch M-format*	8.00	1/2-inch	2400**	100.0
1-inch C*	9.61	1-inch	2883	240.3
1-inch B*	9.65	1-inch	2895	241.3
2-inch Quad*	15.00	2-inch	4500	750.0

*Broadcast videotape format included for comparison.
**20-minute maximum for cassettes of this format is 800 feet.

wrapped at more than 180°. When the video-head change is combined with the size reduction of the loading mechanism, the result is a smaller overall size for the recorder—a camcorder that is light-weight and more portable.

JVC's VideoMovie—JVC used a different approach to reduce its VHS camcorder size. For VideoMovie, the 62mm conventional scanner was reduced to 41mm. As with Betamovie, VideoMovie reduced scanner and loading-mechanism size by using a tape wrap that is more than 180°. The difference in the JVC design is the development of a new sequential recording system.

In Chapter 2, we told you that both Beta and VHS use a pair of video heads set apart from the center by offsetting degrees—6° for VHS and 7° for Beta. The combination of the "A" head's track and the "B" head's track gives you a full picture. VideoMovie's sequential recording system uses four video heads. (Although standard VHS machines may have four video heads, they are not used the same way as the four heads in VideoMovie.)

In VideoMovie, there are two "A" heads, which we'll call *A1* and *A2*. There are also two "B" heads, *B1* and *B2*. Although these are smaller, they work well because each head records only every other full video track. Instead of

recording tracks as A1/B1/A1/B1, VideoMovie records A1/B1/A2/B2/A1/B1/A2/B2.

The result is a camcorder with a smaller recording and loading mechanism and compatibility with other VHS machines.

JVC used another trick to achieve VideoMovie's incredibly small package. The VideoMovie is designed to accept only the VHS-C cassette, a compact version of a standard VHS cassette. VHS-C is discussed in Chapters 2 and 4.

The VHS-C cassette contains 1/2-inch-wide tape that is packed in a shell about the size of a deck of cards. To play a VHS-C cassette that has been recorded by either VideoMovie or a VHS-C portable VCR in a standard VHS machine, you must use an adapter that resembles the shell of a standard VHS videocassette.

8mm VIDEO

In some ways, 8mm video systems operate like Beta and VHS, using a helical-scan, azimuth recording technique with rotating video heads. And, 8mm records information on magnetic tape in a cassette. The major difference between 8mm and 1/2-inch systems is the width of the tape. Beta and VHS tapes are 12.65mm wide; 8mm is just 8mm wide.

Other differences also contribute to the small size and light weight of 8mm camcorders.

How It Came About—To understand 8mm video better, it's helpful to know that this format's development is different from that of Beta and VHS.

Beta and VHS are incompatible formats developed by Sony and JVC, respectively, which grant licenses to other companies to manufacture equipment in their formats. The 8mm format was established by the 8mm Video Standardization Conference in Tokyo on March 28, 1983, and agreed to by 122 companies representing the world's leading manufacturers of home-video hardware and videotape.

All 8mm video equipment currently being manufactured adheres to the format specifications. This is important because, if all manufacturers continue to follow the standard, 8mm will avoid a format war similar to the one between 1/2-inch Beta and VHS manufacturers.

However, the 8mm standardization is *not* binding on conference participants. And companies that didn't participate certainly aren't bound to the standards. So, there's no guarantee that all 8mm video systems entering the market will be totally compatible.

Japanese companies will be doing a lot of OEM work. As this book went to press, many of the OEM agreements were not firm enough to offer you a comprehensive listing of who is making what for whom.

Inside 8mm—As already mentioned, 8mm systems include not only a narrower tape, but also a new tape formulation. The new format operates with metal-particle or metal-evaporated tape. These formulations are similar to metal tapes available for audio recording.

Recording Process

A new type of tape was needed to allow greater packing density than available in conventional Beta and VHS ferric-oxide or chromium-dioxide tape. With increased packing density, more information can be recorded on a given area of tape. The 30% to 50% packing-density increase in 8mm tapes makes it possible for the new format to use a slower tape speed for recording. This change translates into a longer recording time on a shorter length of tape.

METAL-PARTICLE TAPE AND METAL-EVAPORATED TAPE

Manufacture of metal-particle tape is similar to that of conventional Beta and VHS tape. For all tapes, the magnetic material is prepared in a mixture that is then applied to a polyester film base, as discussed in Chapter 4. The difference is that the magnetic material in 8mm cassettes is made of pure iron treated to prevent oxidation.

Metal-evaporated tape has a mirror-like finish. To make this tape, treated cobalt-nickel material is evaporated onto a polyester film base in a

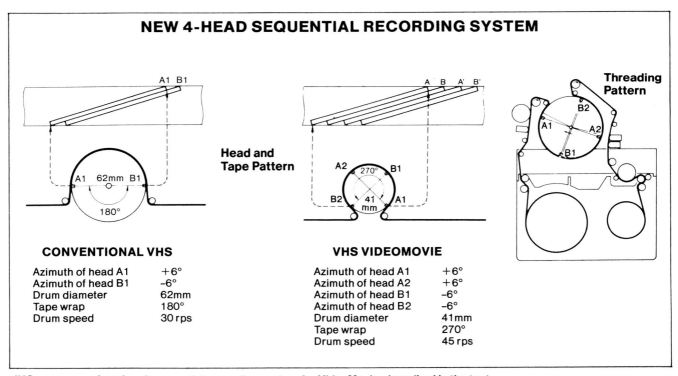

NEW 4-HEAD SEQUENTIAL RECORDING SYSTEM

Head and Tape Pattern

Threading Pattern

CONVENTIONAL VHS

Azimuth of head A1	+6°
Azimuth of head B1	−6°
Drum diameter	62mm
Tape wrap	180°
Drum speed	30 rps

VHS VIDEOMOVIE

Azimuth of head A1	+6°
Azimuth of head A2	+6°
Azimuth of head B1	−6°
Azimuth of head B2	−6°
Drum diameter	41mm
Tape wrap	270°
Drum speed	45 rps

JVC uses a new four-head sequential-recording system for VideoMovie, described in the text.

vacuum chamber. This is in contrast to the more conventional approach of coating tape with microscopic particles.

Because 8mm camcorders can use two kinds of tape, you might expect a tape-selection switch, as is common on some audiocassette recorders.

To eliminate the need for this switch on the camcorder, the 8mm cassette's shell includes a recognition indentation. The indentation allows the camcorder's recording mechanism to sense the type of tape and adjust its electronic and mechanical operations. The 8mm standardization agreement included specifications for this tape-sensing device.

Image Recording—8mm uses a recording system similar to Beta and VHS. Azimuth recording for 8mm systems has 10° offset from one track to the next. Two heads are used for recording, with a third available on some models for clearer still-frames and picture-scan.

One difference from 1/2-inch is that 8mm doesn't use a fixed control track or fixed audio head. Control-track pulses, the electronic equivalent of sprocket holes in film, are recorded as a series of pilot frequencies by the video heads in 8mm. When played back, these frequencies guide the system's internal electronics.

Audio Recording—The 8mm standardization agreement permits audio to be recorded in one of three ways. At present, it's likely that all 8mm camcorders will use only one method, the one that includes a single-channel audio track. Sound is recorded by multiplexing the audio in the video signal. This means that the audio is recorded with the video signal.

As a result, 8mm's audio-recording process is similar to the Beta Hi-Fi system, explained in Chapter 2. Although the two processes are similar, there is a big difference. 8mm systems, as currently planned, don't offer stereo, let alone the near-digital quality delivered by Beta Hi-Fi

VCRs. 8mm does include automatic noise reduction that can't be turned on and off. It always operates.

Future 8mm systems could offer stereo sound providing true pulse-code modulation (PCM)—digital audio recorded by a separate rotary video head. In addition, 8mm has provisions for an auxiliary audio track, which could be recorded using a conventional fixed audio head.

The "Camera"

The small size of the 8mm video camera contributes to the camcorder's overall light weight. Manufacturers are using smaller imaging devices such as the newly developed 1/3-inch Newvicon tube and solid-state imaging chips.

CONFIGURATIONS

The main difference between camcorders and separate camera and VCR units is that the camcorder shoots and records in one integrated unit. When we explained earlier the different ways you could work with a tabletop or portable VCR and camera, we were telling you about *configurations*—how the equipment is arranged in a system.

Record Only—Currently, this configuration is available only with Betamovie. You don't have to worry about a tuner/timer because Betamovie provides no video inputs. And, because Betamovie doesn't play back tapes, you need a separate VCR to view your tapes, and a tuner/timer for time shifting.

In addition, you do need a capability that a tuner/timer in conventional portable VCR packages provides—battery charging. Thus, with Betamovie, you also have to purchase an accessory battery charger.

Record/Play—Currently, the ability to record and play is available or planned for VideoMovie and 8mm. With these camcorders, you can play back what you have just shot through the camcorder's viewfinder.

With VideoMovie, you use an adapter to play the VHS-C cassette in a standard VHS deck. VideoMovie units include video and audio outputs so you can play a cassette through the camcorder to a video monitor. With an optional RF adapter, you can view tapes on a standard TV.

If you already have a VHS VCR, it's probably more convenient to use VideoMovie for shooting, and the VCR, which is already hooked up, for screening what you have shot. You can use a tuner/timer with VideoMovie because the camcorder has video and audio inputs, but you

BASF plans to launch an 8mm videocassette line.

CAMCORDER- AND STANDARD-FORMAT COMPARISON CHART

	8mm	BETA (X2)	BETAMOVIE	VHS (SP)	VIDEOMOVIE
TAPE SPEED (ips)	.56	.79	.79	1.31	1.31
HEAD-DRUM DIAMETER	40mm	74.5mm	44.7mm	62mm	40mm
AZIMUTH ANGLE	+/−10°	+/−7°	+/−7°	+/−6°	+/−6°

ips = inches per second

This chart shows that 8mm uses a slower recording speed than Betamovie's X2 and VideoMovie's SP speeds. And, despite a different head-drum size in both Betamovie and VideoMovie and standard Beta and VHS formats, tape-recording speed and azimuth angle remain the same. This ensures compatibility with the parent format—Beta and Betamovie, and VHS and VideoMovie.

probably would find this process impractical because the VHS-C cassette records only 20 minutes maximum.

As with Betamovie, you will need an accessory battery charger.

Camcorder Record/Cradle Play—This is unique to 8mm. Although all announced 8mm camcorders permit playback through their viewfinders, they currently don't have direct video, audio or RF outputs. Thus, if you use a camcorder to tape a family gathering, you won't be able to show the instant movies on a TV with the camcorder alone. You must bring along a *cradle,* which is an important part of your setup.

The cradle provides AC power and charges the camcorder's battery. Most importantly, it converts the camcorder's signals to video, audio and RF outputs. Without a cradle, you are limited to shooting with the camcorder and playing the pictures back through the small viewfinder.

If a camcorder is your first piece of home-video equipment, you should consider seriously a model such as Kodak's Kodavision. Its cradle includes a power supply, charger and connections. And the company offers an optional tuner/timer. Kodak may also offer an accessory power/RF adapter. Although recording time is limited to about 90 minutes, you'll be able to do off-air recording.

If you like the camcorder concept and own a VHS or Beta VCR, you don't have to worry about a cradle for time shifting. You already have the option of recording off the air, and for a considerably longer time than allowed by 8mm's 90-minute cassettes. In this case, look for an 8mm system that offers an accessory power/RF adapter similar to a power-supply adapter used to connect a video camera to a tabletop VCR. This was discussed in Chapter 3. When available, this lightweight, inexpensive option will allow you to play 8mm tapes on your TV without using a cradle.

FEATURES

A camcorder is a combination VCR and camera, so its features are similar to many of those discussed in Chapters 2 and 3. Features such as auto-focus, auto-white balance, viewfinder indicators and character generators found on conventional home video cameras appear on camcorders as well. *VCR* features, such as picture-scan, freeze-frame and tuner/timer programmability are also part of some 8mm units.

Base your choice of camcorder features on the same criteria outlined in Chapters 2 and 3. It's especially important to remember that when you add features to a camcorder, you probably will add weight. Remember that lightweight design and portability are the main reasons you may be considering a camcorder in the first place!

Some features are more important when you consider a camcorder instead of conventional video equipment. The *Camcorder Buying Checklist* on page 160 lists these and other features you may want on your equipment.

Controls—Study the controls. Although they are similar to separate camera and portable VCR combinations, camcorder controls assume different roles.

On a conventional VCR, the controls are on the VCR itself. Remote control is wired or wireless, basic or full-function. A camcorder has different requirements. For example, Kodavision has a full set of controls on the camcorder as well as on the front panel of the cradle. And the wired remote control also has a set of controls.

RCA's 8mm camcorder has a standard stop/start trigger with a full set of controls on a separate remote. A simple design without a full set of controls keeps the camcorder's weight down.

Although Betamovie has a remote control—used mainly for a convenient way to start and stop the camcorder when it's mounted on a tripod—the only on-camera functions are start

To play VideoMovie tapes, you can view them through the camcorder's viewfinder or on a TV connected to the camcorder's outputs. To watch tapes using a standard VHS VCR, you need a special cassette adapter (above).

and stop. This isn't a drawback. Because there is neither playback nor fast-forward with Betamovie, you need only the simplest kind of control.

Counter—You don't need a counter on Betamovie because it has no rewind or fast-forward modes. There's no way to locate a portion of what you've recorded, let alone play it back.

VideoMovie and 8mm can rewind and play back. Therefore, these should have a counter. Apply the same criteria to a camcorder counter as you would to one on a standard VCR.

Batteries and Power Supply—These features are especially important with camcorders. Consider batteries and power supply with great care. Find out how long the battery will last on a single charge and how easy it is to recharge. And, see if the system can charge a spare battery outside the camcorder.

It's helpful if the system can operate from a car's cigarette-lighter jack. Because a camcorder is no doubt destined for a lot of outdoor shooting, this may be important.

How to Buy a Camcorder

When considering purchase of a camcorder, an important point may be whether you already own a Beta or VHS VCR. You'll be going through many of the same steps as a first-time buyer of conventional video equipment.

For example, ask people who already own camcorders or portable systems about their experiences. It's important to know if they are new to video or already own Beta or VHS machines. However, it may be difficult to find people with camcorder experience because this equipment is so new. Sometimes it's nice to be "the first one on your block," but that isn't necessarily the best way.

Read about the latest products in home-video magazines. Test reports tell you if the equipment has any basic drawbacks.

Visit dealers, ask questions and get product brochures. Study the specs. Camcorder spec sheets will provide much of the same information as VCR and camera spec sheets, such as signal-to-noise ratio, picture resolution and power requirements.

When you go to a dealer, it's important to get a hands-on demonstration. Try different camcorders to see how comfortable they are to use. Be cer-

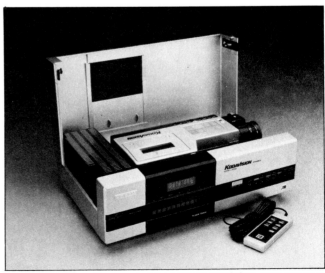

To play back an 8mm cassette with Kodavision, you can use the b&w viewfinder. But if you want to share the image with others, the camcorder must be placed in a cradle/adapter and connected to a TV.

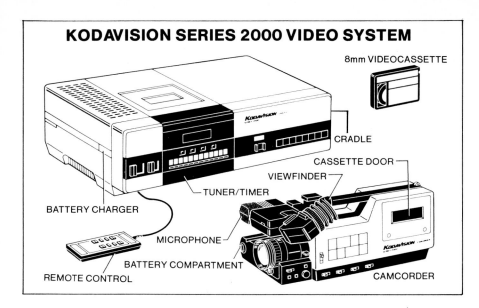

KODAVISION SERIES 2000 VIDEO SYSTEM

8mm VIDEOCASSETTE
CRADLE
CASSETTE DOOR
VIEWFINDER
TUNER/TIMER
BATTERY CHARGER
MICROPHONE
BATTERY COMPARTMENT
REMOTE CONTROL
CAMCORDER

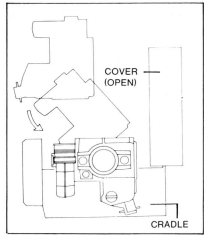

COVER (OPEN)
CRADLE

This illustrates parts of camcorder and cradle, and how the camcorder fits in the cradle.

tain that the model you're interested in offers what you want in a camcorder.

Once you've made your brand and model selection, shop around for price. Don't ignore other factors, such as dealer reputation and access to service and parts.

CAMCORDER CONSIDERATIONS

Several factors will affect your camcorder purchasing decision. One of them is the probability that there will be shortages for a while—especially with 8mm systems. This means that "street prices" for any format camcorder will be closer to suggested retail price than is common for other video products. As camcorder makers learn more about manufacturing the new systems, they will develop ways to cut production costs. And as production increases, you'll see more competitive pricing.

So, if you're trying to decide between a conventional portable VCR with camera and a camcorder, you'll probably be comparing a heavily discounted deal with a package selling close to list. For the price of a camcorder and its power supply and/or cradle, you no doubt could buy a more fully featured camera and high-end portable VCR with stereo sound and more.

A Camcorder for You?—What's all the excitement about? Isn't a camcorder just a combination of functions that you can already buy in separate units, and probably for a better price? If you're seriously considering a camcorder, here's some advice:

• There's no need to consider buying a camcord-

To record off the air with Kodavision, you must use this optional tuner/timer. It plugs into the cradle/adapter.

Kodavision model 2400 8mm camcorder.

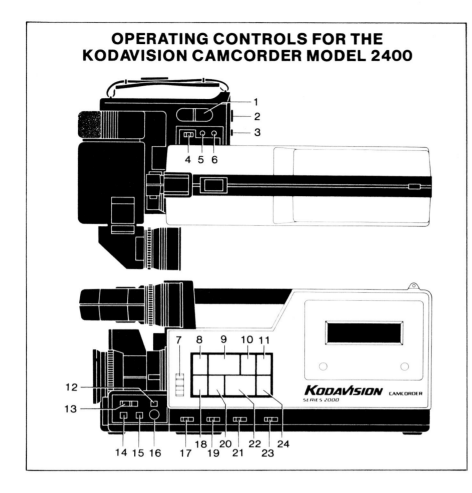

OPERATING CONTROLS FOR THE KODAVISION CAMCORDER MODEL 2400

1 POWER-ZOOM CONTROL
2 CAMERA-RECORD/PAUSE BUTTON
3 RECORD-REVIEW BUTTON
4 DATE-SELECT/COUNTER SWITCH
5 SELECT/MEMORY BUTTON
6 DATE-SET/COUNTER-RESET BUTTON
7 DAYLIGHT/TUNGSTEN-SELECT SWITCH
8 FAST-FORWARD/SEARCH CONTROL
9 PLAY CONTROL
10 REWIND/SEARCH CONTROL
11 RECORD CONTROL
12 NEGATIVE/POSITIVE SWITCH
13 AUTOMATIC-FOCUS SELECT SWITCH
14 FADE-IN/FADE-OUT SWITCH
15 BACK-LIGHT BUTTON
16 MANUAL WHITE-BALANCE CONTROL
17 AUTOMATIC WHITE-BALANCE SWITCH
18 PAUSE/STILL CONTROL
19 STANDBY/OPERATE SWITCH
20 SINGLE-FRAME ADVANCE CONTROL
21 CAMERA/PLAYBACK/CRADLE SWITCH
22 STOP CONTROL
23 ON/OFF POWER SWITCH
24 EJECT CONTROL

Kodavision model 2400 camcorder offers auto-focus, power zoom, fast-forward scan control and negative/positive switch—all features found in traditional separate camera units.

er if you don't want to create home movies.

• Some people love to have the newest electronic devices on the market. If that's you, a camcorder is a must.

• Camcorders are small and lightweight. And they don't need connecting wires. There's no VCR to sling over one shoulder while you're balancing the camera on the other. Camcorders are great for travel and outdoor shooting. They are more portable and convenient than separate camera/VCR packages.

• If you own a tabletop VCR and want to get into home moviemaking, don't just consider camcorders. A lightweight camera/VCR package may be what you want instead. Just as camcorders are reaching the market, so are newer and lighter camera/VCR packages. If you decide on a portable VCR with a camera, you don't need a tuner/timer, which is built into the tabletop.

• With 8mm and VideoMovie, the camcorder doesn't have to be the same format as your VCR to copy tapes you make. With Betamovie, there is no way to make copies with another VCR because Betamovie can't play back.

• If your main interest is videotaping events and people, and you're not interested in time shifting or renting prerecorded movies, a camcorder may be what you need.

• Camcorders have limitations that could make you consider a lightweight camera and portable VCR. This is important if a camcorder is to be the only piece of video equipment you plan to buy, and if home moviemaking is your main consideration.

• At this time, there is no prerecorded 8mm programming. And cassettes currently are limited to about 90 minutes. Two 8mm cassettes would be required to record most feature films.

• It's expected that blank 8mm cassettes will be more expensive than those for Beta and VHS.

• VideoMovie and Betamovie can't be used to play back movies you rent or buy. Betamovie can't play back at all. And because VideoMovie uses VHS-C cassettes, it's unlikely that movies would be released on cassettes that hold only 20 minutes of material. This limitation is similar to 8mm. If you like Betamovie or VideoMovie and want to play back prerecorded cassettes, we suggest you buy a VCR of the same format. The same is true if you want to record off the air.

• VideoMovie only records for 20 minutes on a single cassette. Although professionals using portable 3/4-inch-format VCRs are limited to 20-minute cassettes, you may find the recording time too short for home needs.

• No first-generation camcorders offer stereo or hi-fi quality sound. However, there's no technical reason why these features can't or won't be available in the future. If you want to add narration to the audio you've recorded, you can't do it with Betamovie or 8mm. With VideoMovie, you can place the VHS-C cassette in an adapter and add narration using a VHS VCR offering sound-on-sound, as discussed in Chapter 2.

• Cassettes for Betamovie are standard Beta cassettes, and are easy to purchase. Cassettes for VideoMovie and 8mm may be more expensive. Sometimes they may not be available. This is important to remember if you live in a small town or intend to travel with your equipment.

• When price is a consideration, a camcorder may be a good idea but not the best value. Don't expect the same type of deals that are available for conventional VCRs and cameras.

• With some camcorder systems, the camera must be in a cradle to record off the air, and you may need an additional piece of equipment for time shifting. This means that you won't be able to record your favorite soap opera while at the beach shooting with your camcorder. Even if an 8mm system doesn't require a cradle, the power adapter for off-the-air recording requires that the camcorder be present to tape TV shows.

Camcorders are new and wonderful! Make sure the one you're interested in meets your needs and pocketbook. To make the correct decision, you must filter out any hype and misinformation accompanying their introduction. Some would lead you to believe that home-video moviemaking is arriving for the first time. As you already know, it has been with us since the late 1970s.

Hooking Up a Camcorder

You may think that this is unnecessary when talking about a one-piece, integrated camera/recorder system. But this equipment is designed to do more than just shoot with tape. VHS and Beta camcorders supplement capabilities of current 1/2-inch systems. Some 8mm systems allow you to play tapes on your TV and record cable or broadcast signals.

BETAMOVIE

Betamovie is a record-only unit. By itself, all

RCA plans to reduce weight of its 8mm system by placing most transport controls on a remote control (not shown).

you can do is record live images. To play back the cassette, you must place the tape in a Beta-format VCR. Currently, Betamovie records only at X2 speed. You can't play a Betamovie tape on an industrial Beta machine limited to X1 for playback.

Assuming your Beta VCR is hooked up and ready to go, Betamovie requires no extra connections or adapters. Just pop the cassette into the VCR and follow usual procedures.

VHS VIDEOMOVIE

With the VHS VideoMovie camcorder, you simply aim and shoot to record, much like Betamovie. However, you can play back what you have recorded through the electronic viewfinder. Tape playback is controlled by buttons on the camcorder.

To view VideoMovie recordings on a TV or monitor, you can connect the camcorder by wires. If you have a monitor/receiver—TV set with separate video and audio inputs—you'll use separate audio and video wires. This approach offers the best-quality picture and sound, and is possible because VideoMovie has individual audio and video outputs.

For conventional TV, VideoMovie offers an optional RF adapter that sends visuals and sound through one wire.

Another option with VideoMovie is to play the VHS-C cassettes in a standard VHS VCR. But first you must place the VHS-C cassette in an adapter that fits in all VHS tabletops and portables, except VHS-C portables.

Photographic-equipment dealers are now selling such video items as VCRs, TVs and 8mm video.

8mm VIDEO

As with VideoMovie, 8mm allows immediate playback and viewing through the camera's electronic viewfinder, using controls on the camcorder. To view 8mm cassettes on TV requires more hooking up than with Betamovie and VideoMovie. With first-generation 8mm, the camcorder is the only machine available. There are no stand-alone 8mm VCRs.

The first generation 8mm camcorders have no video, audio or RF outputs, so you need a cradle or power adapter for viewing 8mm cassettes on a TV or monitor. Plug the camcorder into the cradle or adapter. To connect the cradle or adapter to a TV, follow the appropriate hookup diagram in Chapter 7. The same applies for connecting a cradle or adapter with a tuner/timer to an antenna or cable-TV hookup.

Camcorder Accessories

The list of accessories for these new systems is growing fast. Some items, such as the cradle, are for accommodating the size and operational requirements of camcorders. Others already on the market for standard cameras and portables work well with camcorders. These include lights, tripods, microphones and mixers, discussed in Chapter 5.

Shoulder Frame or Brace—Camcorders have a flat base. A shoulder frame is shaped so a contoured, padded piece fits over your shoulder. The flat top of the brace mates to the bottom of the camcorder through a tripod-mounting screw.

Cassette Rewinder—Betamovie doesn't rewind cassettes. A cassette rewinder, which any Beta VCR owner can use, will do it if you don't want to use your Beta VCR for this function. The rewinder can also erase the cassette. Cassette rewinders aren't new. Until recently, they've been most popular with video dealers who rent videocassettes.

Cases—A hard-shell case protects a camcorder from the hard knocks of travel. A soft case is a good cover for a camcorder while shooting. This is important in wet or dusty conditions that may damage the equipment's internal parts. A case can also act as a blanket, a vital function because batteries lose power quickly in low temperatures.

Batteries—The standard battery pack for most systems allows only one hour of use. Because the camcorder is designed for use away from home and outdoors, you might want an extended power supply. Accessory batteries and belts allow up to four hours of operation with one battery.

The Future of Camcorders

Camcorders are relatively new, so it's difficult to predict their future. Until 1983, camcorders were the future!

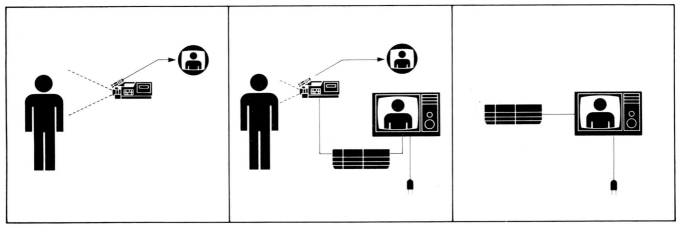

Battery-operated camcorder.   **Subject viewed through viewfinder/TV.**   **Playback through TV or record from TV with tuner/timer.**

We observe trends, listen to what the major hardware and software manufacturers and distributors are saying, and visit trade shows where new models and prototypes of new systems are displayed. Here are our observations about the near future for camcorders.

BETAMOVIE

Betamovie is useful only to someone who already owns a Beta-format VCR. If you love Betamovie and don't own a VCR, you'll have to spend about $1500 for the camcorder and an additional $400 or so for a leader-model Beta tabletop—just so you can play back what you record.

Sony, initially the only company manufacturing Betamovie, may be able to make its camcorder even lighter, by using a solid-state imaging device instead of 1/2-inch tube. With the weight saved, Sony might add a playback function. If Beta-format companies that are currently selling a Sony-made camcorder—NEC, Toshiba and Sanyo—decide to make their own, playback could be a competitive feature they might add. An electronic viewfinder would no doubt be offered with the playback function.

VIDEOMOVIE

The VHS camcorder offers almost everything you could want in a one-piece system. Thus, changes would probably be subtle.

Although JVC designed and manufactures VideoMovie, Zenith was the first company to formally introduce the system in North America. It was part of Zenith's format switch from Beta to VHS at the beginning of 1984. Initially, JVC and Zenith are selling VideoMovie. If the system catches on, other VHS manufacturers or marketers may join in.

One objection to VideoMovie is the relatively short recording/playing time. The VHS-C cassette records for only 20 minutes. It's conceivable that they will find a way to add a second, slower recording speed to increase recording time on the T-20 cassette. They could also add stereo sound.

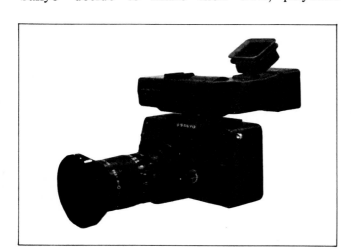

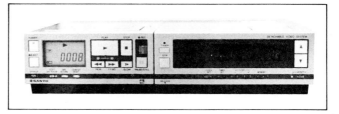

This Sanyo prototype 8mm system offers an 8mm VCR (above) that docks with a tuner/timer. The camera (left) looks similar to a 35mm SLR still camera. Both components are light, but separate.

8mm VIDEO

Important future changes are likely to involve parts of the system other than the camcorder, which could enhance 8mm's appeal and increase its popularity.

We expect stand-alone 8mm VCRs that probably will resemble dockable VHS portables. Then, users will have a full-featured VCR for off-the-air recording, and a light portable for recording with a light camera. This approach may seem to violate the camcorder concept for which 8mm was developed, but could help expand the format's popularity. Not only could you consider buying an 8mm camcorder, but also a compact 8mm portable that could be connected to a palm-size camera. Some of these cameras may look like 35mm SLR cameras.

The Future in Video

Anyone who has followed the development of home video will quickly point out that many features available today were unheard of a few years ago. If you have charted price changes in VCRs, you know that even with inflation, you get much more for your money today than five years ago.

When considering camcorders, keep in mind that you are looking at the system's first generation. Based on past video history, what manufacturers offer tomorrow will probably be much different. The same applies to price.

As the camcorder market matures, we expect to see units with character generators, stereo and hi-fi audio, low-light imaging devices and interchangeable lenses. It's safe to say that almost every feature you now find on a conventional camera and portable VCR eventually will be incorporated into a camcorder.

Beta and VHS videocassettes are available almost anywhere.

ABOUT SONY'S MAVICA CAMERA

Sony has demonstrated a video *still camera* called *Mavica.* Instead of film, it uses a magnetic disk to capture still images. Because electronics are used, no developing is required. The still images can be recorded on a VCR, viewed immediately on a TV or transmitted over telephone lines. With a Sony-developed printer, full-color hard copies can be produced from the disk. The Mavica camera, which looks like a 35mm SLR camera, uses a solid-state imaging device.

Sony has coined the term *Mavigraphy* to describe their magnetic video photography system.

Sony's Mavica electronic still camera records images on disks that can be played back instantly on a TV. When this book went to press, the unit was not yet available to the public.

Maybe you're ready for a camcorder today—or perhaps tomorrow. It's also possible that you'll never need one. Camcorders aren't the only game in town. There's a range of systems for making home-video movies.

Most people who get into video are actually more interested in recording off the air. Movies on cassette rent for reasonable prices. Programs include not only movies, but how-to tapes and video-music titles. And the list is expanding to meet almost every need and taste.

The same could be said for today's home-video hardware, and systems on the way. When selecting home-video equipment, we suggest that you examine *your future needs.* Will you want to record off the air, play back prerecorded programs, create home-video movies? There are systems that allow all of these options.

Unless money is no object, you should buy a home-video system that best meets your needs today and allows you to expand tomorrow.

Source List

RECORDING EQUIPMENT MARKETERS
These companies market video equipment in North America. An asterisk (*) indicates those companies that have announced plans but are not yet offering video equipment as of April 1984.

Aiwa America, Inc.
35 Oxford Drive
Moonachie NJ 07074

Akai America Ltd.
800 West Artesia Boulevard
Compton CA 90220

Canon USA, Inc.
One Canon Plaza
Lake Success NY 11042

Curtis Mathes Corp.
1311 Greenway
Irving TX 75062

Eastman Kodak Company
343 State Street
Rochester NY 14650

Elmo Manufacturing Corp.
70 New Hyde Park Road
New Hyde Park NY 11040

Emerson Radio Corp.
1 Emerson Lane
Secaucus NJ 07094

Fisher Corp.
21314 Lassen Street
Chatsworth CA 91311

General Electric
Video Products Division
1 College Boulevard
Portsmouth VA 23705

Hitachi Sales Corp. of America
401 West Artesia Boulevard
Compton CA 90220

Jensen Sound Laboratories
4136 North United Parkway
Schiller Park IL 60176

JVC Company of America
41 Slater Drive
Elmwood Park NJ 07407

Kenwood Electronics, Inc.
1315 East Watsoncenter Road
Carson CA 90745

Konica Audio-Video Division
Konishiroku Photo Industry USA
440 Sylvan Avenue
Englewood Cliffs NJ 07632

Magnavox
NAP Consumer Electronics Corp.
I-40 & Straw Plains Pike
Knoxville TN 37914

Marantz Company, Inc.
20525 Nordhoff Street
Chatsworth CA 91311

Minolta Corp.
101 Williams Drive
Ramsey NJ 07446

Mitsubishi Electric Sales of America
3030 East Victoria Street
Compton CA 90221

Montgomery Ward
535 West Chicago Avenue
Chicago IL 60607

Nakamichi USA Corp.*
1101 Colorado Avenue
Santa Monica CA 90401

NEC Home Electronics Inc.
1401 West Estes Avenue
Elk Grove Village IL 60007

Nikon Inc.*
623 Stewart Avenue
Garden City NY 11530

Olympus Camera Corp.
Crossways Park
Woodbury NY 11797

Panasonic Company
1 Panasonic Way
Secaucus NJ 07094

Pentax Corp.
35 Inverness Drive, East
Englewood CO 80112

J.C. Penney
1301 Avenue of Americas
New York NY 10019

Philco
NAP Consumer Electronics Corp.
I-40 & Straw Plains Pike
Knoxville TN 37914

Pioneer Video, Inc.*
200 West Grand Avenue
Montvale NJ 07645

Quasar Company
Matsushita Electric Corp. of America
9401 West Grand Avenue
Franklin Park IL 60131

Radio Shack
1500 One Tandy Center
Ft. Worth TX 76102

RCA Consumer Electronics Div.
RCA Corporation
600 North Sherman Drive
Indianapolis IN 46201

Sansui Electronics Corp.
1250 Valley Brook Avenue
Lyndhurst NJ 07071

Sanyo Electric, Inc.
1200 West Artesia Boulevard
Compton CA 90220

Sears, Roebuck & Company
Sears Tower
Chicago IL 60684

Sharp Electronics Corp.
10 Sharp Plaza
Paramus NJ 07652

Sony Consumer Products Company
Sony Corp. of America
Sony Drive
Park Ridge NY 07656

Sylvania
NAP Consumer Electronics Corp.
I-40 & Straw Plains Pike
Knoxville TN 37914

Teknika Electronics Corp.*
1633 Broadway
NY NY 10019

Toshiba America, Inc.
82 Totowa Road
Wayne NJ 07470

Video Concepts
7600 East Orchard Road
Englewood CO 80111

Zenith Radio Corporation
1000 Milwaukee Avenue
Glenview IL 60025

BLANK TAPE VIDEOCASSETTE MARKETERS
These companies are manufacturers and/or marketers of blank videocassettes.

BASF Systems Corp.
10 Crosby Drive
Bedford MA 01730
Beta, VHS, 8mm

Canon USA, Inc.
One Canon Plaza
Lake Success NY 11042
VHS

Certron Corp.
8929 Wilshire Blvd.
Beverly Hills CA 90211
Beta, VHS

Eastman Kodak Company
343 State Street
Rochester NY 14650
Beta, VHS, 8mm

Fuji Photo Film U.S.A., Inc.
350 Fifth Avenue
New York NY 10118
Beta, VHS, VHS-C

Irish Magnetic Industries
270-78 Newton Road
Plainview NY 11803
VHS

JVC Company of America
41 Slater Drive
Elmwood Park NJ 07407
VHS, VHS-C

Konica Audio-Video Division
Konishiroku Photo Industry USA, Inc.
440 Sylvan Ave.
Englewood Cliffs NJ 07632
Beta, VHS

BLANK TAPE VIDEOCASSETTE MARKETERS continued

Magnavox
NAP Consumer Electronics Corp.
I-40 & Straw Plains Pike
Knoxville TN 37914
VHS

Maxell Corp. of America
60 Oxford Drive
Moonachie NJ 07074
Beta, VHS, VHS-C

Memtek Products (Memorex)
Div. Tandy Corp.
Box 988
Santa Clara CA 95052
Beta, VHS

Minolta Corp.
101 Williams Drive
Ramsey NJ 07446
VHS

NEC Home Electronics, Inc.
1401 West Estes Avenue
Elk Grove Village IL 60007
Beta, VHS

Panasonic Company
1 Panasonic Way
Secaucus NJ 07094
VHS

PDMagnetics
Box 4499
Wilmington DE 19817
Beta, VHS

Polaroid Corp.
549 Technology Square
Cambridge MA 02139
Beta, VHS

Quasar Company
Matsushita Electric Corp. of America
9401 West Grand Avenue
Franklin Park IL 60131
VHS

Radio Shack
1500 One Tandy Center
Ft. Worth TX 76102
Beta, VHS

RCA Consumer Electronics Div.
RCA Corporation
600 North Sherman Drive
Indianapolis IN 46201
Beta, VHS

RKO Tape Corp.
3 Fairfield Cresent
West Caldwell NJ 07006
Beta, VHS

Samsung Pacific International, Inc.
600 Wilshire Blvd.
Los Angeles CA 90017
VHS

SKC-Sunkyong International, Inc.
30 Congress Drive
Moonachie NJ 07064
Beta, VHS

Sony Tape Sales Company
Sony Corp. of America
Sony Drive
Park Ridge NJ 07656
Beta, VHS

TDK Electronics Corp.
12 Harbor Park Drive
Port Washington NY 11050
Beta, VHS, VHS-C

3M
Magnetic Audio/Video Products
3M Center, Building 223-5
St. Paul MN 55144
Beta, VHS

Zimag
Magnetic Tape International
14600 South Broadway
Gardena CA 90248
Beta, VHS

PRERECORDED VIDEOCASSETTE MARKETERS

You can buy or rent videocassettes containing theatrical and television programs, how-to shows and other types of programming. This is a list of some companies marketing these videocassettes through retail stores and by mail-order. For catalogs listing their offerings, ask your videocassette retailer. If not available locally, write directly to the companies.

CBS/Fox Video
1211 Avenue of the Americas
New York NY 10036

Embassy Home Entertainment
1901 Avenue of the Stars
Los Angeles CA 90067

Family Home Entertainment
7920 Alabama Avenue
Canoga Park CA 91304

Karl Video
899 West 16th Street
Newport Beach CA 92663

MCA Videocassette
70 Universal City Plaza
Universal City CA 91608

Media Home Entertainment
116 North Robertson Boulevard
Los Angeles CA 90048

MGM/UA Home Entertainment
1350 Avenue of the Americas
New York NY 10019

National Telefilm Associates
12636 Beatrice Street
Los Angeles CA 90066

NFL Films
330 Fellowship Road
Mount Laurel NJ 08054

Nostalgia Merchant
6225 Sunset Boulevard
Hollywood CA 90028

Pacific Arts Video
Box 22770
Carmel CA 93922

Paramount Home Video
5555 Melrose Avenue
Hollywood CA 90038

RCA/Columbia Pictures Home Video
2901 West Alameda Avenue
Burbank CA 91505

Thorn EMI Video
1370 Avenue of the Americas
New York NY 10019

Vestron Video
911 Hope Street
Stamford CT 06907

VidAmerica
235 E. 55th Street
NY NY 10022

Video Gems
731 North La Brea
Los Angeles CA 90038

Walt Disney Home Video
500 South Buena Vista Street
Burbank CA 91521

Warner Home Video
4000 Warner Boulevard
Burbank CA 91522

ACCESSORY MANUFACTURERS/MARKETERS

Many accessories for video are also used in conventional photography. The companies listed here sell photographic and/or video accessories direct or through selected dealers. In addition to these companies, video-equipment marketers also sell accessories.

Ambico, Inc.
101 Horton Avenue
Lynbrook NY 11563

Amaray Sales Corp.
2251 Grand Road
Los Altos CA 94022

Arel, Inc.
4916 Shaw Avenue
St. Louis MO 63110

Argraph Corp.
111 Asia Place
Carlstadt NJ 07072

Brandess Bros.
5441 N. Kedzie
Chicago, IL 60625

Coast Photo
555 E. 242nd St.
Bronx NY 10470

Comprehensive Video Supply Corp.
148 Veterans Drive
Northvale NJ 07647

General Photo Products, Ltd.
1350 Birchmount Road
Scarborough, Ontario
Canada M1P 2E4

Gusdorf Corp.
6900 Manchester Ave.
St. Louis MO 63143

Hervic Corporation
6910 Hayvenhurst Ave.
Van Nuys CA 91406

Ideal World Marketing, Inc.
900 Broadway
New York NY 10003

Jasco Products Co., Inc.
217 N.E. 46, Box 466
Oklahoma City OK 73101

Kalt Corp.
2036 Broadway
Santa Monica CA 90404

Kiwi, Div. of Northern Mercantile
1030 E. 30th Street
Hialeah FL 33013

La Grange, Inc.
13209 Saticoy Street
N. Hollywood CA 91605

Louis Lefkowitz & Brothers, Inc.
50 Washington Avenue
Milltown NJ 08850

O'Sullivan Industries, Inc.
19th & Gulf Streets
Lamar MO 64759

Photoco, Inc.
4347 Cranwood Parkway
Cleveland OH 44128

Radio Shack, Div. Tandy Corp.
1500 One Tandy Center
Fort Worth TX 76102

Rome Photo, Inc.
3445 N. Broadway
Chicago IL 60657

Reeves Photo Sales
9000 Sovereign Row
Dallas TX 75247

Saft America Inc.
931 Vandalia Street
St. Paul MN 55114

Satter Dist. Co., Inc.
4100 Dahlia
Denver CO 80207

Showtime Video Ventures
2715 5th Street
Tillamook OR 97141

Slik Div.
Berkey Marketing Companies
25-20 Brooklyn-Queens Expressway West
Woodside NY 11377

TVS Total Video Supply
9181-A Kearny Villa Court
San Diego CA 92123

Uniphot-Levit Corp.
61-10 34th Ave.
Woodside NY 11377

Video Products of America, Inc.
4849 N. Western Ave.
Chicago IL 60625

Vivitar Corporation
1630 Stewart Ave.
Santa Monica CA 90406

Welt/Safe-Lock Inc.
2400 West 8th Lane
Hialeah FL 33010

Index

A

Accessories, 58-59, 107-115
   camcorder, 151
   manufacturers/marketers, 156
AFT, 29
Assemble editing, 51
Audio dub, 45
Audio head, 23-25
Audio-level control defeat, 45
Auto capping, 83
Automatic features
   fine tuning (AFT), 29
   focus, 75-77
   gain control, 45
   iris, 74-75
   pause release, 50
   volume control, 45

B

Backlight switch, 80
Backspace editing, 52
Batteries, 38
Batteries, camcorder, 147
Beta and VHS comparison, 16
Betamax, 8-9
Betamovie, 140-152
Blank tape marketers, 154-155
Brand names, 13

C

Cable-readiness, 30-31
Camcorders
   accessories, 151
   batteries, 147
   buying checklist, 160
   configurations, 145-147
   controls, 146-147
   counter, 147
   hookup, 150-151
   operating controls, 149
   power supply, 147
   record/cradle play, 146
Camera
   as live monitor, 135
   buying, 86-94
   buying checklist, 159
   features, 77-85
   high-end models, 88
   leader models, 87
   Mavica, 153
   super-high-end models, 88-89
Cartrivision, 8
Cassette tab, 99
Cassette vs. cartridge, 96
Cassette-size comparison, 141
Channel lock, 47
Channel settings, 137
Character generator, 81-82
Checklists
   camcorder, 160
   VCR, 158
   video camera, 159
Chrominance, 56
Clock, 136-137
C-mount lens, 71
Color vs. b&w, 64-65
Color-adjust control, 80
Color-control setting, 69
Companding, 44
Compatibility, 18, 89-91
Computer "videotape," 97
Computer hookup, 135-136
Connecting Kodavision, 152
Connections, 122-136

Connections, portable, 124-125
Controls, camcorder, 146-147
Cost, 4-5
Counter display, 69
Counters
   camcorder, 147
   electronic, 44
   linear time, 44-45
   mechanical, 40
Counter-memory, 40
Cue and locating systems, 52

D

dbx, 44
Dealer, choosing, 59-61
Dew warning, 53
Disc hookup, 135-136
Dolby noise reduction, 42-44

E

Earth-station hookup, 135-136
Editing, 50-52
8mm video, 10, 140-153
Electro-mechanical features, 47-53
Electronic features
   clock, 30
   counter, 44
   exposure control, 74-75
   tuner, 28-29
   viewfinder, 67-68
Equipment marketers, 154
Erase head, 23-25
External filter, 74

F

Fade in/fade out, 78-79
Features
   camera, 77-85
   VCR electro-mechanical, 47-53
   VCR electronic, 40-47
   VCR mechanical, 39-40
Freeze-frame, 48
Frequency response, 57
Frequency-synthesized tuner, 39
Future of Beta, VHS, 119-120

G

Gain-boost control, 81
Great Time Machine, 9
Grundig V-2000, 9

H

Head drum, 20-21
Head-gap width, 23
Helical-scan recording, 17
Hi-Fi sound, 41-42
Hookups
   camcorder, 150-151
   camera, 133-135
   computer, 135-136
   disc, 135-136
   earth-station, 135-136
   VCR, 125-132
Horizontal resolution, 57

I

Imaging devices, 69-77
Indicators, viewfinder, 68-69
Inputs, 57
Insert editing, 51
Interchangeable lenses, 69-71
Interference, 136
Iris scale, 69

K

Kodavision 8mm video, 141

L

Lenses, 69-77
   focal-length, 69
   speed, 73
   zoom, 71-73
Linear time counter, 44-45
Live monitor, camera hookup, 135
Loading, 39
Low-battery indicator, 69
Low-light indicator, 69
Luminance, 56

M

Macro lens, 74
Market-share chart, 32
Mavica camera, 153
Mechanical tuner, 28
Metal-evaporated tape, 140, 144-145
Metal-particle tape, 140, 144-145
Microphone, 84-85
Modulators, 136
Multi-motor transport, 40

N

Noise reduction, 42-44

O

OEM, 31-32
One-touch recording, 52
On-screen timer, 83
Operating controls, camcorder, 149
Optical viewfinder, 65-66
Original equipment manufacturer
   (OEM), 31-32
Outputs, 57

P

Pause, 45-46
Pay-TV channels, 129
PCM output, 46
Pickup device, camera, 91-92
Portable VCRs, 11-13, 36-38
   high-end models, 38
   leader models, 37
   step-up models, 37-38
   "wireless," 138
Positive/negative switch, 79
Power consumption, VCR, 58
Power-saver switch, 78
Power supplies, 77
Power supply, camcorder, 147
Powering up, 125
Prerecorded videocassette
   marketers, 155
Prices, 59-61

Q

Quasar Great Time Machine, 9

R

Record-only, 145
Record/play, 145-146
Recording indicator, 68
Recording process,
   camcorders, 144-145
Recording speeds, 18-19, 56
Recording times, comparison, 18
Remote control, 53, 83
Renting equipment, 116-120
Rewind time, 58
RF, 125

S

Sanyo V-Cord, 9
Scanner, 20
Sensitivity control, 81

Settings, channel, 137
Signal-to-noise (S/N) ratio, 56-57
Soft-touch controls, 53
Sony Mavica camera, 153
Sony developments, 7-10
Sound-on-sound, 45
Source List, 154-156
Special effects, 47-50
Specs
   camera, 91-94
   tape, 102-105
   VCR, 54-60
Standards, television, 11
Stereo adapter output, 47
Stereo sound, 41-42
Still-frame, 48
Stopwatch display, 82-83
STV hookups, 131-132
Styling, camera, 85-86

T

Tab marker, 50
Tabletop VCRs, 11-13, 35-38
   high-end models, 36
   leader models, 35-36
   step-up models, 36
Tape
   metal-evaporated 140, 144-145
   metal-particle, 140, 144-145
   standard vs. high-grade, 104-105
Tape-efficiency chart, 143
Tape-remaining indicator, 46
Timer, 29-30, 137
   back-up, 46-47
Tracking control, 137-138
Transport motors, 25-26
TTL reflex viewfinder, 66-67
Tuner types, 27-29

U

U-Matic, 7-8
Unpacking equipment, 122

V

V-2000, 9
V-Cord, 9
VCR
   buying checklist, 158
   controls, 33-35
   specifications, 54-59
VHS and Beta comparison, 16, 19-20
VTR vs. VCR, 10
Video cameras, 13-14, 62-94
   buying checklist, 159
   heads, 21-23
Videodisc, 14
VideoMovie, 140-152
Videotape brands, grades, 99-104
Video vs. audio, 17-18
Viewfinder, camera, 65-69
Viewfinder indicators, 68-69

W

Warranties, 59-60
Waveform display, 68-69
White-balance
   control, 79
   indicator, 69

Z

Zoom lens, 71-73

VCR BUYING CHECKLIST

	VCR #1 Brand: _____ Model: _____	VCR #2 Brand: _____ Model: _____	VCR #3 Brand: _____ Model: _____
ITEM			
Format			
Tabletop			
Portable			
Recording Speeds			
Playback Speeds			
Tuner Type (mechanical, electronic or frequency-synthesized)			
Tuner Number of Days			
Tuner Number of Events			
Cable-ready			
Channel Lock			
Stereo or Hi-Fi Stereo			
Noise Reduction			
Audio-Level Defeat			
Audio-Level Indicators			
Audio Dub			
Sound-on-Sound			
Fast-Scan Forward			
Fast-Scan Reverse			
Slow-Scan Forward			
Slow-Scan Reverse			
Variable Slow-Scan			
Pause			
Freeze Frame			
Frame-Advance			
Automatic Pause Release			
Loading: top or front			
Counter Type: mechanical or electronic			
Time Counter			
Auto-Rewind			
Sleep Switch			
One-Touch Recording			
PCM Output Switch			
Insert Edit			
Camera Plug			
Remote Type: wired or wireless			
Remote Functions			
Power Consumption			
Weight			
Length of Warranty			
Price			
Standard Accessories			

ADD YOUR OWN POINTS:

_____

_____

_____

_____

CUT HERE

CUT HERE

VIDEO CAMERA BUYING CHECKLIST

	Camera #1 Brand: _____ Model: _____	Camera #2 Brand: _____ Model: _____	Camera #3 Brand: _____ Model: _____
ITEM			
Zoom Range	_____	_____	_____
Zoom Ratio	_____	_____	_____
Lens Speed	_____	_____	_____
Macro Focus	_____	_____	_____
Auto-Focus	_____	_____	_____
Auto-Iris	_____	_____	_____
Power Zoom	_____	_____	_____
Fade In/Out	_____	_____	_____
Imaging Device	_____	_____	_____
Negative/Positive Switch	_____	_____	_____
Interchangeable Lenses	_____	_____	_____
Auto-White Balance	_____	_____	_____
Back-Light Switch	_____	_____	_____
Power-Saver Switch	_____	_____	_____
Gain Boost	_____	_____	_____
Mike Type	_____	_____	_____
External Mike Jack	_____	_____	_____
Viewfinder Type	_____	_____	_____
Built-In Indicators	_____	_____	_____
Orientable Finder	_____	_____	_____
Tally Light	_____	_____	_____
Counter Display	_____	_____	_____
Waveform Display	_____	_____	_____
Character Generator	_____	_____	_____
Stopwatch/Timer Display	_____	_____	_____
Remote Control Functions	_____	_____	_____
Styling	_____	_____	_____
Power Consumption	_____	_____	_____
Weight	_____	_____	_____
Price	_____	_____	_____
Standard Accessories	_____	_____	_____

ADD YOUR OWN POINTS:

_____	_____	_____	_____
_____	_____	_____	_____
_____	_____	_____	_____
_____	_____	_____	_____
_____	_____	_____	_____
_____	_____	_____	_____
_____	_____	_____	_____
_____	_____	_____	_____
_____	_____	_____	_____
_____	_____	_____	_____
_____	_____	_____	_____
_____	_____	_____	_____

CAMCORDER BUYING CHECKLIST

ITEM	Camcorder #1 Brand: _____ Model: _____	Camcorder #2 Brand: _____ Model: _____	Camcorder #3 Brand: _____ Model: _____
Format	_____	_____	_____
Weight	_____	_____	_____
Playback in finder	_____	_____	_____
RF Output	_____	_____	_____
Video Output	_____	_____	_____
Audio Output	_____	_____	_____
Recording Speeds	_____	_____	_____
Playback Speeds	_____	_____	_____
Rewind	_____	_____	_____
Fast-Scan	_____	_____	_____
Slow-Scan	_____	_____	_____
Freeze Frame	_____	_____	_____
Frame Advance	_____	_____	_____
Full Controls on Camera	_____	_____	_____
Remote: wired or wireless	_____	_____	_____
Remote: standard or optional	_____	_____	_____
Imaging Device	_____	_____	_____
Zoom Range	_____	_____	_____
Lens Speed	_____	_____	_____
Interchangeable Lenses	_____	_____	_____
Viewfinder Type	_____	_____	_____
Macro Focus	_____	_____	_____
Power Zoom	_____	_____	_____
Auto-Focus	_____	_____	_____
Negative/Positive Switch	_____	_____	_____
Auto-White Balance	_____	_____	_____
Orientable Finder	_____	_____	_____
Tally Light	_____	_____	_____
Built-In Indicators	_____	_____	_____
Character Generator	_____	_____	_____
Stopwatch/Timer Display	_____	_____	_____
Mike Type	_____	_____	_____
Tuner Type (mechanical, electronic or frequency-synthesized)	_____	_____	_____
Tuner Number of Days	_____	_____	_____
Tuner Number of Events	_____	_____	_____
Stereo or Hi-Fi Stereo	_____	_____	_____
Inputs	_____	_____	_____
Price (camcorder only)	_____	_____	_____
Price of cradle/adapter	_____	_____	_____
Price of simple adapter (no tuner, for power and RF)	_____	_____	_____
Power Consumption (camcorder)	_____	_____	_____
Standard Accessories	_____	_____	_____
ADD YOUR OWN POINTS:			
_____	_____	_____	_____
_____	_____	_____	_____
_____	_____	_____	_____
_____	_____	_____	_____

CUT HERE

CUT HERE

8.41289302773